# Lucky Thirteen

## D-Days in the Pacific with the U.S. Coast Guard in World War II

# Lucky Thirteen

## D-Days in the Pacific with the U.S. Coast Guard in World War II

### Ken Wiley

CASEMATE

*Philadelphia*

Published by CASEMATE
1016 Warrior Road, Suite C
Drexel Hill, PA 19026
Phone: 610-853-9131
www.casematepublishing.com

Typeset and design by Savas Publishing & Consulting Group


ISBN 10: 1-932033-53-X
ISBN 13: 978-1932033-53-3

First edition, first printing

Cataloging-in-Publication data is available
from the Library of Congress



Printed in the United States of America

For my wife Deane and my family.


For my mother Gold Star Mother Dora Thompson Wiley,
and my father Troy Wiley. They gave up their five sons, volunteers all,
to serve and save our country.

For the small town of Itasca, Texas (population 1,758 in 1941) and the
thirty-three Itasca High School students and alumni, including my
brother Joe, who gave up their lives in World War II.

Ken Wiley, United States Coast Guard, July 1943. *Author's Collection*

# Contents

Contents (continued)

# Contents (continued)

# Illustrations

Miscellaneous illustrations appear throughout the book,
with a photo gallery following page 144

Preface

# The Last Seven Miles

This story is about the U .S. Coast Guard's role in World War II, as told from the perspective of a teenage boy who played a part in that great global struggle. It is also about an unheralded boat that played an insignificant and yet very important role in America's response to restoring freedom to a part of the world enslaved by an evil tyranny. Lucky 13—my boat—was a weapon specifically designed and mass produced in the United States to bridge the 6,000-mile ocean gap and carry the war to the shores of the enemy. The "Higgins" boats were lowered from troop ships with one mission: to carry the infantry and equipment the last seven miles of the long and perilous journey onto the beaches of enemy-held islands.

I grew up in the U.S. Coast Guard. Although I was only a kid of seventeen when I enlisted, I was a man when I left the service at twenty. You grew up quick in those days and under the circumstances so many of us experienced. I spent six short weeks in Boot Camp in St Augustine, Florida, where I saw my first ocean; nine weeks in Landing Craft School with the Marines at Camp Lejuene, North Carolina, where I saw and was given my first landing craft and on to a waiting Attack Transport, and where I was hoisted aboard my first ship as a Cox'n of an LCVP (Higgins boat). Six months after I joined the Coast Guard I was heading for

Kwajalien in the Marshall Islands—my first invasion in the Pacific theater of war.

I was one of five brothers who served in the military during WWII. We all volunteered. One of us did not come back. The three older boys were in the Army Air Corps, one younger brother was in the Army, and I served as the only sailor in the family with the unheralded amphibious forces that island-hopped its bloody way to Japan. The environment of the world, the times, the war, and most of all the shaping of the minds of the 15 million young people in uniform is the key to understanding how it was back then. Most of us were teenagers. We couldn't legally drink or vote. We were the children of the 1930s and we carried our experiences from childhood and the Great Depression into the Great War of the 1940s.

On December 7, 1941, the Japanese bombed Pearl Harbor, where they destroyed a number of our capital warships and killed thousands of men. We were not at war when they attacked, and there was no advance warning. By the spring of 1942, the Japanese had conquered the Philippines, Singapore, much of Southeast Asia, Guam, Wake Island, and New Guinea. In less than four months they had effectively built a wall around the vast central and southwest Pacific ocean. They had killed, driven out, or captured Allied forces in order to do so. Imperial Japan was well positioned for further conquests. After Pearl Harbor, American isolation was no longer an option. Our choices were limited to fighting for our freedom and utterly defeating our enemies, or surrendering to them. There was no middle ground.

On the other side of the world in Europe, Nazi Germany had enslaved France, Poland, Czechoslovakia, Austria, Romania, Holland, Belgium, Norway, Finland, Greece, and Ethiopia. Most of western Russia had also fallen to invading Axis forces. England, driven off the European mainland in 1940, was locked in a death struggle to stave off a German invasion of its homeland. Would it survive long enough to turn the tide with the help of American troops and equipment? No one knew the answer to that question. The Free World had reached its nadir.

The Japanese intended to take all of Burma, India, Australia, Midway, the Aleutians, and Hawaii before forcing us to surrender to avoid an invasion of our western states. Japan and Germany were allied in their war against the Western democracies. Japan had nine million men in the military, twice as many fighting ships and aircraft carriers as we did and perhaps more importantly, a home field advantage. Our troops numbered fewer than one million at the beginning of the war. After losing most of our battleships and fighter aircraft at Pearl Harbor, the United States Navy was hard pressed to carry the war against its Pacific enemy.

We had to do the impossible, and do it immediately: carry the war into Japanese waters while assisting England in defeating Germany thousands of miles away. The specter of a two-front war was a daunting one, but the alternative was unthinkable. In order to stop Japan, we had to move our troops and equipment 6,000 miles across the ocean in ships we didn't have to fight an enemy already firmly entrenched on scores of islands with air fields, supported by a powerful navy several times the size of our own battered fleet.

And we did it.

*Lucky Thirteen* is the story of how we achieved this remarkable feat, as told through the eyes of a teenager in command of his own boat.

## Acknowledgements

For *Lucky 13*, the list of contributors is long because it spans a half-century of my life. It begins in the first third of the last century with family, followed by my friends, my shipmates, and business associates. Many do not realize the contribution they supplied. The greatest help came from those who were honestly critical of my effort, but gave me encouragement along the way. My greatest fear is that I overlooked someone. If I did, and you don't find your name here, please know I appreciate your efforts.

First, I want to extend thanks to David Farnsworth of Casemate Publishing for taking a chance on an unheralded author because the humane nature of this book and its illustrations tell a story that needed to be told.

I also want to thank David for selecting Theodore P. "Ted" Savas of Savas Publishing and Consulting Group to edit and design this book. Ted is the type of editor who completely submerges himself in the storyline until he thoroughly understands its environment—every character, event, photo, and illustration. Once he understood my story, he set about organizing it, polishing it, and presenting it in a format I know readers will find pleasing. You will enjoy this book more because of Ted Savas' efforts, and I am proud to have him as the editor of my book.

My family, to whom I owe everything, was a tremendous help. I wrote the original manuscript ten years ago, but it was my family who encouraged me to publish it because it opens a door to an area of WWII known to so few. The story of the APA, the LCVP, and the Coast Guard's participation in the war needs to be widely told. Although I am a prolific writer and have been accused of being a good storyteller, I needed a lot of help to complete this book. I could never have done it without the help of my family.

My wife Deane is my best critic. Deane not only stood by me while I labored to finish this book, but also helped by offering many valuable suggestions for improving *Lucky Thirteen*. Although we met late in life, she is my life and has been throughout the preparation of this work. Deane has always been there when I needed her, and you would not be holding this book in your hands without her loving assistance.

Our daughters Lisa and Sandra supported my writing and veterans programs and responded to my needs with encouragement and the proper equipment, work space, and even airline tickets when needed. When I needed someone who could actually decode and read my handwritten manuscripts and type it into a computer, Deane and Lisa found the person in Terri Miller.

Terri Miller deserves a special acknowledgment. Every word of the original manuscript for *Lucky 13* was handwritten on airplanes across a period of nearly 25 years. My "daytime" career required me to traveling about 70 times each year. I am grateful to my company LTV and a dozen or so airlines for providing a prime time studio for writing. Although I know all the problems Terri faced trying to decode this faded old manuscript, being the gracious lady that she is, she in never complained. I ask each of you reading this to join me in gratitude for my friend Terri Miller.

Ken Riley's illustrations (only a few of which grace these pages) add so much to *Lucky 13*. I am grateful to have served on the same ship with such a famous and good person and for the privilege of using his work in my book. Ken wished me success with this project, and I am grateful to him for originating his priceless images that document the story of the *Arthur Middleton* as it unfolded more than sixty years ago.

I would also like to extend my thanks to my shipmates on the USS *Cambria* and all of the crewmen who served about the *Middleton*. Paired off we were brothers; together we were a family. We looked after each other in combat and behind the lines. I am grateful to have been associated with these American heroes. We shared intimate details of the lives we left behind and our dreams of the future. These contributions provide the thread of humanity in the book you are now holding. My two closest friends and "buddies" during my life in the Coast Guard were Charles Doll and Bill Miller. Bill passed away a few years ago. I so wish he could have lived long enough to read this book that helps commemorate his role in the war. Bill and Doll contributed so much to *Lucky 13*.. I miss those guys and will remember that life forever.

I would also like to acknowledge two very important "veterans" of World War II. The Higgins Boat Company and the Chris Craft Boat Company designed and built the LCVP, (the Higgins Boat). Many lives, including my own, were saved because of the ingenuity of the design and the dependability and durability of the LCVP

Chapter 1

# The Attack Transport Emerges

Fighting and defeating the Japanese in the Pacific Theater during World War II offered many difficult challenges for America. Existing equipment would not suffice. We had to have a weapon that could move across 6,000 miles of ocean, slip through enemy defenses undetected, and land divisions of troops on raw beaches within minutes before enemy reinforcements arrived. Our aircraft and bombers during that time had a limited range, which meant they would have to operate from aircraft carriers. The enemy, however, could operate from their carriers as well as from island bases.

American ingenuity responded nearly overnight by developing the Attack Transport system. This "system" consisted of a ship that could carry 1,400-1,500 assault troops and all of their gear to within seven to ten miles of their target, deploy the men and their gear, and then land them in a powerful assault quickly and with as little risk as possible. The ship carried approximately 30 specially-built boats that ran at 10-12 knots fully loaded. These boats could drive all of the way up on a beach, unload within two minutes, back off, and repeat the process. The boat was called the Landing Craft Vehicle Personnel (or LCVP for short), which became famous as the "Higgins" boat, named after Andrew Jackson Higgins, the craft's designer.

There were three versions of the Higgins boat. The LCVP was 36 feet long, built of plywood with a steel plate on each side to protect the troops crouched inside. It had a steel ramp in front that lowered to let troops run out, and allowed small vehicles like jeeps pulling 37mm howitzers to drive out onto dry land. The steel ramp also served as protection for the troops against small arms fire. The combination of a barge-like boat with a shallow draft that could travel fully loaded at 10-12 knots and drive its nose onto dry land required an ingenious design. The ingenuity centered on the bow, which rode above the water while the stern traveled slightly submerged. Even when fully loaded, the bow (or nose) was above the water level. The speedboat bottom had a skag that ran all the way to the stern to protect the screw and rudder above it. The boat was built to run up on the beach. The commander in the boat, the coxswain (or cox'n), had to see over the ramp to drive the boat. He stood up in a "drivers" area just behind the troop compartment. Two gun pits with 30-caliber machine guns were at the very rear. In Landing Craft school, cox'ns learned how to put the bow right up on a wave and ride it in. This helped lift the boat and get the front end as far up on the beach as possible, straight and firmly grounded. This was important because when the boats were unloaded they had a tendency to float. When it was time to back off, the engines were reversed and full power was employed, with the screw protected by the skag in "floating" water.

Another version of the Higgins boat was the Landing Craft Personnel (LCP). This was built of plywood and used as a control boat. Its nose was like a speedboat, but it did not have a ramp like the LCVP. The third revised Landing Craft Tank (LCT) was 56 feet long, all metal, and could carry a Sherman tank. Like the LCVP, it also had a ramp in front to allow the tank to drive out.

Once the design was perfected, construction began. However, there wasn't time to wait for new ships to be built that would carry these Higgins boats. Instead, twenty-seven cruise ships and luxury liners were converted to haul the new boats that Higgins, Chris Craft, and other boat builders were turning out. Seven months after Pearl Harbor, the Coast Guard—called upon for its knowledge of small boats—landed Marine assault troops and Navy Seabees on Guadalcanal and Tulagi in the Solomon Islands to establish an airfield. This operation marked the birth of the American amphibious force. This was the way we were able to fight the war. History has earmarked "D-Day" as June 6, 1944, in Normandy. In the Pacific Theater there were many D-Days and H-hours. Allied forces established "stepping stones" across the south and central Pacific, the Mideast, North Africa, Sicily, Italy, and eventually France. Even after an official D-Day landing, Higgins boats were used to rescue trapped troops and move assault forces around the enemy. If a single weapon could be credited with winning the war, Dwight D. Eisenhower explained, it was the Higgins boat. The amphibious force was never given an official emblem.

The LCVP landed assault troops in more than 100 invasions during World War II. With a speedboat bottom, large carrying capacity, and under skag screw and rudder, the boat could almost dig its way on and off any beach. Built to withstand virtually any kind of weather, heavy seas, and operate on shallow beaches without grounding, it was the true "all -terrain" vehicle of the sea.

Each invasion was planned and practiced in minute detail, and took into consideration issues relating to weather, tides, enemy defenses, and the element of surprise. The primary purpose of each landing was to establish an air and logistic base in a strategic location so our aircraft, naval, and ground forces could operate within range of the enemy. The Task Force for each invasion consisted of transports, other amphibious ships and boats, aircraft carriers, battleships, cruisers, destroyers, submarines, mine sweepers, tankers, cargo vessels, hospital ships, and PT boats. They were massive operations, and a sight to behold.

Once a Task Force was formed, it moved by convoy toward the target. A convoy never traveled a straight course. Instead, moved in a zig-zag pattern to make it difficult for enemy submarines to track and sink the ships. With perfect timing, every ship made pre-programmed turns simultaneously at prescribed intervals. Final destinations were not revealed to us until after the ships left port and joined the convoy. During the days or weeks they were underway, we engaged in intensive training. We memorized every detail about the beach we were to land upon and got a good feel for the campaign's overall strategy. This schooling continued right up to D-Day. On the evening before the landing, a special meal (sometimes dubbed "The Last Supper" by the men who ate it) was served to troops and crew. Ideally, air superiority was established prior to the invasion, which continued once a land-based airfield was established. Submarines carried Underwater Demolition Teams (UDT, or frogmen) close to the shores to clear routes through coral reefs and other obstructions to the beach so our boats could reach the shore.

Early on D-Day morning, heavy artillery from battleships, cruisers, destroyers, and rocket boats pounded the beach area to kill or drive away the enemy. Aided by aircraft, the intent was to clear an area for the landing. There was never a standard time for H-Hour, but it was normally 7:00-8:00 AM. On the APAs, meanwhile, the Higgins boats were put into the water in a record thirty minutes or less. Two or three cargo nets were dropped from the deck along both sides of the ship. The boats circling the ships peeled off and slipped alongside each cargo net. The troops climbed down the nets, four abreast, until each boat was loaded. Cargo booms were used to lower jeeps, heavy equipment, and tanks into the waiting boats. As each boat was loaded, it pulled away and resumed circling. Once every boat was loaded, they formed in waves of five to six boats each. Each ship had four to six waves of boats. Each ship had a designated area of the beach upon which its boats would land. Each ship also provided a beach party of communications technicians, hospital corpsmen, and beach fire spotters and directors who landed with the first assault waves to establish a beachhead.

The initial landing in an invasion was only the beginning. The boats unloaded all of the ships and supplies necessary to support an invasion. They performed rescue operations and special missions whenever necessary, but usually worked as as a water taxi service. The first Higgins boats had some problems, including gasoline engines that stalled because of water submersion issues. The improved boats had Gray Marine Diesel engines, which were much more dependable. The majority of these improved boats were built by Chris Craft. My boat, number 13 ("Lucky 13," as we came to call her), was one of these improved boats. The improvements saved a lot of lives, including my own. As insignificant as it was, I was in command of Lucky 13. She was my boat.

D-Day, H-Hour: The spear tip of the invasion. An LCVP carries assault troops the last seven miles to the enemy beach. An illustration by Coast Guard combat artist Ken Riley.

A chief I had aboard my first ship, *USS Cambria* (APA-36) explained what the Coast Guard did during the war in relation to these invasions in the Pacific:

> The Guadalcanal and Tulagi operations was all Coast Guard and Marines. We had to load these Marines, go 6,000 miles on ships and then take 'em that last seven miles in some kind of boat that could run right up on the beach, under fire, unload and back of to go get another load. And this wasn't just troops you put ashore. It was all the support equipment and supplies to support 'em, 'cause these guys had a one-way ticket. The Attack Transport also provides the beach party. That's me and a hundred other guys right off the ship. The beach party goes in with the first waves, sets up communications, a beach hospital and medical corps to bring back and treat the wounded. The Coast Guard ranks right up there with the Marines for being

ready when the call came. It was the same up the Solomon chain, New Guinea, North Africa, Sicily, and Italy. The Coast Guard led the way.

I recall a friendly argument between some soldiers who were questioning sailors about what the Coast Guard did. The discussion occurred on the main deck right outside my boat, which was stowed on the outboard davit. The chief, who had been one of the instructors in landing craft school, jumped in with both feet.

I was at Algiers when the war started and the word was they needed an amphibious force to take the war to the Japs and Germans. This involved ships and boats. We were experienced in both, so they called on the Coast Guard to take the Marines in ships and boats to the beach. The first attack transports weren't new transport ships like the one we're on. Why, the *Cambria*, which is Number 36, just came out of the shipyard. All of the first APAs were conversions. Look at the numbers: *Leonard Wood,* 14; *Hunter Ligget,* 12; *Arthur Middleton,* 25; *Chase,* 26; *Climber,* 27. All these are converted passenger ships cause we had to hurry.

Then the chief added his punch line: "The Coast Guard and Marines stopped the Japs," he explained, "while the Army and Navy mobilized."

Chapter 2

# Children of the Thirties

I was five years old in 1930. My family lived in Itasca, a small cotton farming town in north central Texas. The summers were long, hot, and dry. Although short, the winters caught the tail end of the bitter cold weather that sweeps across the Rocky Mountains to plague the rest of the central Midwestern states.

There were eight in our family and we lived in a wooden frame house with two bedrooms, a living room, and a kitchen. I have very few memories of the first five years of my life. America was slipping into the worst depression it, and perhaps the world, had ever faced. There had been many years of hard living from the turn of the century, but this was depression at its worst. Of course we did not have a television (that came in the late 1940s after the war), but we also did not have a radio, either. In fact, we had no electricity and used kerosene lamps. Refrigeration consisted of blocks of ice in an old fashioned icebox.

With the blistering hot Texas summer weather, the "Ice House" was one of the most popular stores in town. The Ice House delivered the ice daily by sending a horse-drawn and wood insulated covered wagon around to all the streets. The women had cardboard signs they put in the front window. The signs were divided into four sections with the numbers 25, 50, 75, or 100. The number represented the size, in pounds, of ice they wanted. Kids flocked out to the wagon and followed it for a block or two, knowing that Mr.

Gibson, the driver, would let us have ice chips that popped loose from the larger ice blocks as he chipped away to produce the size desired.

We had natural gas, but only had one space heater, which we hovered around in the living room during the winter months. There were no inside toilet facilities, so we used an outhouse at the back of our lot. The only paved street downtown was main street. A few of the main roads running through the town were graveled. The rest and all of the side streets were just dirt roads. Each fall we picked cotton for the farmers so we had some money to buy our clothes, which we would wear for the rest of the year. We were poor and we knew it, but so was most everyone else in 1930 America.

As a kid I never knew anything but the hardship of the Depression years. I was not unique because everyone was alike and we thought everyone was poor. I was the fifth of five boys and had one sister, and our family existed only because of an iron-willed mother and father. My mom's name was Dora, and my dad was Troy. Our names, in order of birth, were as follows: Victor Dudley, Ailene, Joseph Wade, Troy Jr., myself (Kenneth Edwin), and Billy Donald.

These times were especially hard on grown people because their responsibilities were awesome. My father, a natural carpenter, worked 10-12 hours every day for anyone he could, whether loading, driving, and unloading a short-haul truck, shoveling cottonseed or grain, or digging foundations and ditches.

As hard as the Depression was on men, it was even harder on women. Washing clothes, for an example, was an all-day affair. Lye soap had to be cooked beforehand. All the work was outside, regardless of the weather. Clothes were boiled and stirred in a large cast iron pot with a wood fire roaring beneath it. Next, the clothes had to be scrubbed on a scrub board by hand in a #2 wash tub. After rinsing the clothes (which was also laborious), they were wrung by hand and hung to dry from a wire clothesline with clothes pins. The #2 tubs we used for clothes doubled as bathtubs. We boiled water on a stove, poured it into the tub, and stepped in. We took most of our baths inside the house.

In addition to laundry, women also had to cook three meals a day for the family, serve as a doctor to the children, wash the dishes, clean the house, can fruit and vegetables, and everything else you can imagine.

The long wooden table, built by my dad, seated ten people comfortably and on any given day it was full. As I noted, my dad was a natural carpenter and all five of his sons followed suit. We built our own toys from scrap wood, and quickly became the town manufacturer of cowboy 45s (wooden rubber guns that shot rubber bands cut from old auto inner tubes, with leather holsters made from old boot tops), airplanes, boats, and ships. I had always had a passion to drive or fly something of my own and put myself into these crude toys as if they were real.

There always seemed to be spares waiting around to get in on my mother's cooking. I remember one day it was two of Vic's friends, Boone Bradley and I. C. Curtiss from Bynum. Vic and both of his friends were sixteen, which at only eight years old seemed full grown to me.

I was troubled because Vic had just told me he was twice as old as I was, but he never would be again. I remember trying to figure that out. The other thing that troubled Troy, Bill, and me was his friend Boone. Troy asked him where he got his name, and he said that his parents lost him one time in Kentucky and the Indians got him. The only white man name they knew was Boone (for Daniel Boone), so they named him that. We were beginning to get a little suspicious of all three of these roustabouts. It seemed to us that the only thing they cared about was girls, and they stayed out late every night "sparking" with them. Most of the time, they talked way above our young heads anyway.

"Hey Dudley!" (Vic's other name). "Did you wash your hands after last night?" asked my sister Ailene.

"With lye soap," answered Vic, his reply nearly smothered by loud guffawing.

"Oh, you boys!" Ailene turned red with embarrassment as the Don Juans jeered even louder. "Troy, when you and Ken finish, take your wheelbarrows and go to the ice house. Here's a dime. Get us 25 pounds of ice and we'll make some ice cream."

Vic extended the dime to Troy, who eagerly took it and stuck it in his pocket. Our wheelbarrows were our pride and joy. It was 1933, in the midst of the Great Depression. Very few young boys had anything "store bought," and bicycles were out of the question. Instead, we built wheelbarrows. They were our race cars, boats, trucks, airplanes, or trains—whatever we fantasized at the time. We built them from wooden apple boxes. Two long handlebars (from 1 x 4 lumber) protruding at an angle from the back; two more extended straight out from the front bottom, supporting a wheel salvaged from some long ago retired tricycle or little red wagon. From that basic point on, we displayed our ingenuity with mirrors, old license plates, reflectors, and levers on the handlebars that activated another lever providing braking action on the wheel.

It never dawned on us to take one wheelbarrow. When driving our wheelbarrows, or whatever we chose to call it, we were in command. Each of us took our wheelbarrows and headed across town for the icehouse. Today we were World War I pilots, flying our bi-wing Sopwith Camels across the German border in search of Fokkers. It was Sunday, a hot Texas summer day with the temperature hovering around 100 degrees. We met A. J. Lambert, Tom Hollimon, and Stanley Ketchacombs coming back from town with their wheelbarrows, each full of ice. After a couple minor dogfights, we left them behind and crossed the mythical German border. We saw what looked like one Fokker about two block away, but he was also heading the other way, so we went on to the ice house without further incident.

We got the ice without incident and started for home. When we reached the Baker house, a group of boys were playing football on their big lawn. They yelled at us to join them.

"We could play a few downs," I suggested.

"Well, OK, but we have to get home," answered Troy.

Football was the love of our lives. We envisioned ourselves playing for the best team in the world, which was Army, with Notre Dame and Texas A&M almost as good. We quickly got involved and forgot about the ice.

It was Troy who finally said, "Hey! We better go."

The wheelbarrow seemed lighter, but we didn't bother to check the ice packed under an old toe sack. Vic and his friends were really anxious by the time we got back home. In fact, their girlfriends were there and they were all downright mad. Of course, that was nothing compared to their moods after they looked for the ice and discovered only eight or nine pounds of it and a very wet wheelbarrow. Troy and I set a new wheelbarrow record on the follow-up trip to the icehouse.

Dramatic changes occurred in those years. Electricity spread across much of the country, first in cities and towns and then in rural areas. Radios, refrigerators, washing machines, and automobiles became a standard part of most households. Even with the accelerated growth in technology, the economic situation didn't change until war broke out in Europe in 1939.

As the world chose sides and began the massive build-up for the spreading conflict, we children of the 1930s found happiness anywhere we could. Moving pictures became commonplace by the late 1930s and Hollywood brought the rest of the world to us. It was entertainment, geography, history, books, stories, and news events brought to life—the opening of a dramatic revelation for us. The money needed to see the movies, however, seemed like the pot of gold at the end of the rainbow. Finding money for the movies was always difficult. We collected and sold bottles and scrap metal and worked for local farmers for the little money we had. We made our own toys and bought our own clothes. There were seasons for everything. Depending on the season, we flew kites, played marbles, spun tops, cracked pecans, played football, baseball, basketball, or track. There were some things, like cowboys and Indians, sword fighting, World War I movie reenactment, and building model airplanes and toys that ignored the seasons and provided year-round fun.

The millions of men who fought World War II were mostly between the ages of five and fifteen years old in 1930, their lives shaped largely in and by that decade. School was the heart of the community. In many ways, it was "home." Sure, the children of the 1930s knew poverty, hardship, pain, suffering, and frustration, but we also knew freedom and never lost sight of hope. Looking back, it seems we lived a lifetime during those ten or twelve years.

My brother Troy and I were inseparable growing up. He was only one year ahead of me in school and we were about the same size. In fact, many people called us twins. Sandlot football, fishing in the small creeks around Itasca, and hunting rabbits and squirrels with dad's old double-barreled shotgun was our entertainment until football season rolled around and we could see our school team play. We looked forward to the day when we would be old enough to try out for the team.

"Pat and Mike" provided our transportation—a favorite way of saying your left and right feet. We walked everywhere we went because we didn't have cars. No wonder I relished the idea of driving. Very few people had cars to drive or to ride in. This may have been responsible for the burning ambition I had to drive a car, airplane, boat, or anything that moved. I wanted to control and feel the power of an engine respond to me. My father drove trucks for a living, and since we did not have a family car, we rode in the back of the truck to visit relatives on weekends.

I had dreamed from my earliest years of owning an automobile. Some of the lucky older boys were salvaging worn out Model T's and fixing them up. Once, when I was a freshman, thirteen years old, we went to the county seat at Hillsboro for a track meet. Bud Meyers and I were in front of the school building waiting on the school bus when I saw my dream car. It was a 1925 Model T Roadster. It was red and white, the Hillsboro school colors. There were three high school boys in it and several girls trying to get in. I had never felt so envious.

"Wow! Just to be able to drive around in that. To have all the girls notice you and all the boys look on with envy," I remarked to Bud.

I heard later that one of the boys' fathers had found the car and fixed it up for him. Someone said he paid all of $15.00 for it.

I was working in various jobs, making about ten cents an hour. I saved my money and finally scraped $9.00 together. I was a sophomore before I had my opportunity. A friend wanted to sell his Model T. We drove around town negotiating the sale and finally he agreed to accept the $9.00. He tried to show me how to drive it, but I couldn't get the starting procedure down. He got the car going and climbed out on the running board, letting me slide over in the driver's seat. I drove slowly past his house and he jumped off without my having to stop, and then I drove home.

Unfortunately, the old car was just plain worn out. My friends and I spent more time cranking it than driving it. My Uncle Clyde finally sold it for me to some people who had to tow it away. I was nearly broke and somewhat wiser, but not dismayed. The dream persisted.

I got my second chance later that year. I was caring for a family's lawn and milking their cow while they were on vacation when I noticed an old Model T Ford in their barn, I asked if I could buy it. Mr. Innis, the owner, surprised me when he answered, "If you can take the wall of the barn down and then put it back, you can have it. There's no door to that barn anymore."

The car was a 1927 coupe with only two years on it before Mr. Innis put it in the barn. It was in great shape except for the battery and the tires, which had rotted away. I cut off the top, removed the trunk lid and built a "rumble seat" in the back. Then I painted it black and gold, the Itasca school colors. Money was always a problem. I found some old used tires and tubes, barely better than the ones I took off my "new" car. I couldn't afford a battery, so I ran it on the Magneto (electric generator). We were able to get "burnt" (used) oil from a service station. It took me two weeks to get the car running. White gas (regular) was eleven cents a gallon and the old car got good mileage.

By pooling our money, Bud and I had eleven cents. "Let's get some girls and go riding," he suggested one day. We walked to town, carrying a gallon can and bought a gallon of gas, then walked back and put it in the car.

We decided to go to where the girls were, and drove the five miles to the Presbyterian Home. It was after curfew and we weren't even supposed to be on the grounds, but we managed to get some encouragement from some adventuresome girls who slipped out the back door and joined us. We left thinking no one had noticed us, and did not give much thought to the fact that a Model T with a hole in the muffler is anything but silent.

We drove around all over the "mountains" and then came back about midnight. The campus of the Home had a circular driveway around the administration building. Mr. Hawkins ran out on the porch. It was a hot night and he heard us and ran outside without taking time to dress. He was in his shorts. He obviously didn't know we had girls in the car.

We let him chase us around the circle twice, flashlight in hand and yelling at us to stop—or else. When I finally stopped he charged up to the driver's side of the car. It was then he saw the girls' long hair and realized his mistake.

"Why, Mr. Hawkins, you don't have on your pants," Bud teased.

He was so embarrassed he turned and walked backward to the house, trying to hold his hands in front of himself for protection. "I'll have you arrested for this!" he shouted. "You take those girls back immediately! Do you hear me? Susy! Is that you? Estelle, I know that's you! Now you get in that house and get in bed!"

I took advantage of the opportunity to drive the girls to their dormitory, where I dropped them off and sped back by the administration building. We didn't see Mr. Hawkins this time around. We made it back home and ran out of gas as we coasted up to my house. It was a typical Model T night. The next day we pushed the car down to the service station to get another gallon of gas. We were only there a short time when Mr. Hawkins drove up. He walked around our car, studying it closely.

"Were you boys out at the home last night?" he asked.

"What home?" Bud asked.

"There was a car just like this one out there disturbing the peace last night."

"Why, we weren't disturbing the peace last night," I replied, skirting the truth again.

Mr. Johnson, the service station attendant, couldn't keep quiet any longer. "What I heard was there was a grown man roaming around in his undershorts in front of some girls out there last night. That couldn't have been these boys."

A model T is not a very heavy car. The method for starting it on the magneto was to lift up a rear wheel, and put a rock under the axle so the wheel is off the ground and can spin when it is cranked in gear. Once up on a rock, we put the car in gear and cranked fast enough for the magneto to supply the electrical spark to start the engine. Likewise, when we had a flat tire, which was often (indeed, it was probably the most dependable feature of the car), we lifted up the wheel, took off the tire and tube, located the hole, and applied a cold patch to it. Then we reassembled the tire, tube, and rim, put the boots back in place, and pumped it up with a hand pump while one of us held the corner of the car with the wounded tire off the ground.

Jacks, like batteries, were an expensive and unnecessary commodity. A flat every three miles was about average. Gear bands on the Model T were highly expendable items. The drive gear belt would go first. We used leather belts as replacements. When there were no more belts and the drive gear started to slip, usually while going up a hill, we turned the car around and drove up the hill in reverse. We did this because the reverse gear was the least used and more dependable!

Then there was the day Janie Phillips came to town. The boys of Itasca were never the same again. Janie came to visit a girl named Marge, who was also visiting her stepfather next door to our house. My childhood sweetheart was Marge's half-sister Jean. She had lived there but moved away with her mother when her parents divorced. I had dated Marge once or twice before when she visited, so my friend James and I bought a gallon of gas and took Marge and Janie for a ride. Janie, warned my mother, "is a girl with just the right amount of everything in all the right places." She was also cute, petite, intelligent, and confident.

Communication, normally slow in Itasca, spread like a roaring fire because of Janie. Itasca was a small town, and Janie was a sex bomb. The problem was that no one knew how long or short her fuse was. Within a few blocks, seven or eight boys had "joined up" and were hanging all over the car. At various times during the evening there were as many as thirteen people aboard the "T" with ten of them clamoring to be closer to Janie. She loved every second.

It was a beautiful night. We drove down every street in town and most of the country roads, singing all the popular songs. There was plenty of help to fix flats, crank, or donate leather belts. Because of the magneto, the lights brightened or dimmed depending on the speed of the engine. Finally, I pulled up to what always seemed to be our final destination—the high school football field. Couples everywhere ducked under their blankets, which was standard equipment for every car, until my engine stopped and the lights went out.

The boys got out of our car and spread the blankets on the grass. Being experts on astronomy, they were all trying to explain the stars, comets, and brilliant heavens to the girls. Janie was a very experienced sixteen-year-old and she loved all the attention and playfulness. The girls were busy giggling and trying to act as if they should not be here.

"Aunt Frankie is going to be out of her mind. We should go soon,"Marge exclaimed. (It was never, "We have to go now! It was always "soon.")

"Don't do that. You're naughty," Janie said unconvincingly as I looked to see who was the latest hero in the group.

By default, "Margie" was considered my date, a fact that all the other guys enjoyed. I wasn't so sure. I knew Margie wanted to move in on my relationship with Jean. We looked at the stars and talked. Marge talked of officers she had dated. I talked of my intent to get in the Naval Air Corps. We kissed, but it was like teenagers kissing; we did it but were not sure why.

Janie, on the other hand, had every one of the boys in the palm of her hand. The ones who were a little bit smoother got quick passionate kisses and warm embraces. She culled the others out of the group, who were lucky to get into the conversation thereafter. I found myself wishing I was in her group. I was staring at her when she caught my eye and smiled.

A bright light flashed from the end of the field. "OK everyone!" shouted Mr. Connally, the school's night watchman. "It's time to clear the field and go home."

The rule was that school property had to be cleared by 11:00 p.m. Mr. Connally always gave us until about 12:30, and no one seemed to question it. Figures came alive all over the field. Subdued voices grumbled and protested the order. Dark figures everywhere stood up, folded blankets, and moved around. Car lights popped on, engines started, and within fifteen minutes the place was empty.

I dropped the guys off at various places on the way and the girls and I rolled the "T" up into my yard. I walked both of the girls to their house next door. When we reached the small front porch I kissed Margie goodnight and turned to leave. Margie was turning to go inside when Janie suddenly turned and threw her arms around my neck and planted "The Kiss" on my lips. I had never been kissed like that before! It seemed that her whole body was a part of it. The kiss had a start, a warm passionate middle, and after what seemed an eternity, a lingering finish.

"Good night, Ken, I really had a good time."

Somehow I managed to walk across the yard to my house, find the front door, and step inside. I couldn't sleep. Instead, I lay there for hours thinking about Janie. Why had her kiss been so different? It wasn't even a real French kiss, because she barely used her tongue—or did she at all? It was just so perfect.

The next day was Sunday. After church and "dinner" there was a knock on the door. My mother answered it. It was Janie. "Is Ken here?"

My mother showed her into the living room and called me. My little brother Bill, who had been peeping through the hall door, ran back to the kitchen where the rest of the family was gathered.

"Hey! There's some girl here to see Ken!"

At the height of embarrassment, I got up from the table and went into the living room. My mother grabbed Bill by the ear and marched him back into the kitchen. She closed the living room door so Janie and I had some privacy from the rest of the family. I was still embarrassed and hardly knew what to say. We sat on the couch. She spoke first.

"You hardly noticed me last night. I was so jealous of Margie. Are you going steady?"

"No. We're just good friends."

"That's not what Margie said. But she did say that you were so in love with Jean that you hardly noticed anyone else."

"Really? No, as a matter of fact, I don't go steady with anyone. Jean and I still write each other, but that's all there is to it."

With this news, Janie slipped closer to me. She was not at all like the fun-filled girl at the football field. She seemed so serious now. As she came closer, I knew she was going to kiss me. I met her this time and felt that same sensation of the night before. I was drifting away into dreamland. We kissed again and again. It was the same each time.

She told me about working as a carhop in Ft. Worth and asked me to come and see her. We spent most of the next hour talking and kissing. I had never felt this way before. I was reaching a point of sheer passion when there was a knock on the door. It was Margie, and she didn't look so happy.

"We have to leave, Janie," she said coldly. "Aunt Frankie is ready to take us home."

And just like that Janie was gone, leaving me alone with a confused feeling. Had the past hour really happened, or was I dreaming? Janie Phillips was a topic of conversation for a long time in Itasca. I never saw her again, but I never forgot her, either.

In the 1930s, worldwide communication was severely limited and environments were built around small sectors of the country. Poverty always has a negative impact on environment. Democracy was still new and untested in most of the world. World War I was the beginning of the great battle for freedom. Unfortunately, it did not resolve it and we all knew it. We were aware of Germany's resurgence to take over the world under Hitler's ironclad rule, of Japan's militaristic conquests in Southeast Asia, of Italy's puppeteer government, and the Soviet Union's oppressive domination over most of Asia. The news we got came to us through the newspapers and later the newsreel clips at movie houses that came to life in the mid-1930s. Hollywood opened the door to the world for the millions of Americans. It glamorized geography, history and war, and fantasized about life in every aspect. Above all, it brought us closer together, a decent substitute for the travel most of us could not afford.

We sensed by the late 1930s that war was inevitable and America began to prepare for it. For most young men reaching the age of 17 or 18 years old, there were few choices. College was limited to those with means. Jobs were few and far between, and no one I knew had money. We planned our careers over days or weeks, not years or decades. Facing this frustration, the military offered travel to places you would never get to see otherwise, food, clothing, and a home, plus the glory associated with heroism. The Wiley family had five boys, each of whom would soon face that decision.

Vic, my oldest brother, was born in 1917 and graduated from high school in 1935. He wanted desperately to go to college, but every door closed in front of him. After two frustrating years of hard labor jobs, government work programs, and failing to find a career opportunity, Vic found a home in the Army Air Corps. If it was hard for boys back then, it was doubly hard for girls. My sister Ailene graduated in 1937 and had no chance to go to college or find a job. Joe, who graduated in 1939, followed the same pattern as Vic. He joined him in California in early 1941 and enlisted in the Army Air

Corps. Both were assigned to the 36th Bombardment Group, which was being transferred to the Philippine Islands. Most of the group was already there. My brothers were on an unguarded troopship, one day out if Honolulu and heading for the Philippines on December 7, 1941. The ship zigzagged its way back to San Francisco. Vic and Joe both applied for cadet pilot training and were accepted. I was a senior in High School, sixteen years old.

The Great Depression was all but over after Pearl Harbor. With young men leaving in masses for the service and increased government spending, jobs were suddenly plentiful. After graduation, my brother Troy and I drove the old "T" 180 miles to Wichita Falls and worked through the summer at the Coca Cola plant. Troy joined the Army Air Corp in September. I was still to young and so returned home and worked for the Soil Conservation Service. It was now just a matter of months before I could join the service. With time and money on my hands, I bought a Model "A" roadster with a real rumble seat and enjoyed the last few innocent months of my life.

Anyone under 18 needed his parents' permission to enlist in any branch of the military. The news, movies, and propaganda were loaded with recruiting data for all of the services. Like millions of other young men, we flipped from one day to the other on being a pilot, a navigator, a gunner, a sailor, a merchant marine, a marine, or a soldier. I wanted to fly and it didn't matter whether it was Army, Navy, Marines, or Coast Guard. My father, however, refused to let me go. When Troy, the next oldest, joined the Army Air Corps and went to gunnery school, I launched a frantic campaign to enlist. I visited recruiting offices of every branch of the service and brought home papers for my father to sign.

I chose the Coast Guard almost by accident. During one of my regular visits to the recruiting offices, I spoke with a Coast Guard recruiter. He went over all of the things the Coast Guard was doing. I knew the Navy had taken the Coast Guard over when the war began, but I wasn't aware of all of the things the Coast Guard did. I heard for the first time that its members drove the landing craft that deposited the Marines on Guadalcanal. I was impressed with their flying submarine patrols and saw an opportunity to be a pilot. The recruiter assured me I could go to their pilot training school and become a pilot on submarine patrol. Two of my closest friends, Tom Hollimon and Billy Buck Blair, went with me to Dallas. Billy, who had tried to enlist at each of the recruiting offices, tried to enlist on the spot at the Coast Guard office and told the recruiting officer he was 18. He was actually only 14. The officer told him he would have to bring his birth certificate back with him.

To my surprise, this time around my dad agreed to let me join up. I was approaching the age of 18, and he knew I would be drafted without choice into the Army or Navy. The Coast Guard sounded better to him. Neither of us knew what was really happening.

As it turned out, the United States was building up the greatest amphibious force the world had ever known, and the Coast Guard had a key role to play in it.

# Chapter 3

# Seventeen Going on Maturity

T he bus driver closed the doors and sat down in the driver's seat. The engine started, and I could hear him above the roar of the motor. "We'll be in Dallas in about an hour."

It was July 15, 1943. I had won my battle to enlist and was finally going to war. Jean had come back to visit her aunt, and when I told her I was leaving we spent three days together. She was no longer a little girl. Her fiery red hair and freckles had blended her into a beautiful young woman at 15.

I thought of her as I searched out a vacant seat and sat down. I looked out the window and spotted my mom and dad standing on the corner. Jean was there, too. When she saw me, she raised her hand in a quick motion and slowly waved as the bus began to roll. I waved back until I could no longer see her. When the bus rounded the corner, I settled back in my seat and began to think.

I could feel the bulge of papers in my inside coat pocket. It took two days of red tape to get all those papers signed, take my physical, and so on. Essentially, what the papers said was something like "Kenneth E. Wiley, 588-757, United States Coast Guard Reserve."

I was a sailor and I had never seen an ocean. Three days before, I would not have believed it if someone told me that Thursday I would be on my way to Florida. Sure, I wanted to get into something—what self-respecting seventeen-year-old kid didn't? I thought it would be with the Army Air Corps, where my three older brothers served. Vic and Joe were already cadets; Troy was in gunnery school. Joe's last training was with bombers and he was already overseas. Troy would be joining him soon. Vic was in Albuquerque at Sandia.

When I was in school, I had three ambitions: get a car of my own, make the high school football team, and become a pilot in the Army Air Corps. (I had one other desire, but she moved out of town before I could make it come true.) After the Army Air Corps came the Marines and the Navy. My pick of the latter two was the Navy. When I finally got dad's permission to investigate them, I discovered there was too much red tape (about a month's worth) when it came to joining the Air Corps. Once I was 18 and drafted, I wouldn't have any choice in the matter. The Navy had a draft leaving in two weeks, but I couldn't make up my mind. It was at this time I saw the poster in the hall in front of the Coast Guard Recruiting Office. One of the pictures on it was a flying seaplane.

It was customary for everyone who went in the service to spend a number of weeks in "boot camp" learning how to be a soldier. Once that was over, nearly everyone enjoyed a short leave home before being posted somewhere. New recruits, complete in their crisp new uniforms, were the toast of the town. Everyone admired them, and most of the girls relentlessly pursued them. That alone was one of the major reasons many boys enlisted. It was the "utopia" period of a young man's life. I reveled in the thought of that trip back to Itasca. The war was worth it, I naively believed. The recruiting officer assured me that I would get boot leave. "Why, everyone does!" was what he told me when I asked about it.

Well, not exactly. A few notches up the totem pole, unbeknownst to mere mortals like recruiting officers and new recruits, the high brass was putting extreme pressure on the Coast Guard to supply more amphibious personnel. Ships and boats were coming off the assembly lines at an amazing pace. Someone had to man them. The Guard was amassing large numbers for some of the greatest invasions ever witnessed by mankind. Boot camp was cut to six weeks, and most of the boat graduates were sent immediately without leave to landing craft school, where a normal 26-week course was condensed to nine weeks, and the graduates immediately assigned to a brand new ship just out of the shipyard.

Still, the opportunity to learn how to fly and spend six weeks in uniform back home had persuaded me that the Coast Guard would be the right choice. So here I was, sitting in a hot bus on the way to Dallas, where I would be sworn into the Coast Guard and catch a train to St. Augustine, Florida. I thought again about Jean. She looked cute standing there with the wind blowing through her copper red hair. She was my girl, I guessed. We had been childhood sweethearts, but she had moved away when I was thirteen and she was just eleven. I had known her quite awhile, but had not seen her for more than four years until a few days ago, when she returned to Itasca to see me off.

I had spent those three days with her night and day, neglecting my other farewells. We tried to revive those childhood feelings, but at seventeen and fifteen we were different people than we had been. Still, we had fun and pledged a new relationship. I was excited about going into the service and all of the adventures awaiting me. Many boys were leaving almost every day, so my departure wasn't anything unusual.

My ever-loving shadows, Tommy and Bill, spent the entire night with me before I left. When the sun rose, Jean asked to come to the bus station with me and my parents, so Tommy and Bill volunteered to stay home with my sister, who was expecting a baby at any moment. I didn't know exactly what they could do if anything happened, but they seemed confident.

There was nothing definite between Jean and I, but I reasoned that a man who was going out to win the war for his country needed to have a special girl back home. All the other guys had some special girl, and it seemed like the thing to do. But Bill, Tommy, and I didn't go in for that steady girlfriend stuff. One or two dates with the same girl was about all we could take. Every once in a while, Tommy would get a slight case of heart flutter, but it didn't take Bill and I long to take care of that.

Now it was different. So at the old age of seventeen, I decided my life had been fairly complete and henceforth I would get more serious about it, be more reserved in my actions. Just before I got on the bus, Jean kissed me right there in front of my mom and dad. Hell, it was as if I was going to be gone for a couple years or something.

"I'll be back in about six weeks, as soon as I get out of boot camp," I assured everyone.

When the bus pulled into Dallas I got off at the station. There were plenty of taxis, but it wasn't very far to the recruiting office and I had plenty of time so I decided to walk. I didn't even know the name of the building I was looking for, but I knew where it was. Before too long I was on the elevator going up to the fourteenth floor of the U.S. Post Office Building.

I stepped out of the elevator and walked down the corridor to the Coast Guard Recruiting Office. Inside were the four other boys I would spend the rest of the war with. I sat down with them and we exchanged greetings.

"You must be Wiley, the other fella," said one of the guys.

"That's right," I answered.

We all introduced ourselves. There was Bill Miller, a seventeen-year-old from Riverside in Ft. Worth. He was about 5 ft. 8 in. tall and weighed 140 lbs., with brown wavy hair and a long lean face. Some people always have a smile on their face. Bill always had a laugh on his.

Bob Horton, also seventeen and from Ft. Worth, was short, dark, and handsome. Bob had long black wavy hair and was the kind of boy that girls swooned over.

The other two guys, Lynn Britton and John Ligon, were from Dallas. Both were seventeen and high school friends. Lynn was about 165 lbs., stocky, freckle-faced with crew-cut brown hair. John was the picture of the all-American boy. He stood six feet tall, weighed in at 185 lbs., sported a blond crew-cut, and was much more reserved than the others were.

"Hey, Wiley," said Bill. "We've sure got a deal. Just the five of us are going on a Pullman all the way to St. Augustine, Florida. Nobody in charge or anything."

"I wouldn't mind that little SPAR going along," said Lynn.

I looked at the subject of his comment in the adjoining office to see what he was talking about. She was cute, had brown hair, and was rather curvy. She looked up from her typewriter and gave one of those "recruiting office" smiles. I decided then and there I was going to wait until I was eighteen to practice being more reserved. Women in each branch of the services had nicknames. The Air

Corps had the WAAFs, the Army WACs, the Marines BAMS, the Navy WAVES, and the Coast Guard SPARS.

"Here comes the Admiral," announced John. The approaching officer was only a pencil pusher, third class, but the five of us wouldn't have known the difference.

"Okay, you men, come on. We're going down to get sworn in," he barked with all the nautical authority of Horatio Hornblower.

When we stood to leave, Bill and I went back and tapped Lynn on the shoulder. "Lynn, the Admiral is talking to us."

Shaken from his reverie, Lynn took one last look at the delicate little creature banging away on the typewriter, looked up at me and winked, and mumbled something about whether he was going to be issued "one of those."

"Nice thought, anyway," I mused.

The pencil pusher guided us into the basement of another large building. The five of us were standing there wondering what was going to happen next when a door opened. I could tell at a glance that the person who walked in was a real officer. It was obvious not just from his uniform, but his entire demeanor. He was a born leader.

He looked us over and told us to stand at attention. "Men," he said. "You are about to be sworn in." He began reading, but spoke so fast I couldn't understand what he was saying. Once I think I heard the words "United States," so I knew we were still in the right country. Suddenly I felt exhausted and nervous. "Boy," I thought, "If they have much of this stuff, I could be talked into resigning right now."

Just as abruptly as he started he stopped. "Now, repeat 'I do.'"

Somehow we all managed our "I do's."

"O.K.," he said. "Now in case any of you have changed your minds . . ." Here it was, I thought. Now was the time. Did I really want to join this outfit? ". . . Just try it!" the officer finished. Well, that settled that. I was in the Coast Guard.

We had lunch in the lobby of the Baker Hotel and, with a couple hours to kill before we had to board the train, decided to take in a movie.

About 3:30 that afternoon we were on a train headed for the paradise of palm tree and bathing beauties. Our tickets called for seats on the Pullman in the best car on the train. Two girls came in and sat down in the seats across from us. We decided it was high time to begin acting like sailors. The girls had a large basket with them that suggested food. The basket looked better to me than the girls did.

"You girls wouldn't be interested in a card game, would you?" asked Bill.

They looked up with that surprised but "glad you asked" look. "Why, I suppose so," replied one of them.

"What's your name?" I asked as Bill and I moved closer.

"I'm Lois," said the one who had replied. "This is Evelyn," she continued, nodding toward her friend. "We work in the Mercantile Building in Dallas and we're going to New Orleans for our vacation."

"No kidding," I said. "Well, this is Bill, Bobby, Lynn, John, and I'm Ken, and we're all heading for Florida for our vacation."

It didn't take long to get an invite into that basket, which contained fried chicken, cake, and everything that goes with it. In even less time we emptied that basket. As soon as the food was gone, the girls lost their attraction and also their would-be boyfriends, who began to look somewhere else for entertainment.

The next morning Bill and I got up first and walked to the dining car. We sat down at a table with an older woman of twenty-seven or twenty-eight. She was an Army nurse and very attractive.

"Hello," said Bill, "Don't tell me you're what we've go to look forward to when we start gold-bricking and go to the hospital?"

She smiled. "Are you boys going to camp?" The way she said the word "boys" made us realize we weren't such men after all. Oh well, maybe the uniform would change all that. She told us about her husband in North Africa and talked about the service in general. "You won't like it at first," she explained, "but after about six months, everything will be all right."

"Is it true that we'll have to take all those shots and everything?" I asked. "I heard they use a square needle, too."

"You'll have to wait and see," she teased with a grin on her face.

We climbed off the train for about an hour in New Orleans. When we got back on, there seemed to be a big commotion just outside our car. Some guy came in, followed by two porters with their arms full of bags.

"Hey, fellas, that's the actor Phillip Dorn!" John explained. It didn't take a second look for us to know he was right. Any doubt we may have had was erased by the stenciled name on one of his bags. Since the five of us had one extra seat, he asked if he might sit with us.

"Sure," I replied. As he talked, we all decided he was really a nice guy. When we told him we were off for boot camp, he seemed to take a personal interest in all five of us.

"Boy, only one day away from home and here we were, talking to a famous movie star just like he was an old friend or something." I thought,

We arrived in St. Augustine about 9:30 Saturday morning. We got off the train and took a look around. "Boy, they weren't kidding when they said this place was paradise," Bill said as we all gazed at the surroundings. None of us had ever seen a palm tree before. There were palm trees as far as we could see.

"Yeah," Lynn commented as he swatted a mosquito about the size of a Messerschmitt. "They must be having maneuvers; they've got their bombers out."

"Where can we get a taxi?" I asked a porter standing close by.

"There it is, boss," he answered, pointing to what looked like something out of Gone with the Wind. It was an old Southern two-seater buggy with the fringe-on-top and a sleepy looking old nag hitched to it. We got in and rode across town to our destination, the Ponce de Leon Hotel, recently converted to U.S. Coast Guard boot camp. It was our final, if temporary, destination—our home for the next couple of months.

Boot camp. That's where the change began. I might have been born in Texas, but I grew up in boot camp. I was about to learn how they drained the teenage immaturity out of young boys and replaced it with manhood.

# Chapter 4

# Misery in the Making

Boot camp was everything I didn't expect it to be. The Ponce de Leon hotel was absolutely beautiful. Looking back, I can see that the good outweighed the bad, and overall it was a thrilling time for me.

"Boy, they weren't kidding when they said this town was picturesque," Bobby said as we walked up to the main gate in front of the hotel. "Just look at that. I'll bet it cost several hundred even back in peace time."

It was a beautiful scene, palm trees all over the place, archways covered in vines with millions of flowers, and a pool just inside the courtyard. Fountains and statues of all kinds adorned the grounds. The buildings were widely dispersed, with the complex completely covered a large city block. The buildings were a combination of rose and dull rust colors. A solid stucco-type fence, also rose colored, completely surrounded the complex. I couldn't believe this was really the place.

We walked up to the gate and reported to the guard. Things began to become a little more realistic immediately. Hoards of guys in dungarees and white hats crowded around us yelling, "You'll be sorry! You'll be sorry!"

I grinned sheepishly because I was beginning to believe them.

The guard at the gate told us to report to Annex II, leave our bags, and to report to sick bay for our physicals. Before we could move he added, "Take a good look at things on the outside of this gate."

"Why?" asked Lynn.

"Because you won't see the outside of this place again for three weeks!" he snapped.

After going through another bombardment of "you'll be sorry" and "suckers!" comments, we located Annex II. When we reached the sickbay, which was nothing more than a hospital, we found a long line of the other guys in "civies" waiting like we were. All of the windows were open. Just outside the one next to us was a tall sleepy looking guy pushing a lawn mower. It was later when I learned he was appropriately called "Goon."

"Hey, how'd you get stuck with that job?" I called out.

He slowly looked around and drawled out, "Well, I'll tell ya'll. Yesterday at muster, the Chief asked us if anybody had ever had experience with or knew anything about, or wanted to know anything about, a Coast Guard Cutter. I told him I was willing to learn. He said 'okay,' and here I am. Now my advice is don't volunteer for nuthin!" Goon continued. "And don't take orders from just anyone. The officers and chiefs have all the authority and they wear khaki all the time. Everybody else wears blue shirts and dungarees like us." He looked around and pointed. "See that kid over there pushing the wheelbarrow full of cement? He volunteered when they asked for drivers of small carriers."

As I eventually discovered, his advice was pretty sound.

We finally got in and went through a rigorous physical that consisted of removing our shirts and turning around three times really fast. If at the end of this time you were still alive and could see a light bulb burning six feet in front of you, the doc pronounced you physically fit. The next thing we knew, some guy was blowing a bugle and yelling for Company P-1 to muster on the quarterdeck. This muster business had us worried, so Bobby and I decided we would go down and see what was happening. Neither of us had the slightest idea where the quarterdeck was.

"I sure feel sorry for those guys in Company P-1," I said still feeling removed from all this because I was dressed in my civilian clothing. We wandered around, afraid to ask anyone where the quarterdeck was, until we reached the main lobby of the hotel.

"Say," said Bobby, "look at all those guys standing over there. Most of them are in civies, too. Let's watch them and see what they're doing. That big guy with all the stripes on his arm is probably feeding them a line of bull. There's one thing I found out. The officers and chiefs all wear khaki. You don't have to do anything unless they tell you."

"Yeah," I said, leaning against one of the massive pillars populating the lobby. "You are probably right about that."

Bobby lit a cigarette and relaxed as I did. "Look at 'em. Boy, they must be a bunch of dumb dodos to take all that stuff in. They're asking for volunteers."

It was about then the man who had been holding the others' rapt attention noticed the two of us lounging around. He walked over to us, leaving the others standing alone.

"My name's Ritter," he said as he extended his hand.

"Wiley," I answered, looking him over with some disgust. I finally offered my hand.

"And you?" he asked, looking at Bobby.

"Horton," said Bobby making no effort to move.

"Well, Wiley and Horton, won't you fella's join us? I was just telling the new boys some things they need to know. I'm looking for some skilled people for some choice assignments."

"Naw. I'll tell you something, fella," I bravely replied. "If you can shoot these guys a line of bull, it's okay by me, but I just don't go in for that 'ole stuff."

"Yeah," chimed in Bobby, taking a deep draw on his cigarette and blowing the smoke toward Ritter's face. "I may be kinda' new here, but I'm not dumb enough to fall for this stuff of just letting anybody tell me what to do. Go peddle your papers somewhere else. I'll find out what I need to know from someone in authority."

A deep red flush shot across Ritter's face until it looked like he was ready to explode. He was about my size, so I really wasn't too worried if he exploded. Besides, I had already decided I didn't like him. I smiled at him. "Go get yourself a commission and drop back around."

Bobby laughed. Ritter drew a deep breath and began screaming. "God damn it! Where do you think I got these three stripes? Off a blasted zebra? Get over there in that front line before I throw ya'll so far back in the brig, they'll have to shoot beans to you with a bean shooter. In case you didn't know it, these three stripes stand for Petty Officer, First Class, and I'm in charge of Company P-1, which you two blasted dumb imbeciles have been assigned to!"

We set a new record for a fifteen-yard dash, and within a couple seconds were standing at attention in the front line. What followed can only be described as ten minutes of the most vile and contemptible sailor's cussing either of us had ever heard. And there was little doubt to whom it was directed. If we were everything we were called, and Ritter practically had us believing all of it, we couldn't pass an I.Q. test to operate a nickel telephone, and Bluebeard was an angel by comparison.

"Damn," I thought. "It's not just the ones in khaki I have to worry about! I have to listen to all of these guys with the chicken tracks on their arms."

"Now, if it's all right with Mr. Wiley and Mr. Horton, we'll continue our discussion," Ritter finally said, calming down slightly. "And if it's not all right with them, we'll continue without them—permanently!"

Actually, it was quite all right with both of us for him to continue, so we just stood there and didn't say anything, which we figured was the smart thing to do.

Another guy with one stripe on his sleeve walked up with a bundle of mail, and Ritter began calling names and distributing it. I wasn't expecting any because I didn't think I had been gone long enough. Besides, no one knew my address—not even me.

It seemed like every other name was Doll. "He must be some sort of business man, to get all that mail," I naively mused to the fellow next to me. When he stepped forward, however, I saw he was just a kid like me—tall with a dark complexion, black hair, and a G.I. haircut. He had a clean-cut look about him that made him a nice looking kid.

At that time, everyone in the service was divided into two simple classes: kids and men. It wasn't so much the age that distinguished boys from grown men. To be honest, at the time I didn't know exactly what it was, but the moment you saw someone in uniform, you could just tell. I wondered how long it would be before I was recognized as a man.

After mail was distributed, Ritter dismissed us, though not without shooting a few hard looks in our direction. We went back to Annex II, which in English was the second floor of the southwest wing. The guy in charge of our quarters was the Master-at-Arms. He assigned everyone to his bunk, and Bobby and I bunked together. The bunks were two high, one right on top of the other. The Master-at-Arms gave us a manuscript containing things not to do.

"Boy," I thought, "they didn't overlook anything. If you breathed too hard, there was a rule to govern it, and all the Master-at-Arms could say was "extra duty" and "brig." He sounded like a foreigner who only knew those three words.

"His mother was probably scared by a broken record before he was born," Bobby commented.

I laughed. "I don't believe he was born. He was probably issued."

I slept like a log that night, at least until the middle of it, when all hell broke loose. Some idiot started blowing "The Charge of the Light Brigade" in a bugle right in my ear, or so it sounded. The Master-at-Arms ran through the annex yelling at the top of his lungs. "Hit the deck, you boots! Reveille! What do you think this is? A pleasure cruise? Hit the deck, I said!"

I didn't exactly know where the deck was, or what I was supposed to hit it with, but I jumped out of bed and fell to the floor, edging my way under the bed, thinking that Hitler had decided to invade America before I finished my training! I peeped out in time to see Bobby cautiously peeping over the edge of his bunk.

"What happened?" he asked. "Didn't the admiral like his coffee?"

Before I could answer, the Master-at-Arms stuck his head back in the door and yelled so loud I thought the walls were going to move back six inches.

"I thought I told you sleepy heads to hit the deck! I didn't say lay on it, either! What's your name?" he howled while peering down at me.

"W-W-iley." I could barely get the word out of my mouth I was so nervous. I stood there, trembling and wishing it was Smeistmueller or anything other than Wiley.

A smile crossed his face. "Well, now isn't that nice," he answered, turning to look at Bobby, who was trying to crawl back under his blanket. "And yours must be Horton!" A large area of Bobby's southernmost extremity remained exposed. The officer was holding a broom in his hand. Just as was drawing back to let it fly, Bobby straightened up.

"Mr. Ritter told me we had two distinguished guests," said the officer, lowering the broom. "In fact, we had a long talk about you two. I'm sorry if I shouted too loud for you, but some of the other boys had to be awakened."

"Oh, that's all right," answered Bobby.

"Say, what time is breakfast?" I asked.

"The dining hall will be open pretty soon, but first I wish you boys would drop down to the office for a few minutes. I may need your help on a couple of things."

"Sure, be glad to," I replied, now fully awake.

Bobby and I got up and followed the M.A. down to his office. He went inside and came out with two mops and two pails.

"Now men, there's sixty rooms on this floor. I want them and all of the halls so clean the Captain can eat his chow right off the floor." He grinned and bowed politely before shoving the mops and pails at us.

I was about to ask him again about breakfast, but thought better of it. I shot a look at Bobby, we both shook our heads in disgust, and began vigorously swabbing the deck.

As we worked, the M.A. walked up and down the hall, looking into different rooms. He stopped outside the room we were working in and walked in the door on the far side of the hall. A heavy thud hit on the floor and a bullish voice bellowed out, "Hit the deck you horizontal genius! What are you doing, dreaming about all those letters you got yesterday? Now get down here and join these other two playboys across the hall swabbing this place up." The M.A. strode out of the room and down the hall, muttering something about "stupidity in the making."

A few second later the kid named Doll, who had already picked up the nickname "Baby Doll," walked across the hall and into our room dressed only in his B.V.D.s, much the same as we were. Without a word, he picked up a mop and started cleaning the floor.

"Does this happen every morning?" I finally asked.

"He doesn't miss a one," answered Doll. "This is my fourth morning here, and I've had extra duty every day."

"I can see that we're all going to be popular."

"It's too bad when they learn your name because they stay on you all the time," Doll continued. "Say, are you fella's from Texas?"

Bobby answered, "Yeah. Where are you from?"

"I'm from Jacksonville, Florida, just about thirty miles away and I'm the home sickest guy in this place. I'd sure rather be a thousand miles away like you."

I began to think how nice it would have been to go to boot camp just thirty miles from home, like Waco, for instance. "It's not so bad," I replied. "We'll all get boot leave in about six weeks, when we finish boot camp.

Doll looked up from his mop and grinned. "Yeah, they told me the same thing at the recruiting office, but they quit giving boot leave about six months ago. The rumor is that we're heading for landing barge school, either in North Carolina or New Orleans."

"Landing Barge School!" exclaimed Bobby. "You mean like the ones that landed the Marines on Guadalcanal?"

"Yeah, that's what they say, but I'm gonna' put in for some Captain of the Port or patrol boat duty here in Florida," said Doll.

I remembered seeing the newsreels of the landing on Guadalcanal. It looked exciting all right, but they promised me at the recruiting office I could get in the C.G. Air Patrol, or on a sub-chaser—or practically anything that I wanted, just by asking for it. I sighed and leaned on my mop handle. "Guess I'll put in for the Air Corps." Bobby nodded his assent.

About that time we heard a familiar roar behind us, which practically scared us out of our remaining wits. "I thought I told you half-witted dreamers to swab this deck! Get busy! You want to get in the Air Corps? How nice," added the M. A. sweetly, his voice dripping with sarcasm. "I'll write Jimmy Doolittle tonight and ask him if he can use you." I was about to thank him for his consideration, but didn't get a chance. "Listen, you air-minded buzz boys, if you don't get busy, the closest you'll ever get to flying is when I boot you out this window! For your information, this company leaves as a unit for the same place and you'll find out where it is when you get there, even though I could make some good suggestions."

I began scrubbing for all I was worth, wondering why the military always had to be so secret about this stuff. No matter where they were going to send us, I just wanted to get through these next few weeks of boot camp. It was crystal clear already I wasn't going to like it, but I still clung to the hope we would get boot leave and a trip home in my uniform. That visit, I knew, would be the greatest moment of my life.

The next few weeks in that beautiful Florida sunshine weren't what I would recommend to a fun-seeking tourist. It was late to bed and early to rise, each day consumed with marching and drilling. Millions of guys went through boot camp. Most survived the experience. Thanks to Ritter, I discovered I was dumbest creature ever created. He told me that repeatedly. Boy, did he enjoy yelling out, "Wiley and Horton!" You never heard one name without the other, so that soon it sounded like a single name.

The five of us who left Dallas together became profound friends during our boot camp experience. Whenever possible, we made our six-hour liberties on Saturday afternoon together. We admitted Doll to the clique, but his mother and girlfriend came down to see him every time we got liberty. He still received his two letters daily from his girl during the week and everyone kidded him constantly about her. We also teased him about his "Baby Doll" nickname, but he was good-natured kid and it didn't faze him.

After two weeks in boot camp, I still didn't see a lot of glory coming my way. That would change, I thought, after I left boot camp. At least I hoped so. Once I got into the Coast Guard Air Corps and start flying submarine patrol and rescue work, there would be glory enough all around.

We all expected boot camp to be hard, and we were not disappointed. I could hardly wait until my six weeks was over so I could get home on boot leave. I clung to the thin reed of hope that the stories were wrong about boot leave. Everyone always got boot leave, right?

One day I was so deep in a daydream about leave that I didn't notice Ritter pause in his demonstration of the thirty-two sailor knots and edge his way over to me while everyone else watched.

"Wiley!" Ritter bellowed about one foot from my face. "Misery in the making, where the hell do you think you are? Out in the middle of a cotton field in Itasca, Texas?"

Everyone snickered as I snapped to attention. "No sir!" I knew that anything else I said would be wrong, so I dummied up. I was a slow learner, but I was learning.

Ritter strutted around me with his hands on his hips. He jammed his face right in front of mine so close I could actually feel the body heat coming from his enraged features. "So help me God, you and that friend of yours, Horton, are the sorriest excuses for mankind I have ever seen!" The veins bulged on his forehead as he screamed at me. He stuck out his hand and shoved the hemp rope at me. "Take this line and tie me these knots as I call them out!"

I nodded my assent and took the hemp rope from him. My mouth felt like it was full of dust.

"Square knot!" shouted Ritter.

I searched my mind back to my Boy Scout days and somehow managed to tied a perfect square knot. Ritter stepped backward in surprise began gathering himself and narrowing his gaze. He would go the whole distance with this tall, gangly upstart.

"Bowline on the bite!" he snapped.

I looked up at the hemp rope we were supposed to call a line and knew I was licked. The Boy Scouts had not gone that far. It was then I noticed a rough looking Bos'n Mate second-class standing over on the side. As I watched, he produced a short piece of line and unnoticed by anyone except me, began tying the complicated bowline on the bite. I gulped, looked into Ritter's glaring eyes, and began following the Bos'n Mate's every move until I held out a perfect sailor's knot. The bowline on the bite would not slip, but equally important, once the tension was released it took no effort to untie it. Ritter scowled in disgust, surprised I had tied the knot and completely unaware that I had been helped. He grabbed the line and tested it, glared at me as if he could actually stare me to death, and then turned and stomped his way to the front of the group.

"All right men, I have a special treat for you today. See this block?" he said, nodding around the room and waving his arm at the same time. "We're going to march to the end, do an about face, and then march to the other end, do an about face, and continue until I tell you to stop. And get this: we're going to do it double time with full packs and rifles. Get your gear!"

We gathered up our equipment and fell in. "All right, forward! March! Come on. Double time! Come on!"

Ritter fell out as the platoon went running to the end of the block. He positioned himself in the middle of the block and continued yelling out the cadence. After four or five times many of the men were beginning to show fatigue, but Ritter kept up the ferocious pace bellowing, "Come on you soft-bellied plow boys! I said double time. Pick it up!"

As we huffed and puffed our way back across the room, Bill broke the silence first. "That S.O.B. is trying to run us down."

"You think?" answered John Ligon sarcastically. "He ain't gonna run me down. I can run all night if he wants to."

"So can I," I replied. A determined Bobby joined in with an "Aye!"

The pace continued until men began dropping out. Some were exhausted, but others stopped because it seemed like a smart and easy way to stop the punishment. Several minutes passed until Doll, John, Lynn, Bill, Bobby, and I were the only six men left. Up and down the block we double-timed up and down, and all the while Ritter kept up the mad cadence.

"Who's running with these men?" The raw-boned, red-headed Bos'n's Mate had yelled the question out to Ritter.

Ritter shot him an angry look. "This is my business, Thornton."

"Well, some of these men who have fallen out may need medical attention."

Ritter, who may have been looking for a way out of his decision, took it. "All right men, halt! At ease. Dismissed."

As we walked back to the barracks, the red-headed Bos'n's Mate trotted up alongside us. "I'm Tex Thornton." He looked at John and me and added, "That was a pretty good exhibition of endurance you guys put on. How much longer could you have gone?"

"Well, I'll tell you," answered John, who was barely breathing hard. "I had a lot left and if that son of a bitch would run with me right now, I'd run him into the ground."

"Look, we're having a track meet in a couple of weeks. How would you two like to run on our mile relay team?"

"All right," said John.

"Okay by me," I piped in.

"Well, we're going to practice a little each day. See you tomorrow."

Thus began my friendship with Tex that lasted throughout the war. Company P-1 took all the honors at the academy-wide track meet. I ran the third leg in the mile relay and gave John a commanding lead, which he never relinquished. We finished one and two, respectively, in the quarter and half-mile.

After the races, Ritter came up to me. "Good going, boy." He shook his head and snickered. "Frankly, I didn't think you had it in you."

From that day on he never picked on Bobby or me again. It was a turning point. The victory, while mine, was not really me over Ritter, but me over an attitude and it belonged to Ritter, whose job was to make men out of a bunch of school kids in six short weeks. The last four weeks of boot camp were almost enjoyable compared to the first two.

We learned how to march, use gas masks, take a Springfield '03 rifle apart, row boats, and even went out on a cutter on submarine patrol and fired "tin cans" (depth charges). We learned how to identify our own and the enemy's aircraft and ships from sellouts, shown in split-second glimpses. We learned how to run through obstacle courses and we learned semaphore and Morse code.

Finally, after a long six weeks, boot camp training ended and we awaited orders. The last glimmer of hopes for boot leave had long ago dimmed. We knew we were going directly to the next phase, whatever that was. Instead of being distributed to many different locations, as we suspected might be the case, we learned were all going—wherever we were going—as a group, as if there was a real shortage somewhere. Rumor had it that the last four companies had gone to Landing Craft School in groups, and that company P-1 would do the same. As weak compensation, probably for not getting boot leave, we received a special liberty. We were plenty excited because this was not the daylight type of liberty, either. We could stay out all night if we wanted to—which was something young men really wanted to hear. The only requirement was that we had to be back at 0800 the next morning.

The little town of St. Augustine, Florida, was always crowded on weekends and especially for the six hours we had been getting on Saturday afternoons. Usually we hung out at local bars or at the beach. This time, however it was Thursday afternoon.

You cannot remove girls from a teenager's mind. Throughout boot camp we all listened (and shared) the adventures, lies, and stories young men routinely tell when they are separated from the opposite sex. Of course, we had no time to make contact of any kind with girls during our six weeks of training, so Bob and I took our liberty together with nothing in mind except the desire to meet some nice girls.

Everything seemed quiet that Thursday. We spent most of the afternoon at the Blue Moon, a little bar down on the beach, drinking beer (or at least trying to, since neither of us had ever really learned how to drink).

"You know," said Bobby. "I sure would like to see Reba" (his latest girl before leaving). "She sure was a cute little girl and boy how I need some loving. That last night we were together, we parked out at the lake and were in the backseat of my car. Reba put her feet up on the back of the front seat and slid her dress back down around her waist and said, 'Honey, take a good look at the most beautiful set of legs in the world and don't forget what they look like.'" Bobby sighed loudly and shook his head. "Forget, Hell! I see those legs in front of my eyes every time I march a step or tie a knot. And that cute little face with her impish smile." He looked at his beer and then shouted, "Hey, Mac! Let's have another one of those Ballintines!" Bobby gestured with his two fingers to the waitress we all called Mac.

"Maybe we're giving up too easy, Bob," I replied. "There ought to be two nice looking girls in this town somewhere. Let's go out and give it a try."

"Well, we could take five bucks and go over to Jacksonville, like Thurman and some of those other guys did, but I'm not ready for that. I want to talk and dance. I want to meet someone that will enjoy being with me. You know what I mean?"

I knew what he meant and agreed as I slipped the waitress a bill and asked, "Mac, tell me what's wrong with the women situation around here. Too many sailors?"

"Sailors? Hell no!" she replied. "Several years ago this place was loaded with whores and pick-ups. The sailors are fine, but those damned officers came in here and married 'em all!"

I waived the change on that as she walked back to the bar, mumbling something about officers ruining the country. We pretended to be finishing our beers, but neither of us did. We just weren't drinkers. When we left, each bottle was nearly full.

"Take a last look at sunshine, Ken. It may be snowing where we go tomorrow."

"Rain, sleet or snow, take a good look up ahead," I answered. "Did you ever see the sun shine so brightly?" I didn't need to point. Bobby focused his eyes on the same thing that had caught my attention. Up ahead were two girls in shorts that would do justice to Varga or Petty for their Esquire models. Bob let out a long low whistle, shoved his hat back on his head, and said, "Boy, this is it. Come on."

We began to close the gap behind them until they reached an intersection and had to stop. While waiting for the light to change both girls look around, acted surprised when they saw us, and quickly turned their eyes away. It was my turn to whistle now, not loud or flirty, but low and appreciative. One of the girls turned her head around and chided me, "Stop that silly whistling."

"Yes, and come on up here," the other quickly added.

We made it in three strides. The light changed and we all walked across the intersection together. The girls were cousins named Jane and Evelyn. They had been swimming and were on their way home.

"You don't have to go yet, do you?" Bob pleaded.

"Let's all go to the Coral Reef," I suggested, knowing the bar had a band and good dancing. "They've got a good orchestra and we have eight more hours."

"That sounds like a good idea," Bob added in an effort to keep the conversation on the right track.

"Look boys, mother's expecting us home and anyway, I don't think she'd like it much if we went out there. We're really sorry, but we have to go home. Maybe ya'll can come over some Sunday."

Bobby shook his head. "We're leaving in the morning. We've got eight hours left, and that's it. Come on, let's have some fun," he pleaded.

"I'm sorry, but Evelyn's mother is expecting us home soon. We've gotta' go. Bye and good luck," answered Jane.

With that, the girls turned and walked away, leaving a couple of very disheartened sailors in their wake. We watched the girls take about ten steps before Evelyn stopped, caught Jane's arm, and whispered something. Jane nodded her head in agreement and the pair turned and walked back to us.

"Look," Jane began, "Now I know it won't be as much fun as the Coral Reef, but you can walk home with us if ya'll want to." There wasn't one bit of argument over that. I took Jane's hand and started walking on clouds, right behind Bob and Evelyn.

"Were you a cowboy in Texas?" she asked after learning where I was from. "Nearly everyone I meet from Texas lives on a big ranch and rides horses all of the time."

"I'm afraid you wouldn't believe it, but somebody's been kidding you, Jane. Texas is almost as civilized as Florida. Why, we've even got trolley cars in Dallas."

When we reached their home, Evelyn introduced us to her mother and father. They were nice people and immediately made us feel at home. I thought about the times my older brothers had brought their friends from other states home with them, and how my mother and father took them in and treated them like family. I had almost forgotten how nice a family could be. Until that moment, I didn't realize how much I missed families.

Evelyn's parents asked us where we were from, all about our own families, how we liked the service, and all in all made us feel at home. The feeling was almost as good as being there with the girls.

After about thirty minutes, her mother dragged her father away, saying she knew young people could have more fun by themselves. Jane put on a stack of records and we walked out into the backyard. The yard looked like a sunken garden in heaven to a young guy like me. There were palm trees, perfectly manicured beautiful flowers, and a goldfish pool with lily pads floating on it. Under the largest tree was a swing with cushions. All of this under a full Florida moon.

We danced, sat, and talked. Jane was a freshman in college and had to go back next month. How I envied all the boys who would be dating her. That, however, was next month. Tonight was all mine! I was sitting in a movie setting with the most beautiful heroine I had ever seen.

"I heard you say you will be leaving tomorrow," she said suddenly. "We'll never get a chance to know each other better and I want you to know why I was reluctant to ask you home. I have dated two other boys from the Training Center. I liked them both, but we never had a chance to see if it could be love, yet I was devastated when they left. I haven't gone with any other boys from the base since. I guess I'm afraid to let myself care too much for anything so temporary. I always thought I would like to play the field, but I don't. I want something special. Am I terrible?"

"If you're terrible, then we both are," I replied, not sure exactly what to say back to her. "Sure we make a lot of noise about a girl in every port, but deep down we all want someone special. We want a reason for living."

"Then don't look at me as Jane," she answered. "I'm that someone special for tonight. Maybe, you will remember this night one night when you're on the other side of the world and you're lonely."

When it was finally time to leave, the girls drove us back to the base in Evelyn's dad's car.

"This is my address at school. Write me," Jane urged.

She kissed me long and passionately as we got out of the car. I think that both of us knew it was just for tonight, and we were happy with that. This was the mood of the times, when young men were on the move, never knowing where they would be tomorrow and girls understood. We lived for the day.

"I sure hate to leave tomorrow," Bobby said as we hit the sack. "I kinda' like it here."

First thing in the morning, Bob and I read a new notice on the bulletin board: "Company P-1 will muster on the quarterdeck, Friday 1530 p.m. with all gear packed. Uniform of the day for travel will be dress blues."

"Dress blues, that means somewhere up north," I thought out loud. Of course, everyone had the latest "scoop" right from the captain and it ranged all the way from Ice Boat duty in Alaska to a trick to fool the fifth columnists and send us to the Panama Canal. We boarded a train and headed north across Georgia and the Carolinas.

We had three chair cars, which looked like the original Tom Thumb. "This is sure different from the Pullman we rode from Texas," I thought to myself.

After two days with little or no sleep, we arrived in Wilmington, North Carolina. From there they loaded us into trucks and hauled us to Court House Bay, Camp Lejeune, North Carolina.

By this time, we knew we were at Landing Barge (or Landing Craft) school.

Chapter 5

# Guys and Gals and Games

The Marines did not welcome us with open arms. Service rivalry, much more apparent in the States than overseas, was at its peak in Camp Lejeune. The North Carolina base was one of the largest Marine facilities in the United States. There were only about 500 Coast Guard men at Court House Bay to train in landing craft. Marines were also trained with the landing craft. "Swabbies and "Leathernecks" worked together for the first time, and although more than words were exchanged, eventually we all learned to appreciate each other.

I got my first glimpse of the landing barges the afternoon we arrived when they came back in from training at the beach. The L.C.V. (Landing Craft Vehicle) was 36 feet long and resembled a huge cracker box on a speedboat bottom. It had a steel ramp in front that could be lowered to let troops and vehicles spill out onto the beach. The craft had a crew of four men: a Cox'n (the driver of the boat), a mechanic called "motor-mac," and two bowmen or seamen to help tie the boat up, lower and raise the ramp, and provide other needed assistance. The bowmen were also available to man the 30-caliber machine guns in two gun pits. On the L.C.V. models, the Cox'n stood up on the stern of the boat in order to see over the ramp. The steering wheel was up on the rear side of a small wooden compartment, like a minister's pulpit. Except for the steel ramp in front, the boats were made entirely of plywood.

Someone told us our boats would be L.C.V.P.'s. In this model, the Cox'n was down inside the boat, which had steel plating on the sides that helped protect everyone aboard. The larger boats, L.C.M. (Landing Craft Mechanized, called "Tank Lighters") were made of steel. Each had two engines and the Cox'n was enclosed in a steel compartment. These boats were 50 feet long and could carry a Sherman tank. It also had a compartment below deck for the "motor-mac," and carried two 50-caliber machine guns.

The next morning we went out in the boats and our training began. There was a trick to landing on a beach correctly. The Cox'n put the nose on the back of a breaker and rammed the boat in as hard as he could. During the approach and once on the beach, the boat had to be kept straight while waves pounded it from the sides and back. A sideways sweep would broach the boat and push it sideways onto the landing zone.

I loved every minute of it this training. Boot camp and all its negatives quickly faded away. This stuff was exciting, and I threw myself into it wholeheartedly. An immediate attachment flooded through me. I quickly understood the old saying, "The sea gets in your blood."

Court House Bay was the base at Camp Lejeune, North Carolina, where the Landing Craft School was located. Being on a Marine base and in a definite minority, it is not hard to understand why the U.S. Coast Guard Amphibious Forces did not have top priority in anything. The training consumed half a day in the classroom and half a day out in the boats. The boats were the famous "Higgins" boats, designed to carry troops from oceangoing transport ships to a dry landing on enemy beaches. One ship could land more than 1,000 men and their equipment on an enemy beach within minutes.

We studied amphibious tactics, seamanship, communications, and armory. I had always been an average student, pulling down more Cs than As or Bs. The exceptions were in subjects like vocational agriculture, history, and spelling, in which I excelled. Landing craft school fit this category. I scored in the high 90s across the board. This hands-on part of the training in boat handling was a fierce competition. One out of every three men made the cut for the position of Cox'n (the driver and commander of the boat). The

The Cox'n is trying to hold the boat in, with the bowman helping by holding the cargo net during a mercilessly high sea.

other two became seamen. A separate competition for "motor mac," or mechanics, completed the four-man crew.

A deeper explanation of these boats is in order. The bottom of each boat was designed so the front could be driven right up to the beach. The skag was a heavy runner that ran completely under the screw in the rear of the boat. The last foot of the skag was the rudder itself. These LCV's (Landing Craft Vehicles) carried either troops or small vehicles. A steel ramp in the front was lowered (dropped when unlatched) to let the troops run out on dry land. The ramp was hand-cranked back into position. The Cox'n stood on the stern of the boat to drive it. Our superiors told us these boats had been used in Guadalcanal, New Guinea, North Africa, and many other U.S. invasions.

A similar boat had a shovelnose front without a ramp and carried only personnel (used mostly for control boats). These were called LCPs (Landing Craft Personnel). The position of the Cox'n in this boat was down at the front end. All of these landing craft had a single Hall Scott gasoline engine. The third boat of the fleet was the twin engine LCT, or LCM, the famous Tank Lighter, which could carry a Sherman Tank.

The old salts who taught us to handle these boats had been around for a long time. They taught us how to pull the boat alongside a ship and hold it in position in the rough waters while troops climbed down cargo nets, sometimes while heavy equipment was being lowered into the boat. They taught us how to drive the boat up on the beach and hold it straight in rough seas while troops ran out from it. They showed us very quickly the dangers of letting the boat broach sideways on the beach. Being stuck as a sitting duck on an enemy beach under heavy fire was not a nice thought. They taught us to get off the beach and away as quickly as possible, and that a loaded boat always had priority over an empty one.

We also learned how to use, dismantle, and reconfigure our machine guns, rifles, and small arms. A Marine Guadalcanal veteran taught us firearms. He showed us how to fire, disassemble, and reassemble our 30- and 50-caliber machine guns, rifles (Springfields, carbines, and M-1s), and the .45 pistol. He even taught us the Lewis Machine Gun and the Japanese .25 caliber rifle. As our Marine instructor put it, "You never know what situation you might be in, and you grab the nearest thing to you. I killed two Japs on Guadalcanal with their own gun when my Lewis jammed."

We practiced maneuvering and formations for a beach assault. The boats move in waves, timed so that one wave of boats unload and back off the beach while another wave comes in to shore. Each wave had a wave leader, a lead boat everyone keyed on. We learned

Morse code and semaphore to communicate during radio silence. Each day we faced a new challenge and mastered a new password.

"Your life and everyone in your boat may depend on answering with the correct password," barked our instructor over and over, drilling the idea into our collective heads. We all later learned the hard way just how right he was. To pass the class, we only had to recognize and send five words a minute, although he wanted to see ten or more. I was determined and reached ten.

After seven weeks of rigid training, Charles Doll and I were selected as boat Cox'ns. Two others, John Ligon and Lynn Britton, also made Cox'n. Billy Miller was picked as "Motor Mac." All six of us had made it. It was a privilege to serve with five of my closest friends. It was now late fall 1943. German submarines had been mauling shipping off the American east coast since January of 1942. Several ships rested on the bottom just off Moorehead City, North Carolina, the closest town to Camp Lejeune. The war was never far from our minds.

Liberty, which was limited to a few hours on Saturday nights, was finally granted to our company. The Marines, of course, had much more generous passes that usually extended over the whole weekend. When the first pass was issued, three of us went to Moorehead City. About 9:00 p.m. that evening, military buses and trucks roared down the streets of Moorehead City with horns blasting and loud speakers calling for all military personnel to "fall in." MPs and SPs ran up and down telling all military personnel to get aboard one of the buses or trucks to meet an emergency situation. Leave was cancelled. We had no choice in the matter, and within a few minutes were sitting on a bus heading back to Camp Lejeune. It was easy to recognize military personnel during World War II, since we were required to wear our uniforms at all times. We were not allowed to wear any civilian clothing.

Back at Camp Lejeune, we organized into platoons and everyone was issued a weapon and live ammunition. A chief was in charge of several of our platoons. "Men," he began. "I don't know much about this myself, but there are ten unidentified ships heading for the North Carolina coast and we have been rounded up to defend the coast. Does everyone have a rifle and plenty of ammunition?"

This was no drill! For several seconds all you could hear was the clicking and rattling noises as we loaded our weapons. One young man from Brooklyn had particular difficulty with his M-1. He apparently had not paid much attention during training.

"What is your name, sailor?"

"Morganthau, sir," he replied.

"I want you to load that piece and unload it," ordered the chief.

Morganthau fumbled his way through the loading process until he got a bullet into the breach and held the gun in a level position with the barrel aimed at the rank of men in front of him.

"Now, unload it," commanded the chief. Morganthau just looked at him. "Don't you know how to unload your rifle?" the chief asked in amazement.

"Yes, sir," stuttered Morganthau as he squeezed the trigger of the M-1. The explosion sounded like a charge of dynamite. The bullet went between the two men directly in front of him, barely missed the chief, and passed through three rows of troops without hitting anyone. I had spent the last many weeks listening every day to language I didn't know existed. Swearing was common among sailors of every nation. But the words and expressions that exploded from the chief's lips comprised an entirely new realm of communication.

After picking himself off the ground, the chief lunged at Morganthau, who looked as if he expected a reward for doing the right thing. As the chief dove through the air, Morganthau realized what was going on, dropped his rifle, and began running for his life. The butt of the cocked M-1 struck the tarmac and discharged a second time, this time straight up into the air. By this time, however, everyone was scrambling for cover. Morganthau was last seen scampering around the armory and heading for the barracks with the chief in hot pursuit.

An NCO named O'Neal finally got everyone back in formation. We were loaded on trucks and driven toward the coast. Several lines of defense were set up along the coast, and we had orders to shoot anything that didn't identify itself as friendly. During the night, shots rang out when someone spotted an "unfriendly" shadow; otherwise, the night passed uneventfully. About 4:00 a.m., the "all-clear" was sounded and we were transported back to our barracks. As it turned out, the ships were friendly. The great North Carolina Coast Invasion was over before it began. Cooks, yeomen, machinists, signal corpsmen, clerks of all kinds, and many more who didn't know anything about firearms, mobilized to defend the coast. I never did learn the full truth about this little episode, but our superiors would never have issued live ammunition to such an unorganized group of men unless someone really believed an enemy invasion was underway.

My company received a 48-hour pass the weekend before graduation. It was the most time off any of us had ever had, but there was nowhere to go. It was impossible to go home, and I didn't know anyone else within range of a two-day pass. Doll, Blaine Collins, and I went to the bus station in Moorehead City and checked out the bus routes.

"How long does it take to get to Charlotte?" asked Doll.

"Six hours," answered the ticket agent.

We purchased tickets to Charlotte and boarded a bus. A debate arose every time we approached and passed through a town: should we get off here or keep going? When we hit Fayetteville, Blaine decided it was time to debark. With this important decision behind us, we three sailors in blue climbed off the bus. As the smoky machine pulled out to complete the trip to Charlotte, we noticed that everyone around us was in khaki. We walked along the street trying to act cool, but we stuck out like a sore thumb because all around us were thousands of soldiers. There was not another sailor in sight. One of the largest Army training centers in North Carolina was located at Fayetteville. The 82nd Airborne trained there.

Even though sailors were an oddity in this town, and we were expecting the worst, everyone was very friendly to us. We went into a restaurant and sat down. What a great feeling it was to sit at a table adorned with a tablecloth! I ordered a breaded veal cutlet and large-cut French fries. It was the best meal I had eaten in months. Individually-prepared food items, like eggs and steaks, are a real luxury to a guy in the service.

The restaurant had three waitresses. The first was cute and friendly. The second was pretty and shy, but had a wedding band on her finger. The third waitress, Helen, was older than the other two and appeared to be in charge. She walked to our table and smiled.

"Where are you boys from?" she asked. "Do you have a place to stay for the night?"

"Camp Lejeune," answered Doll. "We don't have a place yet, but we'll look for a room later."

"I recommend Travers just around the corner," she answered. "It's a clean little hotel who are nice to service people. In fact, my aunt owns it and if you want to stay, I'll call her now and arrange a room for you." We all agreed. Helen placed the call and came back a few minutes later. "You're all set up. Don't forget that the U.S.O. is having a dance tonight."

The cute waitress was named Betty. "Are you going to the U.S.O. dance?" I asked when she walked by our table and caught my eye.

"I'm going to meet my boyfriend and go about nine," she answered. "Why don't you come too? I know a lot of girls who will be there."

"Well, won't we look funny? Three sailors and a hundred soldiers?" asked Doll.

"My girlfriends all want to go with sailors, everyone is invited," she answered. "Ya'll can come with us. Are you staying at Travers?"

"Yes," I answered.

"Okay. When Bill picks me up, we will come by and get you. You can ride with us."

Sure enough, about 9:15 p.m. there was a knock on the door. I opened it to see a young sergeant with red hair and freckles.

"I'm Bill," he said. "Are you fellas ready to go?"

The U.S.O was not that far away. Bill and Betty took us in and introduced us around to everyone. Soon we were dancing and having a great time. I was dancing with one of Betty's friends when I saw the third waitress, the pretty and shy one with the wedding band on her finger, walk in alone. When the song ended I excused myself and walked up to her. "Care to dance?" I asked.

She looked me over and nodded. "Sure."

"You know, I don't even know your name," I said.

"My name is Julie Reynolds."

"I'm Ken Wiley," I replied as we began to dance.

"I know," she replied, "and you're from Texas. Are all Texans tall like you?"

"No, just one out of each litter. I am the only one in my family over six feet tall. How about you, Julie? Where's your husband?"

"I wish I knew," she said with a sigh. "The last letter I got from him was censored so badly that it looked like confetti. Jack shipped out in April from New York. I just know he is somewhere in England getting ready for who knows what."

"You miss him a lot, I bet," I inquired, testing the waters.

Julie looked at me as if it were for the first time. Tears formed in her eyes. "Yes, I miss him so much that I can hardly stand it. I didn't think I would tell you that, but I hope you understand. I do love Jack. We only had one weekend together after we were married before he had to leave. It is different being married when you are all alone. Do you understand what I'm saying?"

She seemed to move closer to me as she spoke and became softer in my arms. I understood. Julie was lonely, but how lonely I didn't yet know. Blaine cut in and I didn't get a chance to answer her directly. The dance went on.

A girl named Mary Beth kept coming my way and dancing with me. We laughed and talked. Her friend Vicki had become Doll's most frequent partner, while Blaine was spending most of his time with Helen, the older waitress from the restaurant. About midnight, Mary Beth's parents came for her and Vicki. Blaine and Helen had disappeared. Doll and I were talking to Bill and Betty. "We're getting ready to leave. The dance will be over in half an hour. Can we drop you fellas off?" asked Bill.

"No," Doll replied. "Let's walk back, OK, Ken? What do you say?"

It sounded like a good idea to me, so we thanked Bill and Betty, said a few other goodbyes, and walked outside. Julie standing at the corner. "Hey, Julie wait!" I shouted. She stopped and I walked over to her. "Can I walk you home?"

For a moment she looked undecided. "Okay," she finally answered slowly. "But let's hurry away from here. I don't want anyone to see me. They might get the wrong idea."

It was a beautiful November night, just cold enough to make a sweater feel good. For the first time I became aware of just how beautiful Julie was. "Do you live alone?" I asked.

"No, I live with my parents and little brother."

"Tell me about yourself."

"Not much to tell," she answered as we walked. "Fayetteville is my home. I've lived here all of my life. I graduated from high school in June of 1942. Cheerleader, pep squad, and all of that. My dad is a dentist. My mom works for the Army. I've just never been much of anywhere except Fayetteville."

"Do you want to travel?" I asked.

"Oh, yes. I wish I were a man. I'd join anything just to get to see the world. How about you?"

"I grew up in a small town in Texas. I never really left Texas until I joined up. We were in boot camp in Florida for eight weeks and then shipped to Camp Lejeune. We're leaving next week but nobody knows where. I'll probably get to Europe in time for the next big invasion."

She stopped and pulled me off the sidewalk into the shadow of some trees.

"Hold me," she said. "Please, just hold me tight." I was all for that. She kissed me long and passionately. I returned it and squeezed her up against me. I figured the corner had turned. Now, it was just a maneuver for the time and place. "Where can we go that we'll be all alone?" I asked.

"I have got to go inside," she said quickly.

My heart skipped a beat. "Oh, don't go now!" I stammered. "How far is your house?"

"That's it. We're in front of it now," she replied. "I'm sorry. I thought you understood. That's all I want. That's as much as I can do to Jack. Please, I get so lonely for a boy to just hold me. Goodnight."

Julie kissed me quickly and darted across the lawn to the front porch. She looked back once just as she opened the door. The street light illuminated her face briefly. I like to think there was a look of contentment on her face as she slipped inside. I never saw Julie again, and never learned her last name.

I walked back to the Travers. Doll was already there. Blaine was not. He came in the next morning around 8:00 a.m. and slipped into bed. Sunday was a slow moving day for all three of us. We rode the bus back late that afternoon.

On the last night at Court House Bay we had a party. The U.S.O. came out and sponsored a dance at the gymnasium, and female Marines from Cherry Point were imported for the occasion. Women in the Marine Corps were known as BAMS (many of the guys claimed the letters stood for Broad-Assed Marines). Thus far during my brief military career the women I had met were generally nice—the kind of girl you would take home to meet mom. This particular group of BAMS, however, was cut from a different cloth. By 10:00 p.m., everyone was either drunk or moving steadily in that direction. The punch was spiked until it had a higher alcohol proof than Southern Comfort, which was reported to be 100 proof. Outside the gym, knots of people were busily emptying bottles. There was every kind of liquor imaginable being passed around. The BAMS brought most of it with them. A tremendous party was going on in the dormitory.

The MPs started rounding up the girls and loading them on the buses about midnight. Half an hour later, the buses pulled out amid shouting and singing. After several hours, the loud roar of the raucous party finally calmed down to an acceptable level. I wandered back to the dormitory. The lights were out and I made my way to my bunk. Someone was in it. "Hey, Buddy! That's my bunk!" I hissed.

"Shut your ass up," replied a feminine voice. "Come to bed before you wake everyone up."

I nearly fell over! Perhaps it was the liquor. Perhaps it was just the mood I was in. Whatever it was, I slipped off my uniform as fast as I could and climbed into the bunk. She—whoever "she" was—was stark naked. "Hurry," she said. "I'm working my way to the front door."

It was a very different kind of lovemaking, fast and without much passion. When she was sure I was through, she said, "That was nice, darling. Who's in the bed next to you?"

"Blaine," I managed to say before she kissed me and crawled down to the floor and up into the next bunk where Blaine was waiting.

"Don't worry, honey," she whispered turning back toward me. "Kitty will be along in a minute. She's behind me somewhere."

About fifteen minutes later, a form appeared in the darkness.

"Hi, hon, I'm Kitty. Did Maybelle tell you I was coming? That's a good one, isn't it? Baby, I was coming!" She laughed, crawled into bed, and took over where Maybelle had left off.

"How many more of you are there?" I asked.

"Oh, honey, I don't know. Seven or eight. We are working our way through the Coast Guard."

Suddenly, the lights switched on in the dorm and two MPs, three SPs, and a Marine Captain were standing in the doorway. "Some of the girls didn't make the last bus," said the Captain. "I thought I heard some giggling. Are there any girls in the dormitory?"

There were a few muffled groans and stifled laughs, but no volunteers for a bus ride.

"Alright, men," said the Captain. "Everybody up! Inspection!"

We groaned aloud as the inspection team walked down the line pulling back covers and pulling people out of their bunks. The men slowly hit the deck and stood at something resembling attention. I looked around, but did not see a female. Still, there were many beds with strange looking lumps under the covers.

An SP prodded one of the lumps, which screamed out, "Stop it, you son-of-a-bitch!"

That response prompted the inspectors to prod lumpy covers until seven stark naked girls were also standing "at attention."

"Get dressed!" ordered the Captain.

With much exchanging of clothes and new cuss words, the girls finally dressed. A lady Lieutenant BAM arrived. She gasped when she realized what had been taking place. "What the hell are you girls doing here? You, Jill, why didn't you get on the bus?"

Jill shot back, "Why, Lieutenant, we were trying our best to get out. In fact, I was on my way to the door just now when the Captain came in. You see, Maybelle here just had to go to the bathroom and somebody turned the lights out while we were in there. On the way out, we ran into all these bunks in the dark and we were just trying our best to work our way out. Yes, ma'am, you might say, we were all working our way through here trying to get out!"

The room filled with laughter.

Jill, somehow managing to keep a straight face, continued: "We knew that you wanted us on that bus and honestly, with the help of these nice boys, we were all coming as fast as we could."

# Chapter 6

# A Touch of Salt Spray

Company P-1 shipped out the next morning. Perhaps this was the reason there were no reprisals about what took place the prior night. We traveled by train to Norfolk, Virginia, and then by bus to the naval station at Little Creek, Virginia. By the time we got there, word spread that we were going to pick up brand new boats at Little Creek. The next morning we went down to the marina and the selection process began. What a beauty these new LCVP's were. They had Gray Marine Diesel engines and the coxswain's position was down inside the boat. My boat was the No. 13. Doll was assigned to LCM-29, a Tank Lighter.

When everyone was assigned to a boat, the boat group commander, a young Second Lieutenant with a bullhorn, gave the signal to follow him, and away the boats went up the Chesapeake Bay. It was early December 1943. The boats were assigned to the USS *Cambria* (APA-36), which was anchored midway up the Chesapeake Bay. We passed the battleship USS *Texas* and several other ships that had just returned from the North African theater.

The wind was blowing and the temperature was near freezing. The choppy waters of the Chesapeake Bay can be rough even on a calm day. This day was especially bad, with waves as tall as ten feet. Within minutes, everyone in the boats was drenched to the skin. Reaching the *Cambria* did not put an end to our misery. The ship's crew had never hoisted boats aboard before, and Company P-1 had never been hoisted aboard a ship before. As the men on the *Cambria* fumbled and toyed with some of the boats, the remaining boats circled in the choppy icy waters. It took thirty-seven hours to hoist aboard all the boats. Officially, the operation was supposed to take less than one hour. The *Cambria* crew got my boat aboard after thirty-two hours. I had never been so cold and exhausted in my entire life. Once on a steady deck they whisked us below for a shower and a hot plate of spaghetti.

*Cambria* pulled into a dock at Norfolk and took aboard troops from the U.S. Army. The next day we pulled out of Norfolk and headed south. Once a course was clearly established, everyone aboard realized we were heading for the Pacific Ocean via the Panama Canal. The third day out the weather began to warm up and it was hot enough for sunbathing.

A giant sheet of water drenched us. "Damn, what the hell was that?" Bill yelled jumping to his feet. The zig-zagging *Cambria* had changed course, which turned the fine spray of water we had been tossing into the air into the solid sheet that inundated us. But this one felt good. What a difference from the icy Chesapeake water!

"The Zigzag Course." To add further protection against submarines, all of the ships in a convoy simultaneously changed course every ten or fifteen minutes. The program was like a code and changed daily.

Being a sailor aboard an ocean-going ship was the most thrilling experience I had ever known. Doing so as a Cox'n of a landing craft destined to land soldiers and Marines on enemy beaches was icing on the cake. Fortunately I never experienced seasickness, although three out of every four of the men aboard beat a steady trail to the leeward side of the vessel to let fly whatever was still in their stomachs. The "salty" cooks prepared the greasiest foods they could to add to the agony of the afflicted. After the spaghetti they fed us greasy pork chops, followed the next day by wieners and sauerkraut. The cooks encouraged the green troops to "help yourself and have all that you want." For the cooks it was well-planned entertainment. They got a kick going topside to watch and laugh as the men hung over the rails divesting the "all-you-can-eat" special.

The ship stored all of the boats on the decks in permanent boat cradles built for the purpose, except twelve of the LCVP's. Davits were used to hoist them aboard (instead of the cargo boom) and four were stowed on each side of the deck. The last four were suspended from the davits, two boats on each side, hanging outboard of the ship. My boat, No. 13, was one of these boats. That explained why we had been one of the last hoisted aboard. The *Cambria's* skipper was very unhappy about the time it took to get the boats up and stowed away. He told his crew and the boat crews that we had to get that time down to less than one hour—or else.

We had left Norfolk with a convoy of ships and destroyer escorts, but by the time we arrived at Panama, half of the ships had dropped out with some sort of trouble. For most of them, this was their maiden voyage.

Passing through the Panama Canal was an amazing experience. The *Cambria* lowered the four outboard davit boats and crews to the water because the ship and boats together were too wide for the canal locks. My boat and crew followed the ship through the canal. The raising and lowering of the water levels in the locks was exciting to watch. Traveling between the Atlantic locks and the Pacific locks was even more exciting. Left at least partially to our own devices, I sped No. 13 up and pulled away from the slow-moving *Cambria*. Midway across the isthmus we reached an island and pulled ashore. Army and Navy troops were scattered about a lazy cantina drinking

Hoisting the boats aboard. The LCVP was 36 feet long and weighed 26,000 pounds. Twelve of them were brought aboard and lowered by davits on each side of the ship. The other 18 were hoisted aboard, or lowered by giant booms (as depicted in Ken Riley's illustration). The booms had many uses and required an expert to handle them.

---

beer and playing ping-pong as if they were on vacation rather than on the way to war.

"What's this place?" I asked a young soldier who was looking our boat over while sipping a beer.

"We call it Sonova Beach," he drawled. "And if you say it slow enough, you got it right."

I laughed and looked him over. He didn't look like an everyday sailor. "You stationed here?"

"Yeah, for the last twenty months," he replied. "The brass wanted to give everyone some recreation without exposing us too much to the natives. So we have to take most of our liberties here. I haven't been to Panama City in three months." He paused for a while and finally said, "You might as well come ashore and have some beer. My name's Luke."

I hadn't really learned to drink beer yet, but I would never acknowledge that. "Well, I'd really like to, but we're on duty, Luke"

I explained, shaking his hand. "We've got to keep up with our ship."

"Aw! Come on! The ship will be hours getting through the canal," he explained. Something flickered in his eyes. "Are you guys interested in women?"

Pete the mechanic perked his ears up. "There are women here? Count me in!"

"No, not just here, but if you take me back to Panama City, I can show you one of the best cat houses in Panama," continued Luke. "You could still get to the other side ahead of your ship and no one would know the difference."

"Come on, Tex," Pete said turning to me. "Let's go have some fun. We may never get another chance."

I had never been to a cat house before, but I wasn't going to admit that, either. Lloyd, the seaman on my boat, wanted to go, too. I reluctantly agreed, we grabbed several bottles of beer, and took off. Luke provided the directions.

We went to the other side of the island and let the *Cambria* glide past before backtracking to a small settlement on the Atlantic side. We pulled into a small dock area and Luke spoke to two armed MPs. After a minute or two he motioned for us to follow and we left the military reservation, caught a "Publica" (taxi) and fish-tailed our way to a dusty roadside cantina.

I immediately noticed there were no other military personnel around, only native Panamanians and a few civilians we couldn't identify. Several girls were flirting their way from table to table. No sooner had the four of us walked in and staked out a table than one of the girls stood and initiated an intense argument with Luke. I couldn't catch all of it, but caught enough of the mixture of Spanish and English to appreciate the gist of the conversation.

"Off limits to military personnel, MPs and trouble, trouble, trouble!" she screamed, shaking her finger in front of Luke's face. Luke answered her syllable for syllable, and after a heated debate sat down and grinned.

"She really loves me. It's four bucks, and we have to hurry. They'll take two at a time. Who's first?"

By this time I was having serous reservations about the whole idea. I knew enough to know that if we were caught doing this we could be court-martialed. We could also miss the ship and be reported as AWOL—or worse. In fact, wasn't I already AWOL? Pete and Lloyd went first. Right after they disappeared into the backroom with two girls a sudden commotion erupted at the front door. One of the native men ran in yelling, "MPs! MPs! Quick, out the back way!"

Luke and I ran out the back door. There were several little cottages behind the place, so we began knocking on each door and calling out for Lloyd and Pete. They both emerged, pulling on their pants as they hopped and trotted away with us. A jeep with two MPs pulled up in front and got out.

"Damn! I left my hat back there," Lloyd groaned. "My name is stenciled inside the brim!"

"No time to go back," I replied. "Let's go!"

We stopped another taxi and rode to the dock where we left the boat. The two guards waved to Luke as we got in No. 13 and sped off. If we did not make it to the Pacific locks by the time the *Cambria* passed through, we were in serious trouble. Why on earth had I gone along with this hair-brained scheme? Running at full speed, I was beginning to lose hope when we finally spotted the *Cambria* pulling into the lock.

By this time Luke was raising hell about wanting off, but I wasn't about to stop for him. "Get down under the stern gunwale," I ordered as I pulled up behind the big ship just as the gates were closing. "Look, I'm going to ease up to the side when the water is high enough and you can jump out on the side of the lock. You'll have to get back the best way that you can."

At the right moment, I eased alongside a ramp and Luke slipped ashore unnoticed. Once through the locks, the boats were hoisted aboard and the *Cambria* set sail into the Pacific. Boy did I breathe a long sigh of relief. No one was the wiser for our little escapade.

On Christmas Eve, the *Cambria* developed engine trouble and stalled. The convoy continued on, leaving us adrift in the middle of the Pacific Ocean for two full days. On Christmas, the ship organized an amateur program for all hands on the main deck. The level of talent for a group of guys thrown together on a ship was simply amazing. It only needed someone willing and able to organize and promote it. It was a fun day, except the thing foremost in everyone's mind was of the Christmas we were missing back home. All of us thought about our families, our mothers, of Christmas dinners, girlfriends, and wives. Loneliness crept into my mind and the thrill of war, action, and heroism faded somewhat. Being adrift in the middle of the South Pacific with 500 sailors and 1,500 soldiers was a different sort of Christmas.

Aboard ship everyone had to stand some kind of watch. Everyone had four hours on watch, and eight hours off. The routine went on twenty-four hours a day, seven days a week. My assignment was boat watch. The primary objective of the boat watch was to see that the boats in your area were secure and that no unauthorized persons molested them. The soldiers loved to climb up on the boats. The twenty-nine boats stowed on the deck and davits afforded an excellent place for sunbathing as well as a much better view of the surrounding ocean. The *Cambria's* executive officer, a seasoned old salt raised to the rank of Commander during the war, didn't take kindly to this display of the U.S. Army lying around on his boats. The truth is that they were not hurting anything, but the executive officer's rule was to "keep the boats clear" at all times. From the ship's bridge, he had a clear view of the entire ship's topside, so he could quickly spot anyone who was breaking his rule. When he did, he grabbed the public address system and shouted, "Clear those soldiers off the boat!"

The problem became acute when another ship was sighted or when landfall was announced. Everyone tried to get into an advantageous position to be able to see what was transpiring. There is little in life more thrilling than to be at sea with nothing but water in all directions for days or weeks on end, and then see the faintest trace of an island on the distant horizon. When the *Cambria* first sighted the Hawaiian Islands, excitement built to a fever pitch, which kept those of us assigned to boat watch busy.

The inter-service rivalry was always present and offered an escape from the relentless boredom. Sailors called soldiers "dogface" or "doggies," Marines were called "leathernecks," and pilots were known as "fly boys." Sailors were routinely dubbed "swabby" or, if he was a member of the Coast Guard, "hooligan."

The "sparks" (a nickname for radiomen) picked up a Honolulu radio station and put it on the P.A. system. There was no mistaking

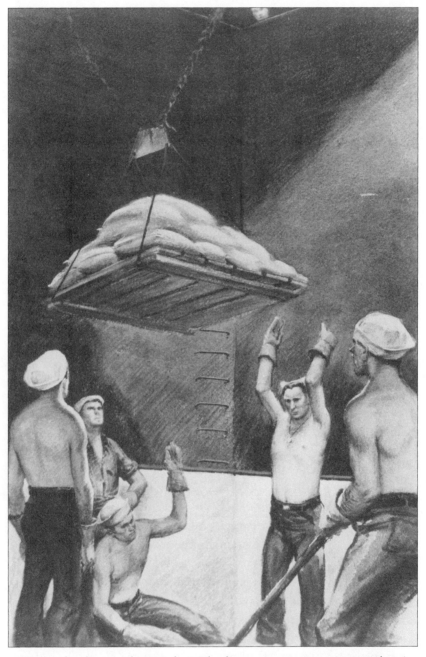

Seamen loading in the "Hole." The boom operator can't see what is going on in the "Hole." The Bos'n Mate on the deck looks down and the seaman with his hands up high is signaling for them to hoist it up, and the Bos'n tells the boom operator.

Hawaiian music. Hawaii had always seemed like such a romantic place, and the soft music complimented that feeling. All of us thought and hoped the same thing: maybe, just maybe, we could get a decent liberty and meet some girls! "Boy, I hope we spend a few days there," Lynn Britton announced.

The *Cambria* pulled into one of the piers and off-loaded the troops. After taking on stores, she pulled out into Pearl Harbor and anchored. Some of the capital ships sunk on December 7, 1941, were now afloat in the harbor. Others were still partially submerged. My boat was lowered and used as a shuttle along with the other davit boats.

Our dream of time in the islands came true, but not exactly as we had been hoping for. Every third day I had liberty in Honolulu. Liberties were only allowed during daylight hours, since curfews and blackouts were still in effect. At this time of the war, Pearl Harbor was the staging area for more than 1,000,000 U.S. servicemen.

Daylight liberty and having to be back to the ship by 6:00 p.m. was bad enough. Being crammed into a place as small as Honolulu with a million other servicemen, however, squeezed all the natural joy out of Honolulu. Our options were limited. We could walk around the streets, eat at the restaurants, drink in the bars, get into fights, or stand in line for the famous "three bucks for three minutes" cat house special. The whorehouses were mostly upstairs. The waiting rooms were always crammed, and the overflow lines stretched down the stairs, along the sidewalks, and around the corners of the block. I saw one line completely wrapped around the block and back again, so it was now a double line. Rumor had it that Eleanor Roosevelt visited Honolulu and asked about the lines. Someone told her that the USO was handing out coffee and donuts for the boys. Mrs. Roosevelt's response made us laugh out aloud every time we thought about it: "Well, it must be a good thing. They seem so happy when they come out."

On the third day in port I returned to the ship and was greeted by an order on the bulletin board: "The following named men are being transferred to the USS *Arthur Middleton*, APA-25 immediately. Please have your sea bag packed and muster on the boat deck at 1400 hours."

My name was on the list with Doll's and Bill Miller's. Our other three comrades (Bob Horton, Lynn Britton, and John Ligon) were not on the list. According to shipboard scuttlebutt, the *Cambria* crew was too green and the *Middleton* was sending over half its experienced boat crews in exchange for half of *Cambria's*. Something big was brewing.

We said our goodbyes quickly.

# Chapter 7

# The Mighty "Middle Maru"

The *Arthur Middleton* was anchored in the harbor close to the *Cambria*. As we walked up the gangplank, I noticed the crewmen of the *Middleton* looked more ragged and salty than the *Cambria's* crew. Several of the men had beards. They lined up on the quarterdeck and a husky old salt addressed us.

"Men, my name is Custer. I'm the Bos'n for Third Division, the boat crew. Attention! This is Commander McKay, the Executive Officer."

A tall, lean man in his late 30s strode up behind Custer. He had on the khakis of an officer but an open shirt and no tie. His face was adorned with a black beard and a mean look. "How many of you men were Cox'n?" he asked. About fifteen of us raised our hands. He walked up to Doll, the tall boy from Florida. "Where did you learn to drive a landing barge, son?"

"At Camp Lejeune, sir."

"How much experience do you have?"

"Nearly three months, sir."

"The rest of you about the same?" Our nods and "ayes" seemed to satisfy him. "Early in the morning, we're going over to Maui for maneuvers. We're going to put all of you in the boats as seamen. You'll have a chance later to regain your Cox'n status, but I'm going to let the more experienced men have the boats right now." With

Busy Hours in Port. The *Arthur Middleton* is drawn here in Honolulu loading up for the Marshall Islands (Kwajalien, Eniwetok) campaign. It is an enormous job loading supplies and equipment for a campaign that lasted almost four months. We had our ship's crew plus 1,500 men of the 22ⁿᵈ Marines, together with all of their equipment.

---

that bombshell, he turned and walked away. Just like that, the whole group was demoted back to seamen.

Custer spoke up. "O.K. men, your quarters are D-1 on the third deck. I'll post boat crews tomorrow morning. While we are on maneuvers, you won't be assigned ship watches. Is that understood? Dismissed."

From the other crew members we learned the *Middleton* was just back from Tarawa, which had been a real rough landing. Someone miscalculated the tides and the boats were not able to get over the reef to land on the beach. The Marines tried wading the last 200 yards to shore, but were picked off like sitting ducks, as were the boats trying to get across the reef. The Japanese resistance was also miscalculated. The island was a nest of underground pill boxes, and naval and air bombardment had not penetrated them as much as expected. The landing forces were pinned on the beach for hours. The slower Amtraks tried to bring the Marines from the stalled boats at the reef, to the beach but were sitting ducks. Hundreds of brave Marines fell on just the first day.

Custer and a seaman named Ken Riley, who I discovered was already a famous combat artist, told us the story of Tarawa. "Everybody's life depends on others doing their job. Tarawa was a failure for the amphibious forces. Our job was to get those Marines ashore, fast and safe. They know what to do then," explained Custer. "Our biggest problem was the miscalculation of the tide," he continued. "The boats just couldn't get over the reef. The Amtraks were not only slower, but they didn't have enough of them and they couldn't carry the number of men the boats could anyway."

Ken Riley was in the beach party, and he finally waded ashore and saw the men being cut down. Custer continued telling the story: "I'm telling you that those guys wading ashore from 200 yards out were like ducks on a duck pond. They say we lost a thousand men on the beach. The Japs had a lot of firepower, that's true, but if we could have put those men all the way ashore in the few minutes we were supposed to, instead of making them wade in, in full view, we wouldn't have lost so many."

Custer paused to let it sink in. "That's how important these boats of ours are. Yes, the brass miscalculated that reef at low tide and that's why we couldn't do our job, but those Marines had to pay the price."

Prior to Tarawa, the *Middleton* had taken part in the Attu and Kiska campaign in the Aleutians, where the ship had run aground and remained there for months. These and other stories convinced we newcomers that these guys were really experienced.

I was assigned to a boat driven by a man named Cahill. He was about 35, small, wiry, and tough as nails. There was another seaman, too. The only name I ever knew for him was "Pissed off Pete." He was a habitual pessimist.

I had never seen so many ships, transports, carriers, destroyers, cruiser, and battleships, not to mention LSTs, LCIs, LCTs, and many other smaller craft. Cahill participated in the briefings for the exercise and told Pete and me our jobs. We were in the first wave of B Group! That meant our wave of approximately nine boats would hit the beach first. This maneuver was like the real thing. For the first time I began to understand the whole picture of what an invasion looked like. Finally, a real-life picture of everything we learned in Landing Craft school.

We conducted our maneuvers on Maui. Aboard were troops from the 22nd Marines. This was their first practice landing. Once lowered, the boats circled around the *Middleton*. One by one they pulled alongside the ship to load up. Cargo nets were dropped over the side. As the boats pulled up, the seamen grabbed the cargo nets to hold the boats in position as the Marines, in full battle gear, climbed down into the boats four abreast.

Loaded boats pulled away and began circling again, waiting for the balance of the boats to take on their troops and cargo. Some of the boats carried only troops, about 26-30 soldiers each. Some carried jeeps, light armored vehicles, or 37-mm howitzers. It only took about thirty minutes to load the boats. The efficiency stunned me. These guys really knew what they were doing. How well I remembered the icy thirty-seven hour vigil of just hoisting aboard all of the boats on the *Cambria*!

The maneuvers at Maui were significantly different from Landing Craft school. The carriers offshore sent in waves of aircraft and dive-bombers. The destroyers, cruisers, and battleships shelled the beach. Smoke screens from ships in key locations completely knocked out visibility at times. When the wave commanders and landing boat leaders signaled for the assault forces to come in, wave after wave of landing craft, all the way from the small LCVPs to LSTs, headed into the beach from about ten miles out. Once the boats were committed, nothing would stop them. If a man fell overboard, he was on his own. Ahead of our boat an LST, which is approximately 330 feet long, hit an LCT broadside and sank it. The 30-man LCT crew was thrown or washed overboard. Although everyone was supposed to wear a life jacket at all times, many of the men did not have them on. The screams for help were heart-wrenching. No one was allowed to stop and help them because the invasion had to continue as if it was the real deal. However, explained the Commandant, a one-star admiral, the men would be picked up later.

After landing on the beach, Cahill, our Cox'n, turned our boat around and headed back to the *Middleton*. Although it was almost an hour after the crash, we could still hear cries from the men in the water. We followed the cries and soon spotted men and the debris floating in the water. Some of the men were wildly splashing the water and yelling, "Sharks! Sharks!"

We picked up one of the survivors. All together the returning boats picked up only five men. Some of them were cut and bleeding. All of them were infuriated at the Navy. "Why had it taken so long to get to us?" many of them asked. According to one of the survivors, after they were in the water they could not see anything because of the smoke. Then the sharks came and began attacking them. Screams filled the air as the sharks ripped men to pieces. They were only in the water about one hour, but 25 of the 30 men were lost, most as a result of shark attack. As the sharks killed their friends, the survivors watched in disbelief as boat after boat motored past without stopping. The Commandant's "maneuver" was too important to interrupt. I had a lot of trouble with this incident, and with the rule governing ships at sea during wartime. If a man fell overboard or a ship sank, you didn't stop to pick him up because it would endanger the ship stopping to assist. War was a serious business.

The fleet remained on maneuvers for about one week, after which time the ships were replenished with fuel and supplies and headed southwest. The convoy was magnificent to behold. It appeared that every ship in the U.S. Navy was involved. The second day out of the Hawaiian Islands, the ships executive officer made an announcement over the public address system:

> Attention, all hands! I know that all of you have been wondering where we are going and I'm sure you are tired of maneuvers. We are heading for the invasion of the Marshall Islands. Our first target will be Kwajalein Atoll. Since we are landing Force B, we will stand by in reserve for the initial invasion. D-Day is set for January 30. We are going to get a chance to meet the Japanese. Remember that we are now in hostile waters. Do not throw anything overboard—not even a cigarette butt—that could give away the fact that our ship has passed. We will be in total blackout topside every night. Smoking on deck is prohibited. You may only smoke and show

lights below decks. I know you men will do well and that the *Arthur Middleton* will do its share. Good luck and smooth sailing.

The response to this announcement was deafening. It was like a crowd at a football game right after the winning touchdown. Everyone joined in to celebrate the news. We were going to engage the Japanese in the Marshall Islands! Most of us had never heard of the Marshall Islands, but they would soon become famous along with Guadalcanal, Tarawa, and all the others.

From that point forward intense preparations began. Top secret maps and photos of the beaches were passed out for us to study. Every man in the boat had to know how to take over in any capacity if needed. A new challenge and password would be issued each day of the invasion. Our orders were to challenge every boat we met by blinking it in Morse code with a red flashlight. If the approaching boat did not answer with the correct password, our orders were to

The Marshall Islands Task Force gets underway. Coast Guard combat artist Ken Riley sketched this drawing of the *Middleton* in convoy from the stern of another ship. All hands are at General Quarters, on the alert for a surprise plane or submarine attack. Dawn patrol planes belonging to the carrier (partially seen at left) are visible overhead.

Anti-Aircraft Battery aboard the *Middleton*. Coast Guard gunners pour death into the skies from a 40mm anti-aircraft battery. Coast Guard combat artist Ken Riley catches the tense action of the loaders, gun pointers, ammunition passers, and communications men as their guns spit fire at Jap bombers winging high overhead.

turn our boat's gun against the other boat and force him to respond or surrender. The same challenge was in effect for boats approaching ships. During daylight hours, the challenge and response was conducted via semaphore.

An invasion depends on intricate timing. Each wave must hit the beach at a certain time and of course, in the correct spot. Tides were calculated beforehand so the boats could get all the way up on dry land for unloading. Coral reefs could rip the bottom out of a boat, and their location and depth played a significant part in the planning. The Navy's underwater demolition team (U.D.T., commonly known as frogmen) went in the night before the invasion, usually dropped off from a submarine. Their job was to find or blast passages through any reefs that threatened to obstruct the boats. Our crash course for the landings in the Marshall Islans consumed five days.

Bill, Doll, and I gathered on the fantail of the ship one night after we got off watch. It was a day or two before we reached Kwajalein. "Well, what do you think?" I inquired of my two closest friends. "Would you like to be back on the *Cambria*?"

"Shoot, no," Doll quickly responded. "You know, Wiley, I'm glad we're on the *Middleton*. Can you believe the way these guys get it done? There's another thing, too. I never felt like the *Cambria* was all together. I mean, everyone was like an individual. There was no feeling of belonging. These guys have been through so much together they are like a family. I like that. I just hope I can fit in."

"Me, too!" chimed in Bill. "The guys down in the boat shop told me the Japanese name for the *Middleton* is 'Middle Maru.' So, here's to you, Middle Maru!"

We all three raised imaginary glasses above us, brought them down to our mouths and tipped a bottoms-up toast to our new home.

"Middle Maru! Middle Maru! Sink or swim, we're with you!"

# Chapter 8

# Fiery Introduction at Kwajalein

Kwajalein is one of the world's largest coral atolls. Part of the Marshall Islands, it is 2,100 miles southwest of Hawaii. The islands are remnants of a volcanic rim formed millions of years ago. The islands around Kwajalein are small, some only a few hundred yards wide. Their length ranged from a few hundred yards to one or two miles. During World War II, they were jungle islands—at least until the heavy bombardments cleared much of the vegetation away. In less than half a day, the bombs eliminated nearly every tree, leaving the scenic islands looking more like mini-deserts in the middle of the ocean.

The *Arthur Middleton* anchored off the atoll. From the relative safety of the ship we watched and listened to what was going on around us while paying close attention to any news piped over the ship's public address system. Occasionally, general quarters sounded when enemy aircraft were sighted. Since we had air superiority, enemy raids were not much too worry about. Only a few planes managed to slip through the protective ring erected by our Navy's fighting ships. During the day, the ships would "make smoke" to completely obscure our anchorages. The sky (at least when you could see it) was almost black with "ack ack," or bursting anti-aircraft shells. At night the transports held their fire to avoid giving away their position.

I was on gun duty the first night of the invasion, manning one of the 40-mm antiaircraft guns aboard the *Middleton*. At first things were relatively quiet. All I could hear and see were the dull roars and flashing lights on the beach ten to fifteen miles away. Several Japanese aircraft flew in to bomb and strafe our men on the beach. The transports, still loaded with troops and waiting out in the harbor, did not respond with antiaircraft fire because it might give away their position. The theory was this: Let the destroyers, cruisers, and fighting ships handle it. That made sense to me.

Suddenly, the drone of engines reached my ears as Japanese aircraft approached. Tracers of antiaircraft fire probed the skies in search of the enemy planes. The destroyers, cruisers, and battleships let loose with a volley so powerful it is impossible to describe. How any aircraft could fly through it was beyond me. The brilliant exploding shells on the beach and tracers zooming into the night skies like Roman candles reminded me of the Fourth of July on a scale I could never have imagined. It was a sight to behold and one I will never forget. Despite the heavy fire, at least one Japanese plane slipped through and dropped its bombs on the beach.

As I sat there in the gun pit witnessing all of this, it suddenly dawned on me that this was the war I had looked forward to for so long. And then, as if my mind had been cleared to receive a message, I knew my brother Joe had been killed. Joe was co-pilot on a B-17 Flying Fortress halfway around the world. It was January 30, 1944.

How I sensed or knew this I don't know, but I just *knew* his plane had been hit by antiaircraft fire over Holland on a flight into Germany. It was all very clear to me. There were no survivors.

I tried to tell myself it was my imagination gone wild, brought on by what I was seeing in front of me, but I knew I was lying to myself. That thought haunted my every hour until I returned to Pearl Harbor three months later in April, where a letter in a stack of mail confirmed my fears.

For the most part, the groups of transports (which included the *Middleton*) sat still in their ringside seats and watched and listened to the deadly entertainment. The news we received from the early stages of the invasion was good. The troops were meeting resistance and advancing. The air raids kept everyone busy, but our carrier fleet did an excellent job of turning back any major Japanese thrusts. Enemy planes that managed to penetrate our naval screen never numbered more than one or two at a time, and they didn't last long.

Bill, Doll, and I came off the four to eight watch and leaned on the rail of the boat deck, watching the tracers and distant flashes of light as shells and bombs exploded on the islands. "Hell, I saw more action than this at the Pike theater," Bill complained.

"Well, I'd sure like to get at least one little look at some action. Do you think that there will be anything left by the time we get in there?" asked Doll.

I looked at him as he spoke. He was serious. We all were. "There'll be other times," I replied. "It's a long way to Tokyo."

The fighting on shore agitated the Marines waiting to join in. They were worried that the fighting would be over by the time they stepped ashore, and their role would be occupying the island and nothing more. The Coast Guardsmen were disappointed, too. No one wanted to die, but the feeling of being left out of the action is difficult to describe. The boat crews made a few runs to and from other ships, and one of the boats was lucky enough to make a trip to the beach. But that was all.

By the third day of the invasion, we were all on edge. The action was out *there* and we were twiddling our thumbs watching it rather than participating in it. My boat, No. 13 with Cahill the Cox'n, was on duty. We had made only one run to the flagship *Cambria*. Suddenly, Custer appeared on the quarterdeck and motioned for us to come aboard the ship. We secured the boat and made our way up the gangplank. He nodded for us to follow him into the wardroom, where the executive officer, a Marine Captain, and four other Marines in full battle gear were waiting for us.

"Men," began Commander McKay. "This is Captain Holland from Naval Intelligence. He needs three boats, one LCVP and two Tank Lighters, for a special mission. Cahill, Boat 13, O'Brien, Boat 30, and Wymer, Boat 29, have been selected because of your experience." McKay nodded at the Captain and continued, "Captain Holland, it's all yours."

The Captain remained seated and began speaking. "Relax men, here's the situation. One of our destroyers patrolling outside the atoll had been getting Morse code signals all day from someone on one of the smaller islands on the North end. The signals are reflections from the sun rather than from a light source, like someone using a small mirror or real shiny stainless steel. A signalman on the destroyer challenged them and got the message: SOS, NAVY PILOTS, SOS!"

He paused and cleared his throat while we waited anxiously for him to continue. "It could be a trap by the Japs, but it could also be a downed Navy pilots who needs our help. The safest thing to do is to wait until the islands are secure and rescue him, but this island is where we suspect the Japs will make their last stand. We know they have a tremendous munitions dump on it. Frankly, the Navy wants to bombard it now. They're giving us until midnight tonight to make whatever rescue we can."

The Captain stood up and pointed to a large map of the islands spread on the table before them. "Here is how we are we going to do it. The Japanese know that all of the landings are taking place from the leeward side of the islands in order for the U.S. Amphibious forces to avoid their fixed shore batteries pointing seaward. That leaves the seaward side virtually unprotected, and that's where we have to come in." He pointed to some photographs. "Here are aerial photos of the beaches taken by our pilots a few days ago. See this inlet? The surf there should be less severe than a more open side of the island. Remember this is a small island. At this point, it's only 300 yards wide. We must depend on surprise."

"How will the pilot or pilots, if they even exist, know we are coming?" asked Cahill.

"Good question," replied the Captain. "We've been sending a coded message from destroyers all day. It's a long shot, but we started sending the password for each day going backwards. When we sent last Saturday's password, we got an immediate response and it was correct. We then sent Friday's, then Thursday's. Every one has been answered correctly by our mirror reflection, as we call him. This tells us the pilots knew the password up until Saturday last, and that gives us much more confidence there are American pilots stranded on the island. Two hours ago we started sending a message, making it look like it was from one destroyer to another, but making sure it was also aimed at the island. The message is 'Boy Scout; Packers; Pepper Upper!'"

We all smiled. Any American boy growing up in the 1930s knew the Boy Scout motto is "Be Prepared." The Captain continued: "We're banking the U.S. pilots know that 'Packers' means the Green Bay Packers, and they are to come to the little bay on the island. The last was a real long shot, but again, most kids listened to the Dr. Pepper cadets or 'Pepper Uppers' and associated it with ten, two, and four. Let's hope they pick out the 10 because that's when we have to be there, 10:00 p.m."

A skeptical Cahill asked the obvious question: "Have we had any answers to the message?"

"Yes," replied Captain Holland. "But, it's only partially deciphered at this point. The message just came back. All it said was Roger!"

Custer spoke up again. "We're taking three boats because we're going to use two of them for protection. O'Brien and Wymer in their tank lighters with their 50-caliber machine guns and eight Marine sharpshooters will cruise just off shore, outside the reef. They will also have small smoke generators for an emergency. Cahill in the smaller LCVP will slip into the bay and try to land unnoticed. We're putting two Marines in your boat and adding Irvin and Baker to man your 30-calibers. Remember though, if you are detected by the Japs, don't spend much time on the beach. If your men don't show up, get out of there fast." Custer rubbed his forehead and added, "Oh, UDT says there is a reef offshore about 80 yards out. They blasted a hole in it just before the main landing on Roi Namur and set out small white buoys. They may or may not still be there. That's the escape route. We should go inside and come around the shoreline of the island. A destroyer will begin a barrage including smoke bombs at that end of the island at 9:15 p.m. The wind is just right to carry you under smoke all the way to the bay and with the destroyer firepower plus all of the other action going in inside the atoll, you should make it all the way undetected. Are there any questions?"

We shook our heads. Custer looked at his watch. "Okay, we shove off from here at 8:00 p.m. That gives us two hours to get around the island and make our rendezvous at 10:00 p.m. I'll be in Wymer's tank lighter and will call signals from there. Total silence after dark. Communications by red flash light to seaward only."

As we walked out of the wardroom, Doll and Bill motioned to me. "Hey, Wiley, I get to go as motor-mac on the Boat 13," said Bill with a grin. "You sure that number is as safe as you said?"

"Safer than the Pike theater on Friday night," I answered back, referring to the well known and popular drive-in theater east of Ft Worth, Texas.

We gathered in the mess hall at the end of one of the tables and talked as we ate. Our meal consisted of a very dry slice of roast beef with dehydrated mashed potatoes, whole kernel corn, and applesauce for desert. "What chance do you think we have of getting the LCVP inside the reef undetected?" I asked.

Well, we'll only be about a hundred yards away if you need help, "said Doll.

"We need to make sure all the boats have marked sounders," warned Cahill.

Every face lit up with recognition when we realized how important that might be. Each boat was supposed to carry a "sounding" line, a line with a weight tied to the end. The line was marked with white paint at every league distance. A man sounded the bottom by lowering the weight until it hit the sea floor and reporting the water depth by the mark—three or whatever the distance was in leagues.

"Everyone check your flashlights and guns," ordered Custer. "I don't think we'll need them, but we better be prepared. And Cahill, you get off that beach fast when you pick 'em up. If the pilots aren't there, don't wait unless you see some sign of them." It was obvious Custer was worried about the mission. He was like a mother hen and we were all his chicks.

Once on the water and after a short rendezvous, we headed our boats away from the ship. Custer was in O'Brien's tank lighter, the lead boat. As we approached the island Cahill stayed close behind Wymer's tank lighter. According to plan, he moved alongside, which made his boat nearly invisible from the island. They proceeded this way until they reached the large reef opening. If anyone spotted them, they would see just two boats.

The smoke from the destroyer smoke shell offered sufficient cover and Cahill slipped his smaller LCVP inside the reef as Wymer followed O'Brien in the larger boats outside the reef running parallel to the shore. From the beach, it would be hard to discern that a third boat was present. Although the diesel engines made lots of noise, the bombing and wave action on and along the atoll drowned most of it out. Cahill moved ahead cautiously, edging along as close to the reef as he dared. I peered intently at the beach for any sign of activity, but could not make out anything of interest.

Beached in a cove of trees was a pair of Japanese barges. We came upon them so suddenly I almost missed them. A lone sentry sat on the stern of one of the boats. My throat tightened when I realized he was a real Japanese soldier. Before anyone could say anything, the Marine sergeant with us yelled out a greeting in perfect Japanese and waved his arm as the LCVP went past. The bluff was perfectly played, and the Jap sentry waved back. In the darkness, he had mistaken the LCVP and two LCMs for Japanese barges. They weren't expecting American boats here. No one else said a word as our LCVP moved as stealthily as possible down the beach. My heart was pounding in my chest so loud I thought everyone around me could hear it.

After about one-quarter of a mile we came to the small bay and silently nosed the boat onto the beach. Just as silently I lowered the ramp and the two Marines moved out in a low crouch and positioned themselves about ten feet in front on either side of the dropped ramp. By this time my heart was beating so loudly I was sure the Japanese could hear it. We waited for what seemed like an eternity, but in reality was only a couple of minutes, before two shadowy figures stepped out of the brush and sprinted toward our boat. The Marine Sergeant stood up and asked in a soft voice, "What's your favorite radio program?"

"The Dr. Pepper Cadets," both men answered as they ran into the boat.

"You better hurry!" one of them announced breathlessly. "There's a Jap patrol that's been chasing us all over this island!"

The Marines were right behind them and as the last one cleared, Cahill began backing the boat off the beach. No one had to say it, but all of us knew it was unlikely we could slip undetected past the two Jap landing barges a second time. We would have to find the hole in the reef the UDT so generously provided us. The tank lighters were already sounding the reef in a frantic attempt to locate the breach. Much to our dismay, the buoys left to mark the small channel were nowhere in sight. Doll and Anderson were standing on the lowered ramps sounding with their marked sounding lines when a flare exploded directly above them. Within seconds we were all exposed just like it was daylight.

And then the firing began.

At first it was rifle fire, but within a short time a machine gun opened on us. A mortar opened on us as well, its shells exploding near the LCMs. We returned fire with our 50- and 30-caliber machine guns, rifles, and BARS, aiming for the small flashes of light on the beach. Our situation worsened considerably when the two Jap barges appeared around the point of the beach heading straight for us. Cahill turned the boat around and was making for the reef as fast as he could go.

Our only chance was to find the hole and go through it. To the left, the way we came in, were the two Jap barges loaded with troops. To our right, the water was shallow because of the reef. The Jap troops on the beach behind us were firing for all they were worth. Returning in that direction meant certain death or capture. It was then I saw the red light. It was Doll blinking out P-O-R-T and yelling the word as loud as he could. With a full throttle, Cahill rammed the boat through a narrow opening in the reef and we joined the two tank lighters, who were giving a good account of themselves with their four 50-caliber machine guns and Marine sharpshooters. Custer sent the prearranged signal to the destroyer waiting offshore that all three boats had cleared the reef. The ship's 5-inch shells thundered past just over our heads. They exploded directly on the beach where we had been just a few minutes earlier.

It was at that point I heard a mortar shell coming. It whistled over my head and struck the corner of the steel ramp from behind, damaging it and breaking the cable. As the ramp plunged down, the quick-thinking Cahill slammed the boat into reverse and gunned the throttle as hard as he could. The boat momentarily folded the ramp back under it and started to nose dive until the reverse screw stopped it. Cahill quickly swung the wheel around, spinning the boat so that its stern pointed out to sea and the nose toward the island. His quick thinking saved the boat from sinking like a large scoop. Moving in reverse was slow, however. The reverse motion caused the ramp to swing back so that it now trailed the boat. Cahill told me to get a line and pull the ramp back up. With the help of the two Marines and the two pilots, we were finally able to raise and secure it. Cahill swung the boat around and once again headed out to sea.

The ramp was up but leaking badly and the sump pumps were not enough to handle the water. Bill and I began bailing as fast as possible with buckets. The two tank lighters were running alongside us now and they tossed over additional buckets for us to use. In this manner, the small flotilla made its way back to the *Middleton*.

One of the pilots told me he and his gunner had been on an observation flight last Saturday when they were shot down by two Jap Zeros. They made a belly landing with their TBF just off the reef and were lucky enough to get out in a rubber raft just before the plane sank. When the Zeros made strafing runs that sank their rubber raft, the men somehow escaped injury and swam ashore. They had been there ever since. Initially they thought they would just wait until the Americans arrived, but they quickly discovered the Japs had underground facilities and troops on the islands. It became clear the bunkers housed an ammunition dump because the Japs returned time and again for load after load of ammunition once the American invasion began. Since the Americans were landing on the leeward side of the islands, the Japanese supply lines were the reef-guarded waterways on the outside or seaward sides.

"After we got you message, we arranged a surprise for them," explained the pilot. "Knowing that you would come at ten tonight, we set off a time fuse which should be happening about now." He glanced at his watch. "Three cigarettes all lit at five minutes to ten, to set off a keg of powder right in the middle of their dump."

He wasn't kidding. The explosion was unlike anything I had ever experienced, and triggered a massive chain reaction. Several small explosions became one big reverberating roar as flames shot skyward right on the beach—exactly where we had landed.

"The dump was right there at the beach where we landed?" stammered the Marine Sergeant

"Yeah," answered the pilot with a questioning look. "But we didn't understand why you chose that particular little bay, unless you wanted us to blow that thing and make our escape easier.

Actually, you slipped in there just like one of their barges. We've seen 'em come and go for days now. I don't think anyone would have detected you if that patrol had not been after us. They saw us messing around the ammo dump and gave chase. We've been leading them around in circles to keep them away from the beach. Knowing that we had to rendezvous with you at ten, we made a break for the beach. I don't know how far behind us they were, but it's a good thing you were here. We figured the three cigarettes would take an hour and the explosion would come between 10:15 and 10:20."

He glanced at his watch a second time. "Damn, we missed it by just five minutes. Since neither of us smoke, it was a really a guessing game."

I looked at this man with awe. Here was the American fighting man. Instead of simply waiting to be rescued after an already narrow escape from being shot down and strafed, he risked his life again and blew up an enemy ammunition dump. Maybe those fly boys weren't so bad, after all. The night mission was quite an introduction to the war for me. Our losses were four men wounded.

We made it back to the *Middleton*, where crewman hoisted us aboard amid cheers from the whole ship. The admiral sent a "well done!" to the whole crew. Doll, Bill, and I sat up late in the boat divisions' quarters, answering questions and telling the story over and over.

I looked at Bill and asked, "How about the 13 boat. Can it be fixed?"

"Like new," he answered, and I'm gonna' request to be the motor-mac on it. Thirteen is a lucky number."

"Maybe we can be together on it, and it's the one I want when I get my own boat."

Finally, when the crowd dispersed, I asked Doll, "How did you find the passage?"

Custer answered the question. "Sounding was too slow," he replied. "We just weren't getting there fast enough. Doll jumped into the water, swam to the reef, and started running down it. The water was only about a foot deep on top of it. When he came to the hole, he dove down and quickly explored it. When he came up, he blinked the message with his red light and started shouting."

Now it was my turn to look at the tall lean Doll with awe. I knew he was an expert swimmer, but he had done this fully clothed, complete with a life jacket and helmet.  "Thanks, buddy." I said.

The shy Doll shrugged his shoulders and answered, "Shucks. I knew that if I didn't find you a hole to come through, we'd have to come in there and get you. I didn't want to be no hero."

The Last Supper. The night before an invasion, everyone received a special meal. In this oil painting by Ken Riley, a new invasion of Japanese-held Pacific territory is only a few short hours away as Coast Guardsmen, Marines, and Army soldiers partake of their "last supper" aboard the *Middleton*. When troops are aboard, the tables are always raised and everyone eats standing up.

# Chapter 9

# Boys Become Men at Eniwetok

As part of the Marshall Island Campaign, Kwajalein was a joint Army-Marine operation. The crew of the *Arthur Middleton* and its troops, the 22nd Marines, were getting impatient. The fighting on Roi and Namur only lasted a few days. The way the Marines put it, it would not have lasted that long if they had been allowed in to help the Army.

One thought crossed all our minds: were we just going to sit here in a backup position and miss the biggest invasion since Tarawa? A few of us got in some duty as the "Duty Boat" crew, and the special mission was exciting, but the Marines just sat there fuming, furious they were not being called upon to kill Japs. Ken Riley, our combat artist, got to go ashore and drew some of his best drawings. The duty boats transported personnel and cargo between ships and the beaches. One day, our boat was dispatched to the USS *Cambria*, which carried the flag for the group. I was hoping to see John, Lynn, or Bobby Horton, but no such luck. Our orders were to pick up the boat group commander, the Beach Master, the Executive officer, and several Marine officers who had been in conference aboard the *Cambria* with the commandant.

One the way back to our ship, the officers said things like, "Pull out at 0700," "Task Force 57, Engebi, Parry," and other names that sounded like some of the islands on the maps on Eniwetok. Finally,

Lt. Hoyle, the Beach Master, looked at me. "Well, son we're finally through waiting."

The following morning, the *Arthur Middleton* and the rest of Task Force 57 pulled out of Kwajalein. The executive officer got on the P.A. system. "Men, I know that it has been awfully hard just sitting back and watching the war. Well, the waiting is over. Task Force 57 is no longer a backup force. We have been selected to be the assault force on Eniwetok Islands. You have two days to review your plans and tactics and check your assignments. I know the *Middleton* will perform with pride and earn a 'Well Done' from the flag." In military jargon, a "Well Done" was the highest verbal compliment given. Getting a "Well Done" was second only to receiving a medal.

The news triggered a current of excitement through the boat division. This was finally it! Cahill had been there before. So had the other seaman, "Pissed Off" Pete. For me, it was a new and exciting time. Our boat would be in the first wave. A young second lieutenant was the Wave Leader. Ironically, the millions of dollars spent bringing our large task force to this point in the Pacific, the hundreds of hours spent in preparation, and the thousands of lives involved, all came down to a single point of dependency. The young second lieutenant Wave Leader was fresh out of Officers Candidate School. He had never been in combat before, but was tapped to lead the first wave in to the beach. His job was to recognize the correct beach and direct the other boats in to follow him. If he failed to hit the "prepared" beach, he might take the men into the strongest opposition and jeopardize the entire landing.

The task force made landfall during the night and as the first rays of morning sun broke, I spotted the islands ahead of us. Eniwetok atoll was also a circular string of islands about twenty-five miles in diameter. Many of the small islands were connected with shallow reefs or shoals. The large Japanese guns on the island were trained seaward to oppose a landing. The US Navy, however, had a better plan than just dumping a bunch of soldiers on a armed beach. The plan was to bomb and shell the large defensive gun locations to soften them up and knock them out. Once that was done we would sail right into the middle of the lagoon and perform

This member of the beach party from the *Arthur Middleton* is fully dressed, with M-1 rifle, canteen. pack, and Ka-Bar knife.  The fiery beach and Japanese enemy await him on Enewitok.

the landing from the inside of the atoll. The entry was a passage less than 1,000 feet wide between two islands.

The convoy passed into the atoll in single file. Mine sweepers went in first and swept away the mines planted by the Japanese. I was on deck on the port side of the ship as the *Arthur Middlton* sailed between Parry and Japtan islands. The former island was a few hundred yards away. I remember thinking at the time that its jungle growth was so thick it reminded me of the Tarzan movies. Thus far, not a shot had been fired and no movement could be seen on either island. Even though we could not see them, everyone knew the Japanese were watching us intently. Our ship passed into the atoll, proceeded to our assigned position, and anchored.

When all of the ships were inside, the bombardment commenced again. I was much closer to the action than I had been at Kwajalein, and it was simply awesome to behold. The carriers cut loose their dive bombers and the destroyers, cruisers, and battleships began a steady bombardment against Engebi and Parry islands. Within a few hours the jungle growth was knocked down and the islands looked like a desert wasteland of broken tree trunks and rough cratered sand dunes.

I didn't believe anyone could live through such a bombardment, but Cahill explained how the Japs hid in concrete bunkers with walls up to six feet thick. "They will be there waiting for us," he assured me.

A schoolmate of mine from Itasca named "Plunket" Powers was one of the Marines on board my boat. He had been in training for six months at Guadalcanal. This was his first real action. I had no idea he was aboard until I ran into him one day in the passageway. After our mutual surprise, we spent hours reminiscing and updating each other on news from home. It was unusual to see someone from your hometown on the far side of the world, especially a town as small as Itasca, Texas.

There were fifteen APAs in the Task Force, plus almost as many AKs (Cargo) and APs (personnel), LSTs (seagoing ships that could also land on the beach, carrying Amtraks, the famous amphibious tractors, or Ducks), LSDs (Landing Ship Docks that carried all types of smaller crafts and boats), and the fighting ships: destroyers, destroyer escorts, cruisers, battleships, and aircraft carriers. Once the APAs and Amtraks put the assault forces ashore and a beachhead was established, all the personnel and the cargo ships were unloaded. The first to touch the enemy beach would be the LCVPs. Boat 13 was in the first wave.

As we all waited, nervous and anxious to get moving, the P.A. system finally announced, "Boat Crews, Man you boats!" The Chaplain got on the system to speak to us. The chaplain aboard the *Middleton* was, frankly, the ship's joke. Everyone had a Chaplain story, and the tales they told of what he did on liberty were probably stretched a little each time, but he always returned to the ship so drunk he had to be helped aboard. I actually saw him hoisted

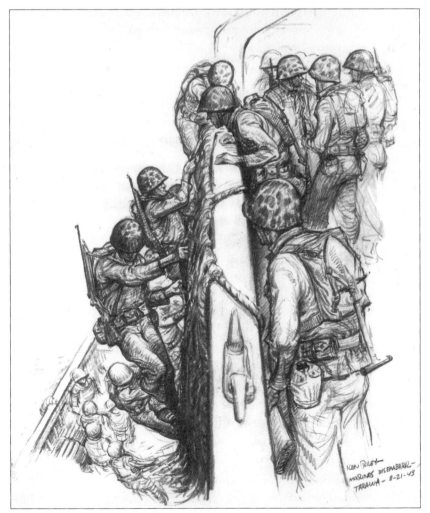

Loading the troops into the landing craft. These Marines go four abreast down the cargo net in a well rehearsed operation. At this point, timing is everything, and the boats must be loaded and formed into waves to land on the beach at a precise time.

aboard in a cargo net because he was too drunk to walk. The Shore Patrol brought him back to the ship on more than one occasion. The Chaplain was Catholic and made no bones about the fact that he was no minister to the Protestants aboard the ship. The funniest story I remember was when he came running out of his quarters, waving his steel helmet, yelling, "What Protestant son-of-a-bitch shit in my helmet?"

Today, the Chaplain addressed the crew and all the troops over the P.A. system. His closing comments helped fan the embers of dislike among the Protestants: "For all you Catholic boys, I want you to know that God is with you. For you Protestants, there is nothing I can say."

Once in the water, the boats rendezvoused and circled, pulling away one at a time to come alongside and take on troops. Cargo nets draped over the sides of the ship on either side. Cahill pulled the boat alongside and Pete and I grabbed the edge of the heavy hemp rope net and yanked it inside. The Marines climbed down the net, four abreast into the boat. At the same time, the ship's cargo booms hoisted the heavy equipment from the ship's hold over the side into the boats. It was an extremely smooth and well organized operation.

Our boat drew a jeep pulling a 37-mm howitzer and about ten Marines. There were three cargo nets dropped on each side of the ship, so six boats could load at a time. In a very few minutes we were loaded and once again circling the mother ship. When every boat was loaded, we took off for the target in waves of six boats. We were now about six miles out. There was one more staging point just offshore. However, this was just to make sure the formations were correct and everything was a "go." It was the Boat Group commander riding in the lead LCVP in the first wave who would give us the final "go" and lead us in.

As we drew closer, we passed LSTs deploying amphibious tractors (Amtraks) and LCIs, which were closer to the beach, firing their rockets. The battleships, cruisers, and destroyers, which had been bombarding the beach with giant shells high above our heads, held their fire when we got about a mile offshore, although the dive bombers continued to provide ground support. I watched Wildcats and Hellcats diving toward the island and pulling up at what seemed like the last second. The explosions created a lot of smoke, but once the heavier ships eased up with the big guns, the smoke began to clear and the island came into view. The Boat Group commander's boat gave the "go" signal and the first wave accelerated for the beach, followed by six other waves.

I was in the starboard 30-caliber gun pit, checking my gun and the belt of shells feeding into it. I had a small Kodak camera in my pocket, courtesy of my friend from Itasca, Bill Underwood, who asked if I could take pictures of the war for him. I held it in one hand and snapped a few shots of the island during our approach. As the beach grew larger, I could make out splashes in the water in front of me. It was still like watching a movie, only this time I was in the middle of it. About this time, the mortar shells began falling around us, splashing alongside and behind and sending geysers of water high into the air. When the shells hit behind us, I really felt for the first time that I was in it the thick of the war. It was no longer a movie. I could be blown to bits any second. I had the 30-caliber on ready, but there was nothing to shoot at. I had always wondered how I would feel about trying to kill another human being, but I knew now that I could and would if they were trying to kill me.

A large LCM (Tank Lighter) carrying a Sherman tank was moving forward to our right. The tank's crew was inside and the hatches battened down, ready to land on the beach. A mortar shell made a direct hit on the ramp in front of the boat and blew it loose. With the ramp gone, the LCM acted like a giant scoop and nosed into the seawater. The boat sank immediately, with the crew locked inside the tank. Those poor boys never had a chance to get out.

Machine gun and rifle fire erupted from the beach. When I saw the line of splashes rake across our boat, I wondered if I was hit. Even though I had no pain, I reached down to feel both my legs because I had developed the picture in my mind that if I were hit, it would be in the legs and not a serious wound. I didn't understand why I didn't feel the pain. Pissed Off Pete, meanwhile, was terrified and lying in the bottom of the boat moaning. The fire from the beach was much heavier now and I could hear it hitting the boat. Lieutenant Ward, the Wave Leader, had made a mistake. Instead of landing the boat on the targeted beach (Blue 1) pulverized by the naval and air bombardment, he aimed us left of Blue 1 directly into the Japanese, who had moved away from the bombardment in that very direction.

Cahill put the boat on the beach and yelled for Pete to lower the ramp. Pete did not move. I climbed out of the gun pit and pulled the lever that lowered the steel ramp onto the sand. The Marines had already started the Jeep and when the ramp dropped, accelerated it out of the boat. The beach was on an incline of about 10 degrees, rising to perhaps eight feet at the top of the crest. Once on land, the firing was so heavy the Marines stopped the jeep and jumped into a large shell crater in front and to the right of the boat. The ramp dropped of its own weight when released, but had to be hand-cranked back up. We couldn't leave the beach until it was up and locked.

Cahill was still yelling for Pete to raise the ramp, but Pete remained huddled against the floor, trying to get as low as he could. I returned to the gun pit, but when I saw the ramp was still down, I climbed back down out of the gun pit and began cranking it up for all I was worth. As I swung the crank around, the handle hit Pete in the rump, which was the highest point of his body sticking up. His ear-splitting scream pierced above the din of all the other sounds that day, and he launched his body over the engine wall and flattened himself on the floor into the now vacated bed of the boat.

"I'm Hit! I'm Hit!" he yelled as he tried to crawl deeper into the boat's floor.

As I raised the ramp, I saw the bravest act I had ever seen. Pinned down in a shell crater directly in front of me about 20 feet away were several Marines. One Marine climbed up and stood silhouetted against the skyline. As he stood tall for a moment, he lowered his rifle and lobbed a grenade over his shoulder. Then he motioned for his comrades to follow and jumped over the ridge. The other Marines scrambled after him. As they were leaving, a mortar shell landed inside the crater and exploded. All of this unfolded almost directly in front of me as I was cranking up the ramp as fast as I could. Once the ramp was up, Cahill backed the boat off the beach and swung it around to head back tor the *Middleton* for another load.

The first loads to hit the beach were troops and fighting equipment. The next loads were cargo from the ships. The system

This live action drawing by U.S. Coast Guard combat artist Ken Riley offers several intimate details. This drawing captures the second wave, which landed just seconds behind the first wave on Engebi island during the invasion of Eniwetok. Troops are temporarily pinned down on the beach as the tanks rumble inland. Note the bare land and rubbish of what was once a jungle island. The Japanese were dug into spider tunnels and popped up through holes in the rubbish behind our troops after letting them run past. We were under heavy fire as we approached the beach. As depicted here, the Marines came out fighting.

was well organized. As the fighting men moved inland, a firm beachhead was established. Navy and Coast Guard beach parties from the ships were always in the first waves with the assault troops. Once the beach was in our hands, they dug in and established communications, field medical facilities, ammunition supplies, and the hundreds of other types of support fighting men required to do their job. The Seabees, also among the first to land, lost no time rebuilding airstrips and fixing or cutting roads. Off shore, meanwhile, control boats monitored the flow of cargo and supplies to the beach. Each boat's Cox'n had a manifest slip describing his cargo and noting where it was to be delivered.

By now, the boat group had established an offshore check point where every boat had to check through before proceeding to the beach. The Beach Master took charge of the beachhead and organized the unloading of the boats. If a boat's cargo was not immediately required, the craft rendezvoused with others in a circle offshore until called in to the beach. As we later learned through hard experience, sometimes the "circle and wait" routine consumed hours and even days. It was during one of these waiting periods later that first day that Cahill and I got into a bit of trouble.

There were several Japanese landing barges partially sunk on a reef just off the beach. As we approached to take a closer look I grabbed the Kodak and snapped another picture. We pulled alongside one of the barges and I climbed aboard it. It was a real mess. A shell had landed right in the middle of it. There was a compartment below deck where the Jap crew slept or worked on the engine. Without thinking, I foolishly peered into it but couldn't see much. Amongst the rubble on the deck was a hand-cranked siren, which had been broken off its mounting by the blast. I picked it up and was about to climb back onto our boat when one of our patrol boats came up. Someone yelled through a megaphone, "Get away from that Japanese barge—it hasn't been secured! We just got a

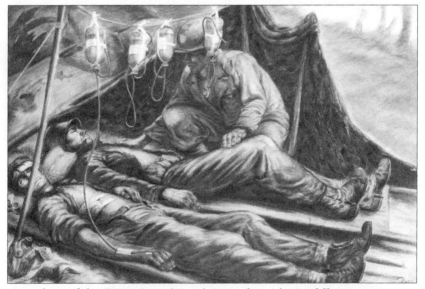

Members of the Coast Guard Beach Party from the *Middleton* prepare a beach hospital within minutes after landing on Engebi. Unless surgery is required immediately, first aid is rendered and the patient is sent back to the ship's hospital.

sniper in one of those barges down the beach. A guy off your ship stuck his head down in the compartment and got it right in the face!" My blood chilled as I waved my understanding and quickly climbed back aboard our boat. I carried the siren with me.

The stench began on the second day. It was everywhere. Bloated bodies, American and Japanese, floated in the water off the beaches. Every aspect of war loomed here, in a small confined 25-mile circle. The hot tropical sun deteriorated the flesh so quickly that within 24 hours the stench became unbearable, even several miles out in the atoll. There is no way newsreels and movies can convey this, I thought. This is what war really is.

Bill Miller, my friend from Ft. Worth, boot camp, and Camp Lejeune, was assigned to another boat on the *Middleton* for this landing. Coming off the beach, an LCI was hit by mortar fire and burning badly. Bill's boat pulled alongside and rescued the whole crew before the LCI exploded. The bravery saved the lives of thirty men. He was later awarded the Army, Navy, and Marine Corps medal for bravery.

After the initial landings, we stayed at Eniwetok several weeks until the islands were "mopped up." The most fighting seemed to be taking place on Parry and Engebi islands. We lived on our boats most of the time because there was the constant need to unload the ships and move troops and supplies from island to island. The Japanese were ferocious fighters, driven by their religion and training to believe that their emperor was a god and that they were destined to be victorious. To die with honor was their highest achievement; surrender was out of the question because it was considered dishonorable. This was one of the primary reasons they were so cruel to their prisoners: they had surrendered. The Japanese were racists of the first order and looked upon other cultures as little more than animals. Surrender only increased their disrespect for others.

We knew the Japs were vicious and cruel because of the stories that poured out of China, Singapore, Pearl Harbor, Wake Island, Corregidor, and Manila. After our military met them face-to-face in the Solomons on Guadalcanal, Tulagi, Midway, the Coral Sea, in New Guinea, and recently on Makin and Tarawa, hundreds of stories about their cruelty to prisoners, their reluctance to take prisoners, and their willingness to choose death over surrender and captivity reached our ears. The Japanese disliked pilots the most because they related them directly to the bombings they were enduring. Many Japanese officers beheaded captured pilots with their famed Samurai swords in public ceremonies. We knew the Japs were cunning and deceptive, and collectively learned to hate the Japanese. Consequently, many American military men acted without compassion in return whenever the opportunity presented itself. Here were the two sides of the war, each believing (for very different reasons) it was certain death to be taken prisoner. Neither side took many prisoners. The hatred brewed on both sides.

The fighting continued on the islands. Planes bombed enemy targets and Navy warships shelled the enemy nearly around the clock. By day, we watched from just off shore where we waited to be unloaded. By night, the fighting resembled a brilliant fireworks display of tracers and exploding shells. At least once each night "Midnight Charlie" made his run above the atoll, strafing and dropping his bomb load while the entire fleet opened up on him with anti-aircraft fire. More often than not, he made his run and got out.

On the island, meanwhile, the Marines were busy battling the Japs, often hand-to-hand in concrete bunkers and inside the "spider tunnels." The latter allowed the enemy to lay low until the Marines passed by, when they popped up from behind and engaged them.

One day, I was back aboard ship for a while and another boat came in carrying a lone Japanese prisoner guarded by four Marines with automatic weapons. They were bringing him aboard for interrogation because there was a Marine interrogating officer aboard. Stripped of his clothing, all the prisoner had on was a filthy jock strap. The guards brought him up the gangplank to the quarterdeck, where a group of officers encircled and confronted him. I had never seen a man so terrified. He reminded me of a rabbit surrounded by hungry wolves. He looked as if he knew they were going to kill him at any moment. His eyes darted back and forth as he sought a means of escape.

By the time the fighting ended, the 5,000 or so Japanese soldiers on the island yielded only 225 prisoners. Our ship was selected to carry them back to Pearl Harbor.

# Chapter 10

# One Punch

He transferred aboard in Honolulu with a group of replacements. He was easily forty years old, but he insisted he was only thirty. He had the build of a boxer, muscular but fighting the flabbiness age inevitably brings. He looked like the typical punch drunk "has been" boxer. His name was Morris, and his nickname was "One Punch."

At one point he had been a pretty good welterweight. At least he carried several old and ragged newspaper and magazine clippings in his pocket that showed him in trunks and gloves, and small write-ups about fights he had waged or was going to have. He also insisted he was about to be ranked in the top ten welterweights, but gave up his opportunity when he enlisted in the Coast Guard. "One Punch" also claimed to have been at Guadalcanal aboard the *Leonard Wood* and that he had killed three Japs while in the beach party. He also had a faded news clipping from his hometown paper that claimed the same thing.

He kept a chip on his shoulder and had several fights on the ship. All but one ended with one or two punches. In the exceptional bout, an argument began on deck with a Bosun's Mate who had a 50-pound advantage plus considerable reach and the additional advantage of open space. The rough Bos'n put "One Punch" on the deck with a solid right before the fight was broken up. As you can imagine, "One Punch" did not want the fight to end that way, and as soon as he could, he followed the Bosun's Mate down to his quarters. Once they were in a confined space, he cornered him and began to get to him. Now the fight was completely different. In the cramped quarters, "One Punch" forced a close-in fight and methodically took him apart with vicious stomach and rib assaults, breaking three ribs before they could stop him. The Bos'n went to the hospital and a happy "One Punch" paid a visit to the brig. We all knew he was the kind of guy who would never admit he was whipped unless he was dead. We stayed clear of him because none of us wanted any trouble. He asked for and was given the "beach party."

At Eniwetok, the beach party went in with the Marines in the first waves. They helped fight until the beachhead was established before setting about their chores. The Japs, of course, did not distinguish between Marines and members of the Coast Guard. They also had this little peculiarity in that they would entice the Marines from their concrete bunkers to attack them. When the Marines charged, as Marines are wont to do, the Japs would duck back in and crawl out through their spider web of tunnels. A minute later they would pop up behind the Marines from a pile of debris that had already been investigated, fire, and dive back into the tunnel and pop up in another place.

Everyone was confused as to what was actually happening except "One Punch." After Guadalcanal he was prepared for anything. He and a yeoman named Miller were following the advancing Marines when he saw smoke and heard the crack of a rifle coming from a brush pile in front of him. He watched as two Marines up ahead of him fell to the ground. Miller, who was in front of "One Punch," also saw the ambush and fired his M-1 into the debris pile. There were two Japs hiding in the pile. They turned around in surprise and one of them fired at Miller at point blank range, hitting him the face and shoulder. Miller went down.

"One Punch" came sailing through the air like a mortar shell and landed right on top of the Japs, knocking their guns loose. As he did so, he rolled across the debris pile, pulling both of them with him like pulling buckets of water out of a well. At the end of the roll he was on his feet, and landed a knockout punch to one of them. The second one drew a knife and swung viciously at him slashing his right shoulder. "One Punch" dropped him with a straight left jab and was on top of him before he could get up. He killed the Jap with his own knife. Then he turned back to the other Jap who was still out cold. As he bent over him, a third Jap popped up from another tunnel about twenty yards away and started firing at other Marines farther to inland. "One Punch" yelled at him at the top of his voice and charged him like a raging bull. The only weapon he had was that dead Jap's knife. The surprised Jap spun around and fired twice, miraculously missing him both times. "One Punch" dove into him and finished him with one swift knife stroke to the chest.

By this time, others in the beach party who witnessed most of the action from a distance realized the knocked out enemy was just beginning to come around. They quickly closed in and tied his hands. He was still groggy as they ushered and prodded him back to the beach. They interrogated him there and eventually put him aboard one of the boats to send him to a ship for further interrogation. Japanese prisoners were few and far between because, as I noted earlier, most preferred death to capture. Word quickly spread that if you want a prisoner, just send "One Punch" out unarmed and tell him how many you need. Some of the Marines who had seen part of the action later asked him jokingly if he would like to transfer to the Corps.

"One Punch" didn't take their question in the manner intended. "Naw," he answered. "You guys are too slow for me."

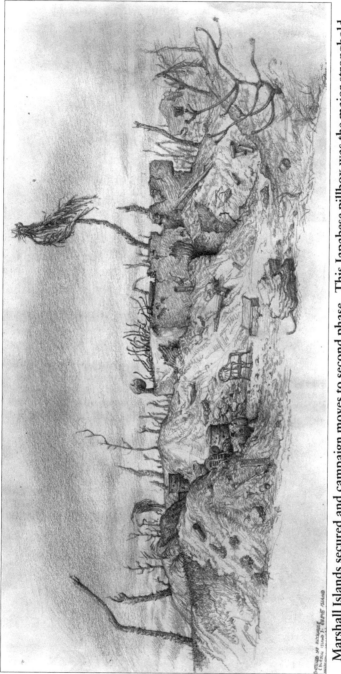

Marshall Islands secured and campaign moves to second phase. This Japabese pillbox was the major stronghold guarding the beach at Ebeye island. A unique meeting in the Marshall Island Campaign of three boys from the same small town in Texas. Two of my High School classmates (from a town of only 1,728 people), one Marine and one Navy rode on our Coast Guard ship and we were together for several weeks. We stopped by Kwajalien, Tarawa, and Makin islands on the way back to Pearl Harbor.

# Chapter 11

# It's a Small World

Word finally came that we were going to pick up the same Marines we had landed on Engebi and head back to Pearl Harbor. On my first trip I picked up a load of the Marines, including my hometown high school friend Plunket Powers. He told me about his experience on the island.

"When you are just charging in from the beach, you shoot a lot but you don't know whether you hit anyone. The only Japs I know I killed was on the second night. My buddy and I dug foxholes and he was asleep. I was on guard and I heard the worst jabbering you ever heard. Here were these three Japs coming down the beach, just jabbering away like they were on Fifth Avenue or something. They were laying land mines. If they had been quiet, I might not have seen them. I dropped two of them before the third could even get his gun up. I killed all three. I took this money off of them," he said, holding up a wad of Japanese Yen.

I felt so far away from home and everything that mattered to me. I had seen war and it wasn't as I imagined it might be. It was a filthy, dirty business. I think we all matured a lot in those two months. The feeling I had when the first mortar shell hit behind me was buried in my soul. It was as if a door had closed, cutting me off from the world, and now I was a part of all those things forever fixed on the movie screen.

Coast Guard combat artist Ken Riley sketched this drawing of a Japanese bi-plane destroyed on Makin island just minutes after it crashed. Pictures and movies of it this illustration made national news. The plane was still there when we came by five months later.

Our boat was back aboard the *Arthur Middleton* and Doll and I checked it over. The Japs had stitched a line of machine gun holes across it. Scratches on the steep ramp and side armor plate also indicated that the gunner had been slightly to our left as we approached, as that was the side showing the most damage. The plywood sideboard above the gunwale was not protected by armor. I wondered how the bullets had missed the Marines crouched in my boat. Just looking at the holes convinced me several of them should have been killed or wounded. My first invasion landing was behind me. It had certainly lived up to my wartime expectations.

Doll wiped his brow and looked me in the eye. "Lord, I thought somebody was pecking away at our tank lighter with a ball pin hammer! Any one of those bullets could have been the one, Wiley. I started confessing about a mile out," he continued. "In fact, I told the Lord some things I didn't intend for him to know about."

"Don't worry, our Chaplain can intercede for you if you're a devout Catholic and ask the Lord to overlook it," I joked in reply.

"Now, if you are a Protestant like me, you'll be up the ole' creek without a paddle." We both laughed.

The loud speaker interrupted our friendly discussion: "Now hear this! Now hear this! All boat crews muster with Custer on the quarterdeck. Must with Custer on the quarterdeck!"

Custer called out the names of seven Cox'ns and their crews. "You men go below and get your gear," he ordered. "You're being transferred to the island's supply depot as a work force to support the Army occupation forces. You have an hour to pack your sea bags and depart the ship. The ship's pulling out at 1400 p.m." The list did not include Doll, Bill, or me. I really felt sorry for the guys who had to stay behind. They would probably be stuck here for the rest of the war.

We were heading back to Pearl Harbor, so the *Middleton* took on some sailors and Seabees with tickets to the same destination. The second day out Plunket Powers came looking for me. "Hey, I'll bet you'd never guess who I just saw?"

"Abe Lincoln?" I joked.

"Not even close. Albert Ellison."

My mouth fell open. It was unbelievable. Three high school friends, a Marine, a Navy swabbie, and a Coast Guardsman from a little Texas school with only 300 students had come together on the far side of the world. The good part was that we would be together on the ship for two weeks, and we spent every minute together we could.

Albert had been on a cruiser, his tour was up, and he was pretty sure he was heading home. The three of us were on the deck talking late that night when Albert told us he was going to marry Marie Sweeny, his high school sweetheart. She didn't know it yet, he admitted, but he sure did. Albert was a grade ahead of me, but Marie was in my class. She was a beautiful girl, shy and very nice. Albert was a lucky guy. We talked about basketball, football, and the people and events at home. Albert had been a standout forward on the Itasca basketball team with a deadly corner shot. We replayed every game for the last five years and exchanged news about the other Itasca boys now distributed around the world in a wide variety of uniforms.

"Remember Tom Wilson? I talked to him just before the Battle of Coral Sea. He was on a destroyer. I think the Japs sank it. Do any of you know anything about him?" Albert inquired.

"No," Plunket answered. "But I heard that Pete Fuller got killed in North Africa. Also, Pete Ivey and James Hargiss."

The news was depressing. These were all guys I had grown up with, had known since I was born. "Itasca is getting hit pretty hard."

I thought about the growing list of casualties that began with Sam Baker and Hatten Sumner. The full significance of the danger I was in didn't hit me right away. I really believed I would survive the war—but then, so too did Sam and Hatten and all the rest. These were guys I had played football with, double-dated with, sat in class with, grew up with. Every time I got a letter from my mother, she added a few more names. It was now the end of March 1944, and we had not received any mail since early January. How many more names would be in my next batch of letters? I thought of my brother Joe and the image I had of his death in combat. I shut the thought out of my mind. Joe would make it, I told myself. For some strange reason I wasn't worried about Troy or Vic.

I shook these thoughts out of my head when Albert asked me, "Who are you going with now? Somebody said you had this girl in San Angelo."

His question caught me off guard. Everybody had to have a girl back home. I had created more out of this thing with Jean than was really there. I really didn't know her. I had seen her once in four years, just before I left. There was no doubt about her being cute. In fact, she was downright sexy. I guess that was one of the problems. The thought of her going out with the soldiers from Biggs Air Force base every night drove me nuts, but I couldn't blame her for enjoying her teenage years. The other part of the problem was that I was rather wild and determined to live life as completely as possible without any strings attached. The truth was that I wished Jean was madly in love with me, would remain true to me—and still let me do what I wanted. Then when the time came, I would decide. I was indeed a selfish young guy. Meanwhile, I was using her because she wrote me letters and I needed a girl.

"Yeah, she's Scrub Young's daughter," I answered Albert. "They used to live next door. She moved to San Angelo in 1939, but we kept in touch and she came to see me just before I left. Boy, would I like to see her right now."

"How much longer ya' think this war is gonna' go on, Plunk? What are they tellin' you guys?" Albert asked.

"Lord, I don't know," answered Plunket. "This was my first time to meet 'em face to face. You know what, though? The bastards won't surrender. After we killed everything on top of the ground, and tossed grenades in all those underground concrete coffins and burned them up with flame throwers, they killed themselves instead of surrendering. We'd find those guys, especially the officers, sitting on the floor of those bunkers with those Samurai swords stuck in their guts. They just sit down with the point against their gut and both hands on the handle. Then they just thrust it clean through themselves. Now, how can you fight something like that?" He stopped speaking for a moment and looked at us each in turn. We just nodded our heads in agreement.

"We had our whole fleet there," Plunket continued. "They didn't have any boats floating. The only airplanes up there in the daytime were ours, and we had them outnumbered five to one, with the Army sitting in the ships out there ready to come help us if we needed them. They still wouldn't surrender." He sighed loudly. "This is what we have to do all the way to Tokyo, and there are thousands of islands between here and there. And, when we get there, that'll just be the beginning. This war will go on for ten more years."

Both Albert and I took in every word and believed every one of them as our minds projected our own futures. Albert might get to go home on rotation, but he knew he would be coming back. Coral Sea, Midway, Guadalcanal, New Guinea, Tarawa, and now this. You'd think he'd had enough. But he would be back. I was just getting started. I had only been overseas three months. If they rotated us at two years, I still had twenty-one months to go. I did not have the opportunity to go home after boot camp. I would not see Jean again until I was 20, at least.

"I guess the old salts are right," I chimed in. "A sailor's home is his ship and you have to take advantage of every opportunity when your ship hits a port. 'Live until you die' is their motto." I added: "Well, enjoy it while you can. Wish I was going to Itasca with you, but since I can't, I'm going to enjoy every port we hit. Course, that doesn't include the beaches."

Chapter 12

# Commit Their Bodies to the Deep

The day started off like any other day at sea. The boat crews were back on our standard shipboard watches of four hours on and eight hours off. I had been on watch since 4:00 a.m., and would remain there until 8:00. From my watch in the 3-inch forward gun turret on the bow of the ship, the view was fantastic. Enewitok and Kwajalein were fast fading out of my mind. It had been different from what I thought it would be, but looking back I realized there were no real surprises. The veterans of the Tarawa operation had filled us in pretty well. The most significant difference between the stories and reality was the death. The awful stench of death permeated the entire atoll. That was something no one could get away from—even aboard the ships.

Once away from Enewitok it was easier to relax. I sat back and enjoyed the cool morning breeze blowing over the bow of the ship with the occasional spray of a fine mist of salt water. It was the most enjoyable thing I had encountered in weeks. My thoughts ran from Enewitok to home and to Joe. I dreaded the message I knew I would get with the next round of mail from home. Then I thought about Troy, who was probably in England now. Troy was a gunner on a B-17. He was supposed to go overseas right after the beginning of 1944. I wondered whether Troy saw Joe before . . . My thought trailed off. I knew Troy was not allowed to serve on the same plane with Joe. After the Sullivan incident, where five brothers all serving on the same destroyer died when the ship was sunk, the military put out an order prohibiting members of the same family from serving together.

The 3-inch gun crew consisted of four persons: trainer, pointer, and two loaders. I was the pointer. Each of us took turns as lookouts, training our binoculars toward distant skies. While one scanned the heavens the others slept or talked. Sometimes the watch was a lively place, with everyone participating in discussions about their accomplishments and conquests at some port. Sometimes we discussed officers, sometimes our food (or the lack of it), but mostly our talks were about women and stateside liberties. This morning had been a quiet one with very little discussion. I just sat there and enjoyed the breeze and the sunrise.

My reverie was interrupted just before 8:00 a.m. when the P.A. system came alive. "Now hear this! Now hear this! All hands not on watch will assemble on the quarterdeck at 0900 this morning for burial services."

I turned to a tall lean Bosun's Mate name Pieteki. I could hardly believe what I was hearing. "You mean we bury them at sea?" As odd as it sounds, I had never really given it much thought. I thought burials at sea were something from the days of sail.

"Yeah, might as well get used to it," he replied. "When these men die at sea, we always bury them as soon as possible. They can't keep them on the ship. We went through this every day after we left Tarawa. I hear we got thirteen this morning."

The bodies, wrapped carefully in white linen and weighed down with iron, were laid out on deck with a flag draped across each corpse. The flag on the ship was lowered to half-mast. We evacuated these men as wounded, but they died before they could get to the hospital at Pearl Harbor. A burial at sea is one of the most dramatic things I ever witnessed. Taps played over the P.A. system. Never before and never since has that trumpet sounded so beautiful, yet so sorrowful. Every one of us felt it. Some mother, some father, wife, sister, or brother would soon get a message that they would never see their loved one again. The Chaplain said a few words over each corpse. His words included the name of the deceased, where he was from, and a short scripture. His final words were always the same:

Coast Guard combat artist Ken Riley displaying his award-winning painting "For Thine is the Kingdom," at the Washington DC Times Herald Seventh Annual Art Festival. The *Middleton's* hospital was large and cared for many wounded and dying young men. The aftermath of each invasion included burials at sea.

"Oh, Lord, we commit their soul to you for all eternity. We now commit their bodies to the deep."

Once these words were spoken, the "pall bearers" lifted the burial boards and each linen-wrapped body, bound with straps and weighed down, slid over the side and plunged into the dark waters below.

These were young boys just like we us, seventeen to twenty-one years old from Kansas, New York, Utah, Mississippi, and even Texas. They would never go home again. All their parents and loved ones would know was that they had been killed in action somewhere in the South Pacific. As the bugler softly played "Taps," I looked back at the spot where the last body had plunged into the water. I wondered how long it would take it to reach the bottom. It was only a body, I told myself. The soul had already departed. I could not shake the thought of how lonely it must be for them to lie at the bottom of the vast ocean, in the dark forever.

"Dismissed!"

As I turned to leave, the Chaplain's words kept ringing in my ears: "We now commit their bodies to the deep."

# Chapter 13

# The Pearl of the Pacific

It was April when we finally arrived in Pearl Harbor. Almost four months of mail was waiting for me. I knew exactly what I was looking for, and I dug through the stack to find the V-mail letters from my mom. The first one was dated early February. According to my mom, the War Department informed them that Joe was missing in action. Two weeks later they were notified he had been killed in action on January 30, 1944. I had known that night that Joe was dead. The letters simply confirmed it, and eliminated any hope I still had my brother was alive.

Joe was the good one of the litter. Why Joe? He had always been the best one of us, and he meant so much to me. Maybe the letters were wrong, I thought, and he would turn up somewhere. Perhaps he was a prisoner of war. I kept this faint hope alive for many years after the war until I visited his grave in Holland. Troy never got to see Joe in England. He arrived too late.

There was a lot of scuttlebutt running around the *Arthur Middleton* that we would be going back to the States to pick up troops. Excitement ran high. In a final gesture of defiance, the Japanese prisoners we were carrying struck one final blow for the rising sun by spreading dysentery through the ship's crew. One third of the crew fell sick with the highly contagious disease and transferred to the naval hospital at Pearl Harbor. As luck would have it, I was included in this lucky group, which eliminated all thoughts of liberty and fun. From the hospital we could see the *Middleton* at anchor in Pearl Harbor. Rumors that the ship was going back to the States ran rampant. When the ship changed anchorage one day, the hearts of scores of quarantined crewmen fell with the thought we were being left behind. I was only sick for a few days, but the doctors kept me in the hospital for six weeks. Meanwhile, the *Middleton*, which was also under a quasi quarantine, was undergoing a complete cleansing and repainting from one end to the other to rid itself of the germs. The crew who stayed aboard later told us they never worked so hard. As it turned out, we were the lucky ones!

A group of Navy public relations personnel walked through our ward one day to pass out Purple Hearts. There were 50 of us from the *Middleton* in the same ward. Someone heard we were wounded at Enewitok. Of course, all of us refused the medal, although you can imagine the fun we had with this snafu.

The ward we were in was in a long low frame building with screened-in windows running along both sides. At the west end of the building was a screen door. The afternoon sun was directly behind the door. One of the highlights of our day was the arrival of the nurses. Each time one came in or out that door, the bright sunlight practically undressed them for us. Fifty cunning minds and 100 eyes jockeyed for position every time this happened. As with any group of gals, one was a real standout. Her name was Lori, and she had the most perfectly curved body I had ever seen. Lori always seemed to linger a while in the doorway, which pleased us greatly. In fact, the guys would take turns calling her and asking her a question at just the right moment to make her pause in the "spotlight." It was strictly "look, but don't touch," however. The guys who mustered up the courage to hit on her were shot down in flames. Rumor had it she was some officer's girl.

The six weeks in the hospital were relaxing, and the docs and nurses did everything within there power to make us comfortable. The truth, however, was after a few days we were bored silly and desperate to get back to our ship. I missed shipboard life and I missed my buddies. My clearance could not come soon enough. Once back aboard, I got liberty in Honolulu every third day. I visited Plunket at his camp and got wind of quite a few Itasca boys rumored to be in Hawaii.

One day Doll, who was rapidly becoming my best friend, took liberty with me. We went to the Royal Hawaiian Hotel to swim on the beach. Honolulu was not a large town at that time, but it was crammed with about one million servicemen from around ten every morning until about six in the evening (liberty hours). The downtown was jammed with bars, shops, and the always popular cat houses. There was no end to the brawls and fights brought on by the liquor and volcanic emotions stored within healthy young men looking for a place to release them. In combat zones, everyone worked as a team toward one objective: killing the enemy. No one noticed any differences when the bullets were flying. Once removed from the combat zone, however—and especially on liberty—it was open season on anyone in a different uniform or branch of service. Not only did the different services fight each other, but even the different ships or outfits in the same branch loved to throw fists. In the middle of this mess was the civilian population. Local Hawaiians appreciated Allied assistance, but developed a strong resentment against the loud, boisterous, drunken U.S. servicemen who took over their city, insulted their women, and picked fights with their young men.

The nice resort hotels were outside the downtown area, scattered along the beach toward the famous Diamond Head Mountain jutting out into the ocean and forming the other side of the half moon bay that included Honolulu harbor. The hotel and beach area were quieter and more sophisticated than downtown. Our submariners practically took over the Royal Hawaiian Hotel, using its quiet setting to relax after their long, silent, and dangerous missions against Japanese shipping and capital ships. None of us begrudged those guys the best quarters they could get. The rooms were restricted to submariners, but the bars and beaches were open to anyone.

Doll and I decided to swim across the inlet. The distance was about one mile, but it looked to be less than that when standing on shore. Doll was an expert swimmer from Florida, and he never thought anything swimming that sort of distance. We had both routinely dove into the ocean all over the Pacific, but I had never tried to swim an extended distance. Without much thought, I jumped in with Doll and set out for the far shore. The weeks of hospitalization had taken their toll on me. Halfway across the inlet, and at the deepest point, I realized I wasn't going to make it. "Doll, I can't do it," I panted. "My muscles are cramping."

"Don't panic, buddy. Don't fight it. Just steady strokes. Don't waste any energy." Then he repeated a phrase over and over as he coached every stroke until after what seemed like an eternity, my feet hit bottom. It was a lesson that has stayed with me forever: "Remember, yard by yard, life is hard, but inch by inch, it's a cinch."

I was still embarrassed by the fact that I hadn't learned to drink, but sitting at the open bars on Waikiki Beach sipping rum and fruit drinks was very close to perfect. There were plenty of girls in swimsuits and shorts for us to drool over. Unfortunately, every one was attached to some other guy, and scores of other guys were standing by to step in and make their move. Still, it was like a little touch of heaven to us.

The first thing I noticed about her as she walked down the beach was her shapely body. She really stood out from the other girls. She was also with two other guys. One was a uniformed naval officer. The other was in a swimsuit, and I assumed he was also an officer. As the trio approached I recognized her. It was Lori, the nurse at the hospital. I was sure she wouldn't recognize me, but as she walked by a hint of recognition and hesitation crossed her features, soon replaced by a fleeting friendly smile as she and the two officers settled down at the other bar. I imagined getting to know her and even being in the place of one of the officers, laughing with her. I carefully assessed my chances. She was beautiful, sexy, and could have her pick of any of the servicemen in Hawaii, where men outnumbered women 100 to 1. However, she was also an officer and I was just a seaman. She lived in a world several plateaus higher than my existence. I smiled into my drink. She offered a nice bit of imagination to take back to sea with me. I always set my targets too high, but if you aren't optimistic, you lead a very dull life.

"Boy, Wiley, did you get a look at that?" exclaimed Doll. "They must have designed the coke bottle after her. And wouldn't you know it, two officers hanging on her like bodyguards. I'll bet she is married to one of them."

"No, she's not married," I answered, lifting my glass to sip some rum. "She was one of the nurses at the hospital. I never saw a ring on her finger."

"You mean you know her? Well what are you waiting for? Go over and speak to her!" Doll punched me in the shoulder to entice me to get up and follow his suggestion.

"She doesn't know me. There were 50 guys in that ward and that wasn't the only ward she worked. She doesn't even recognize me and anyway," I continued, "and she's an officer and I'm not even a Petty Officer yet."

"Yeah, I guess you're right," said Doll with a slow shake of the head. "This damn war has sure classified everyone. It even divides the women up by rank. We can't have the same girls the officers have, but they can sure take ours."

Since he was from the Deep South, I couldn't resist jabbing him a little bit. "Well, now you know how those dark people feel that you guys have been sitting on for so long. How does it feel to sit in the back of the bus, Doll?"

Occasionally, each of the ships would pull away from their anchorage in Pearl Harbor and into a dock at Pearl or Honolulu to take on supplies, stores, and/or troops. When the *Middleton's* time came, two of the other ships from our convoy also moved in and docked alongside. They were the *Monrovia* (APA-31), and *Cavalier* (APA-37), which was the sister ship of the *Cambria*, the ship I had been on originally. The *Cavalier* pulled into the same slip as the *Middleton* and docked directly across from us. The ships were close enough so that you could converse with sailors on the other ship. The sailors on the *Middleton* noticed that a large number of "Wahines" (island girls) were on the dock, screaming and pointing to the deck of the *Cavalier*. One of the *Middleton* sailors who had just come from the dock broadcast the news. "Caesar Romero is on the *Cavalier*!" he yelled. "He's just a seaman first class. Look, you can see him there on the deck."

Sure enough, there sat the actor on the deck, winding up a coil of line, smiling, and occasionally waving back to the screaming girls. Each time he waved the tempo and roar of the screaming picked up.

Romero was surrounded by a several sailors, each of whom also wanted to get in on the attention. Bill, Doll, and I later talked to some of the sailors on the *Cavalier*. They told us Romero had refused a commission and just wanted to be treated like any other sailor. Everyone aboard the *Cavalier* liked him. He was a regular Joe. The newspaper in Honolulu broke the story about his being on the *Cavalier*.

Unlike today, most of the movie stars of the early 1940s went into some branch of the service to serve their country, and the *Middleton* had its share. One young man had starred in several low budget Westerns. The ship, of course, managed to get all of his films and showed them, much to his embarrassment, as the sailors jeered and hooted as he out-drew, out-rode, and out-fought all the bad guys and finally kissed the cowgirls.

One guy who went on to a great career was Wally Westmore, a member of the famous Westmore makeup artist family. After the war Wally went on to become a legend as the number one Hollywood makeup expert. Aboard the *Middleton* in 1944, however, he was just a young 20- year-old sailor everyone liked. He coordinated all entertainment aboard ship, and did a great job, too. Wally was responsible for the excellent amateur shows we enjoyed. A third person who was on his way to becoming a celebrity aboard the *Middleton* was a young combat artist named Kenneth P. Riley. His drawings and paintings of action and shipboard life in the South Pacific won many national awards and claimed a permanent place in the archives of the Navy and Coast Guard's documentation of the great Pacific war.

When our ship pulled out of Pearl Harbor, the first order we received was to catch up with and dispose of all of the Captain's Masts and court-marshal paperwork. Prominent within these legal papers were the names of Gamble and Dees, who were famous on the *Middleton*. Each was an expert in his respective field, but collectively the pair caused the officers more problems than the rest of us put together. Simply put, they had been on the ship for two years, and they wanted off. And they went to wild lengths to get home.

Gamble was sometimes a Bos'n Mate and sometimes a seaman, depending on his latest activity. He was by far the best Bos'n Mate

When 500 guys are together on a ship months on end away from the civilized world, they create their own social life. Jam sessions were common. In this illustration, Ken Riley sketched a group of us involved in a bit of "Boogie-Woogie" on the way to Saipan. Luckily, we had Wally Westmore, one of the famous Westmore brothers, on our ship. His family played a prominent role in the Hollywood make-up industry. Wally planned entertainment programs and developed amateur talent.

on the ship. He was expert in handling the booms, davits, and loading and unloading the ship. He was the most knowledgeable man on deck and the *Middleton* could not operate effectively without him. He was often in the ship's brig. When he was needed on deck, he was brought up to take over until a loading or unloading operation was completed, at which time he was sent back to the brig. Gamble was big and tough. Oddly, he was not a bully. In fact, he was one of the friendliest guys around and was well-liked on the ship. Everyone respected him. His problems got worse every time the ship entered a port—any port.

Dees, his comrade-in-arms, was the best cook on the ship. The Executive officer had written both of these guys up so often that liberty was permanently suspended. Every time they saw a bar, they got rip-roaring drunk and tore up everything in sight. They also had a problem recognizing when liberty was over and it was time to return to the ship.

"Going over the hill" (going Absent Without Leave, or AWOL) was the rule for these guys rather than the exception. They did it in Pearl Harbor, Honolulu, and Maui. The Exec notified the shore patrol, and most of the time they were both picked up and brought back before the ship pulled out. Before long, this became quite a game. Gamble and Dees would wait until the day before the ship was ready to pull out and then find a place to hide. The first few times this happened, the Master-at-Arms went ashore and searched the local jails and late bars until he found them. The Exec finally figured out what was happening and kept them in the brig while in port.

This time, however, these guys were really in trouble. They had gone over-the-hill in a combat zone: Enewitok. Why anyone would go do such a thing during a live amphibious invasion was hard to understand, but Gamble and Dees slipped ashore the day before we left in the hope the ship would leave without them. Dees, who was in the beach party, found a case of Saki and sent the word to Gamble to join him on the ashore. An alert Beach Master returned them to the ship's brig.

Once underway, the Captain decided to hold Captain's Mast to punish them for their crime. The mast took place in the officers' wardroom. The Captain, Exec, and a group of officers were waiting in the room when Gamble and Dees were brought in by the Master-at-Arms. Thinking they would liven the place up a bit, they arrived dressed as ghosts in robes fashioned from bed sheets. Commander McKay took one look and exploded with rage. "What in hell is the meaning of this? You men take off those ridiculous sheets!"

"No, sir, we can't" Dees responded.

"Can't?" shouted McKay. "This is a ship's court and you men are out of uniform. I told you to take them off, and that's an order!"

"Well, if you insist." Gamble replied meekly, but with the glowing look of the devil in his eyes. Both men threw off their sheets and stood stark naked in front of the officers.

Captain Olsen was furious. "Vat is der meaning of dis? Get dose clothes back on!"

With those direct instructions, they both again wrapped the sheets around themselves. McKay was smart enough to realize he was losing the battle, but could not calm himself down. "Where are your clothes?"

"In the laundry, sir," answered Dees.

"Don't you know that you can't come in here wearing sheets?" he screamed.

Gamble and Dees looked at one another, shrugged, and exclaimed in unison, ""All right, sir!" Together, they threw off the sheets a second time.

"Master-at-Arms, you will take these men back to the brig immediately!" ordered McKay, waving his arms in frustration. The smiling men were marched back to the brig. The Captain's Mast was never resumed.

Where the next invasion would be was a favorite guessing game of everyone. In the mind of the average serviceman, the logical steps to take to reach Tokyo were the same ones the Japanese had used to capture the most of the South Pacific: Guadalcanal, New Guinea, Wake Island, Guam, the Philippines, Singapore, and then Japan itself. In the back of our minds, though, we expected we would also have to take Rabaul and Truk, two Japanese strongholds. Word was that Truk was a mighty fortress, and the offensive would meet the Imperial Japanese Fleet head-on. We all expected it would be hundreds of times worse than Tarawa, Kwajalein, or Eniwetok.

The whole crew felt the tension building up. We knew we were approaching another thrust somewhere. We just didn't know where. The day we all knew would come finally did when the ship took on supplies and we headed out to sea. As was the custom, we learned our destination only after we had put to sea.

# Chapter 14

# Idle Time Chatter

The boat division was the "Third Division" aboard ship. Our living quarters in this outfit were on the first deck below the main deck, almost directly below the quarterdeck. The quarterdeck was in the aft section of the ship, immediately behind the superstructure on the main deck. The ship's gangway led off the quarterdeck. When the ship was at anchor or in port, the officer of the deck's post was on the quarterdeck.

A watch post was assigned to each man. It might be a work detail or gun crew, boat watch, or some other duty. The "black gang," or machinists, were assigned to the ship's engines. Pharmacists' mates were dispatched to the ship's infirmary, yeomen to secretarial jobs, signalmen to various radio and communications, cooks to the galley, officers mess cooks to the officers' galley, and gunner's mates to the ship's armory. Seamen, Coxn's, and Bos'n's Mates worked on the decks, stood gun watches, and manned the helm. The public address system coordinated these activities with a shrill whistle followed by "Now Hear This!"

The floor was the deck. Walls were bulkheads, ceiling was overheads, and doors were hatches. Looking forward, the right hand side of the ship was starboard and the left was port. Of course, the front of the ship was the bow and rear of the ship was the stern. Ropes were "lines" until they became big enough to be called "hawsers." When troops were aboard, everyone ate only twice a day except those going on watch, who could always go the galley and get sandwiches and coffee. When not on watch, anyone could sleep, read, write letters, or just about anything he wanted.

The food aboard ship was not very good. Breakfast was predictable. Saturday morning chow was hot beans (like pork and beans), a salty bacon, cornbread, and coffee. On Friday mornings we got the infamous S.O.S. (shit on a shingle). This was a white sauce with bits of beef or ham served on a piece of toast. Most other mornings offered powdered eggs, oatmeal, grits, or French toast, depending on the cook's mood. Coffee and toast were always available, and sometimes if we were lucky sweet rolls and canned juice. The second meal was a variation of wieners and sauerkraut, horsemeat, Australian beef (which was very tough), dehydrated potatoes, and canned vegetables. The pastries they fed us were generally good, and the cooks aboard the *Middleton* cooked a lot of pies and cakes. What we missed were fresh items, like eggs, fruit, milk, and good meat.

Tex Thornton, a Bos'n's Mate Second Class in his mid-30s, had been in the Coast Guard for seven or eight years. He and I became friends at Camp Lejeune. One night he encouraged me to wear one of his uniforms with the Bos'n's Mate 2C stripes on it, and we went to the NCO Club. I would have been court-martialed for impersonating a non-commissioned officer if I had been caught. Tex thought it was all a big joke and more or less took me under his wing. He could tell sea stories with the best of them. One evening we were sitting on our bunks talking with other sailors when a Cox'n named O'Ryan spun off a story about a night in Norfolk and how he was so drunk he couldn't find his way back to the ship. Afraid that he would miss it, he picked a fight with a shore patrol who delivered him to his ship under arrest. At that point, O'Ryan turned to Tex and made some comment about Texas not having any good liberty towns.

Tex arched his eyebrows. "Have you ever hear of El Paso?"

"El Paso?" replied O'Ryan. "That's out west somewhere. I am talking about a place where ships come in and sailors go on liberty."

"Hell, we got shipping at El Paso!" shot back Tex. "The Rio Grande comes right up from the Gulf. Course, if you're ship has a Yankee skipper on it, he may not know about it and he might stop off in Corpus Christi, but let me tell you, we Texans know about El Paso."

O'Ryan narrowed his eyes. "What's so special about that place?"

Tex continued: "You dock on the U.S. side and walk across the border into Juarez. Boy, that Juarez is something else. You pick out girls like picking apples off a tree. Hell, you can have fifteen or twenty in one night, and it will only cost you fifty cents a piece!"

Tex knew he had his audience in his hand. O'Ryan knew it too. "Keep going," urged O'Ryan.

"The last time I went up there, me and the skipper, a fella' name Joe Olgethorpe," continued Tex, "we went over to Monica's, which is one of the best places in Juarez. They have about one hundred girls in there, and you can dance, drink, and take 'em upstairs, one or two at a time for fifty cents a shot."

"Two at a time?" Asked O'Ryan.

Tex just nodded and kept talking. "Well, Joe found someone he liked and he just stayed upstairs. Me, I was passing it around until suddenly, I realized I was clean out of money. I was pretty drunk too, so I decided I would just go outside and wait for Joe. I went across the street and sat down on a little bench by the street. I guess it was for bus passengers. Anyway, I went to sleep. After a while, I woke up to the worst noise I'd ever heard. There were fire trucks and police cars all over the place and smoke was pouring out of Moncia's. The streets were filled with people and the noise was terrible. Everyone seemed to be looking up at the roof. Police and firemen were running around giving directions and pointing up there. I looked up and standing out on the edge of the roof with nothing but his skivvies on, one hand waving a bottle of Tequila and the other one just waving, was Joe Oglethorpe! He was yelling, 'Now, hear this! Fire in No. 3 hold! All hands break out the fire hoses! Stand by to abandon ship! Thornton, where the hell are you?'"

Tex stopped, remembering the event and smiling. "Come on, what happened next?" asked O'Ryan.

"The firemen spread a net under him," continued Tex, "but Oglethorpe kept running back and forth under the edge of the roof. The firemen on the ground were trying to follow him with the net and were tripping over each other. One of the women was down on the ground running around with Joe's hat screaming, 'Captain Joe! Captain Joe! Don't jump! Don't jump!'"

By this time I was laughing myself hoarse. "That must have been some scene," I blurted out.

"Oh, it was," Tex confirmed. "Finally, Joe whirled around and yelled down at the growing crowd, "All right men, we're going down. Abandon ship! Abandon ship! All hands, abandon ship!' Then, he used one hand to grab his nose and he jumped right off the roof, waving his bottle in the other hand. He was up about three stories. The firemen ran the net under him just before he hit the ground and he bounced and came down on his feet right in front of me. He was dazed for a few seconds, but he shook his head to clear it and then spotted me," continued Tex. "Joe looked surprised and yelled out, 'There you are Thornton! Damn, I've been looking all over for you. We're gonna' have to get another ship. That one took a fish right down the gut."

At that, we all laughed and the group broke up for the eight o'clock watch before anyone tried to top Tex's story.

One of the more colorful characters on the *Middleton* was Custer, a Bosn's Mate First Class in charge of the Third Division or Boat Division. Custer was a big guy, standing more than six feet tall and weighing more than 220 pounds. He had a roly-poly face, almost like a baby face, which was deceiving because it did not match his personality. Custer was one tough guy. "Muster with Custer" was a favorite phrase of everyone on the ship. As the P.A. system constantly reminded us, "Boat crew's muster with Custer on the quarterdeck!" or "Third Division muster on the quarterdeck with Custer!"

Because he was the one who passed down orders we pretended to despise him, but we secretly admired him. Like everyone who administers authority, Custer was blamed for every decision and rule handed down. But the fact was that he was good at his job, and could swing a boom, run a davit, and stow for sea with the best of them. As far as I was concerned, he was firm but fair.

Crossing the International dateline had been an event of some note, but it was nothing compared to the crossing of the Equator. Only ninety of the entire crew of 500 had crossed it before. As tradition demanded, these ninety "shellbacks" or old salts initiated the 410 "pollywogs." Strange things happened on the day we were slated to cross. The Chief Warrant Officer was named the *Middleton's* "Sheriff" and his team of Bos'n's Mates were named his deputies. The pollywogs were placed on a list of criminals arrested and brought forth on the deck to stand trial. The Grand Judge was old Neptune himself, played by Lieutenant Hoyle. The judge read outrageous charges against each victim or in some cases, groups of victims. These ranged from insubordination to disrespect for the Grand Dragon, or suspected thoughts about disrespect for any particular shellback. Of course, everyone was guilty and harsh punishment was meted out. The punishment ranged from head shaving to body painting, pushups, and running the gauntlet. The gauntlet was two lines of shellbacks with belts in their hands. As you ran between them, everyone tried to deliver his best lick on the darting twisting prisoner. Occasionally, belligerent pollywogs were carted off to the ship's brig, which became crowded quickly.

The theory of the entire crossing event was that the shellbacks retained control unless the pollywogs mutinied and took control of the ship away from them. About midday, we Pollywogs organized ourselves and, with our superior numbers, began the mutiny. We quietly took positions at the fire hoses. At a given signal, we broke them out and turned them on full power. The move caught the shellbacks completely off guard. And so began an enormous battle all over the ship to control the hoses. We pollywogs had planned our attack well and quickly gained control of the ship.

The Executive Officer, an old shellback himself, saw what was happening from the bridge and got on the P.A. system. "All right, this has gone far enough!" he exclaimed. "All unauthorized personnel are hereby commanded to turn off those fire hoses and surrender them."

His bluff might have worked if it had not been for some smart thinking on the part of a seaman named Murray. Murray controlled the hose on the left bridge and instructed several other pollywogs to do likewise. With the P.A. system still on, he let fly a blast of seawater that nearly washed the Executive Officer off the bridge! Murray and several others washed away a few shellbacks and took over the helm.

After all the gurgling, bubbling, and commotion had settled down, Murray spoke over the P.A. system. "I hereby declare victory for the pollywogs! The ship is under our control. Shut down all fire hoses. Would King Neptune please come to the bridge?"

Several willing sailors ushered Lieutenant Hoyle to the bridge. "Men, by order of the Grand Dragon, I hereby declare you all shellbacks," announced the Lieutenant. "Well done!"

We pollywogs hoisted our colors and flew them until the sun went down. It was a day when thoughts of war and home were far from our minds. We had the time of our lives. It was an event I will remember forever.

The "man-overboard theory" was tested one night before the ship reached Guadalcanal. A man fell overboard from one of the gun pits on the stern of the ship one night. No one saw him after he hit the water. The escort ships were advised of the mishap by red light and Morse code, and one of the destroyer escorts went back to look for him (or at least that was what we heard). I don't recall his name, but we never saw him again. Radio silence and the blackout rules prohibited actions that might otherwise have saved him.

The islands of Guadalcanal and Tulagi witnessed months of intense fighting in 1942. It was the first land battle of the war for American troops, and it took well more than a year to secure completely both islands. I saw many beached Japanese ships lining "Iron Bottom Bay," so named because of the warships that litter the seabed. Bowing to the inevitable, some of the skippers of the Jap ships had pushed their craft ashore. The wrecks were grotesque and even eerie, their bows pointing almost skyward and their sterns partially sunk. The reminded me of ghost ships, and quite frankly, gave me the shivers.

Supposedly, Guadalcanal had been secured, so when we steamed toward our anchorage I was surprised to hear General Quarters sounded and the announcement, "All hands, man your battle stations!"

Suddenly, from the other side of the harbor, there was a terrific explosion and flames shot up into the air several hundred feet. A Japanese midget submarine had slipped into the harbor, apparently using the incoming convoy as camouflage, and torpedoed a tanker full of fuel. The destroyers and destroyer escorts quickly went to work scouring the harbor, dropping depth charges in an effort to destroy the submarine. The search continued for hours. I never found out whether we got it or not. Once we anchored and the "All clear" sounded, life went on as usual.

Our first day at Guadalcanal was a special one, and we eagerly waited for the Bos'n's Mate to call "Attention boat crews, Muster with Custer on the boat deck!" We gathered excitedly. "Men, the new boat assignments will be posted on the bulletin board. New Cox'n's taking on boats are Doll, Wiley, Baker, Lloyd, Myers, McKim, Breland, Stuart, Ryan, Hogan and O'Neal."

Doll and I were ecstatic. We had our own boats! We had made it. As soon as the muster was over we rushed to the bulletin board to read the list. I had Boat 13, an LCVP; Doll had Boat 29, an LCM (Tank Lighter). The fact that Billy Miller was in my crew as my "motor mac" only added to my excitement. Never were two boats in the entire history of the Navy or Coast Guard kept as spotless.

When I was in Honolulu, I visited an auto store and bought a steering wheel knob in anticipation of this day. The knob allowed more control than the stiff steering wheel. I had also pondered long and hard over what I would name my boat. I didn't really have a special girl, but I decided I would name my boat Jean. I thought now of her beautiful flaming red hair and sexy body. "She will do," I said aloud. On many a lonely watch I had dreamed of the day when I would be home asleep on the couch, and Jean would come in and kiss me and tell me she knew I would return and that she had waited for me. Based on these dreams, I named the boat after her and had "Jean" painted on the gunwale beside my position.

Doll and I identified with one another well. Sailors inherently love to gather and brag about their exploits with women, fighting, and drinking. Both Doll and I felt so left out. We listened intently to stories about San Francisco's Market Street, San Diego's beaches, and Hollywood's beautiful girls, but we had very little to offer in the way of experience. When we were alone, we never felt the need to lie to each other. We talked instead about the life in front of us. Doll firmly believed we would find girls when we got home. We had not had a leave to go home or even a decent liberty since enlisting.

Boat duty in Guadalcanal was interesting. Once I had to take a chief across the bay to a Seabee warehouse. Tulagi Bay was the most beautiful thing I had ever seen. The water was between 10 and 30 feet deep, but as clear as the air above it. The beautiful coral flooring looked to be within touching distance. Miles and miles of the bay was this way.

On another trip, with just the crew assigned to my boat, we passed what looked like a mouth of a river. It was a remote part of the island. The river ran under a canopy of trees straight back into the jungle. Curiosity overruled caution and we slowly drove into the river. The waterway narrowed quickly until it was barely wide enough for the boat, but on we motored. The jungle and trees completely engulfed us now. Finally, the terrain opened and we spotted a native village built along the riverbank. When our landing craft beached, the native women and most of the men disappeared into grass huts. After demonstrating that we meant no harm, I was able to coax one of the men over to the boat. To my surprise, he spoke some broken English.

"What's your name?" I asked.

"Taboo," he replied, looking more than a bit apprehensive. The natives were dark with reddish hair and freckles. Taboo looked to be about thirty, but it was hard to tell.

"Why did everyone run?" I asked.

"You see, men tell their women to hide when soldiers approach."

"We are not soldiers. We are sailors." Bill replied slowly.

"Americans?" His eyes narrowed and he took a step backward.

"Did you like the Japanese better?" asked Bill.

He shook his head vehemently. "No! Japanese very cruel. Kill people. Hurt women. American, no kill, no hurt."

"Why don't you like Americans?" I asked.

"Americans bring missionaries," he answered. "Before missionaries, everybody push! Push! All the time! Now no push push! Missionaries tell us push push bad." He shook his head again. "Girls say, 'No more push push! American soldiers come here to push push with girls, but when missionaries came, they say stop. American soldier no stop, so village men make girls hide when solider come."

"Do you like to push push?" asked Bill with a smile.

"O.K., but missionaries scare hell out of girls. Now no more fun. Say gotta' marry to push push!"

The three of us could barely hold back our laughter as we looked around at the thatched huts. The ground in the entire village was packed down tightly by years of treading with bare feet. Not a single blade of grass grew in this area, but a dense undergrowth of jungle rising to tremendous heights surrounded the village. I looked up and scanned the trees. Birds and monkeys were moving in the treetops. It looked just like the Tarzan and Frank Buck movies we watched back home.

I looked back at the huts and spotted two of the young girls lingering as long as they could near one of the entrances, looking at us and offering quick smiles. Neither would ever be confused with Dorothy Lamour in a sarong, but I was beginning to understand what the guys who had been away from women for so long meant when they said, "Your eyes go first. Pretty soon, native girls begin to look like high school cheerleaders."

It was time to go. The narrow river was too narrow to turn around in the normal fashion, so we found the widest spot right in front of the village and used long lines from the shore to spin the boat in the opposite direction. We three adventurers, sworn to secrecy about this little side trip, gave Taboo a few cigarettes and K-rations and headed back to the coast.

Enterprising Americans doing occupational duty in the Solomon Islands devised a brilliant way for battle-worn servicemen to relax and enjoy some of the luxuries from back home. How they did it, I don't know. Somehow, a group of Seabees, sailors, and Marines turned one of the small islands into a small Las Vegas with roulette wheels, poker and black jack tables, and bingo games. The place even had dealers, pit bosses, and of course, Shore Patrol and Military Police to keep order. Boats from the ships brought in load after load of sailors and troops eager to try their luck.

Doll and I took one of our recreation days and headed over to the island. Neither of us had gambled before, but we were the type who got easily addicted to it! We lost a dollar or two on black jack table and roulette wheel, drank some beer, and attended one of the amateur shows. Without women, the men improvised. The shows consisted of small bands, a few pretty good soloists, and some stand-up comedians. All said, it was a pleasant day. I never figured out how "Vegas South" came to be. A few officers and supply types deviated from the book to allow it, but the end result was well worth it. It gave the men a little taste of the good old USA—but where did all that money go?

Finally, the *Arthur Middleton* loaded up a portion of the 2nd Marines and set sail. The 2nd was one of the units that had fought for so long to take Guadalcanal and the Solomon Islands. Guadalcanal was the first American land victory, but the campaign also witnessed some tremendous sea battles between the Imperial Japanese fleet and the bedraggled American Navy. Both sides suffered heavy casualties in terms of ships, planes, and men. The beaches bore gruesome testimony to the water struggle, with grounded and partially sunken vessels of all kinds and buoys bobbing in the bays to represent sunken warships. Japan dominated the sea for a while, but the battles of Coral Sea and Midway shifted that aspect of the war decisively in our favor.

The Marines told us about their long treks through the jungle and swamps fighting the Japanese, of the threat of Jap snipers camouflaged in the towering tree tops, of outflanking the enemy with amphibious landings, and of the constant air raids and strafing by Japanese planes. Even when they thought the island was secure, snipers and Banzai charges killed their buddies as they stood in the chow line or walked to a latrine. The Marines also told us about how the Japanese would call out to them in the dark, when they were in their foxhole. "Hey, Joe. I'm from the section B, let me in."

If a G.I. relaxed and answered or gave away his position in any way, the Jap would toss in a hand grenade. The Marines also related the extreme cruelty practiced by the Japanese. For example, on one occasion the Japanese surrounded a Marine and urged him to give himself up. When he surrendered, they took his rifle and bayoneted him. Any Marines taken prisoner and hauled away had an even worst time of it. The Japanese starved and beat them, and forced them to live in unspeakable squalor. Torture was routine. It was little wonder why American troops hardened their emotions toward this sort of enemy. And it was extremely dangerous to capture men who did not mind dying. Given this, it is easier to understand why most of us believed the only good Jap was a dead Jap.

Chapter 15

# A Rose by Any Other Name

The guessing game was over. We had the 2nd Marines aboard and were heading for Saipan. These were hostile waters, and every white cap and shadow could be hiding a Japanese periscope. The crews manned the gun pits and lookout posts kept sharp watches. None of us believed a Task Force this size could move undetected into the heart of the enemy's stronghold. Each day the planes from the baby flattops in our convoy took off to fly sorties to who knows where, surveying the route ahead of us. When they returned, our spotters picked them up and identified them. Until they were identified, however, they were "bogies" and subject to being shot down with our antiaircraft fire. There was almost constant chatter on the intercom, and it went like this: "Bogies at two o'clock. Five strong. Hell Cats."

Landing on an aircraft carrier was dangerous, and accidents were common. Many planes went over the side into the water. Some planes that crashed on the deck were pushed over the side to clear the deck for other planes waiting to land. When a pilot was in the water, a destroyer or DE usually fished them up.

I remember well the 6th of June 1944. Although we were on our way to our own D-Day, we heard the news from the far side of the world about the landings in France. Tokyo Rose never mentioned it in her propaganda broadcasts.

Approaching Saipan. We carried with us the bloodied 2nd Marines, who had fought on Guadalcanal and Tarawa, and were now preparing for another campaign. In this illustration, Coast Guard combat artist Ken Riley captures three Marines taking a breather. One is reading a letter from home for the tenth time. He will carry this priceless treasure from his wife, mother, or girlfriend in his shirt pocket so he can re-read it every chance he gets. Another Marine is cleaning his M-1 rifle to make sure it will work when he needs it, while his buddy looks on.

Tokyo Rose was the name given to the mysterious Japanese woman we heard on the radio almost anywhere in the South Pacific. She became a legend, and every G.I. recognized her name and despised her. She spoke English almost without an accent, and played popular American songs for the troops. The Japanese used her as a propaganda tool to try to weaken and destroy our morale.

I remember one incident in particular. A group of us was sitting in the chow hall after the four to eight watch one evening eating salami sandwiches and drinking coffee. We were still several days out of Saipan, on the way for what would be one of the bloodiest campaigns of the war for us. We were listening to Tokyo Rose on the radio:

> You American Marines just can't seem to get the message.
> Remember how tough it was on Tarawa, Kwajalein, and

Eniwetok? Remember those Marines lying dead in the surf and on the beach? Well, I've got news for you Leathernecks. That was a cakewalk compared to what it will be when you get to your destination. Yes, we know that you have got a large task force moving west and we know where you are going. We have got some real surprises for you, too. Thousands of brave Japanese soldiers are waiting on the beach for you—if you get that far. You see our big surprise is the Japanese navy is going to cut you off before you get there. Tonight we've already shot down eighty-four of your planes, sunk two of your carriers, three cruisers, and eight of the ten transports in one convoy. So even if your ship gets by, you won't have the support you need. You'll be all alone. Our soldiers are pretty mad about you killing some of their friends on Kwajalein and Eniwetok, and they are going to get even. However, since the Japanese solder is humanitarian, they will not kill you if you throw down your guns and raise your hands when you first hit the beach.

Tokyo Rose continued:

Now don't be foolish and die for all those politicians in Washington. They are the only ones who want war. If you wait until the war is over, then you can go back and join your wife or girlfriend in the states. Think about it. Anything you want to ear or drink. Maybe even meet some nice Japanese ladies. No more K-rations. No more sleeping in foxholes. No more getting shot at or bombed. What do you say, Joe? Remember, just throw down your gun and raise your hands.

As she trailed off her message, the radio began playing "Coming in on a Wing and a Prayer," with Jo Stafford singing it. After the first verse, Tokyo Rose cut in again: "No, I haven't forgot about you fly boys either. If you don't want to die, you can land your airplane at any Japanese landing strip. All of our islands have landing fields and you Americans don't have any place to land since your carriers will be all sunk."

The music switched to country western and one of her favorites, "Somebody Else is Taking My Place." She interrupted again after the first verse: "You didn't think that she was going to just sit and wait for you, did you? I got news for you. The longer this war goes on, the better she likes it. She can have a different stateside Johnny every day while you're gone. You are the dumb one; trying to fight and prolong this war. She's having the time of her life and you're going to help her by dying, trying to steal our Japanese islands. Well, think it over Johnny and don't forget what's waiting for you."

"You know," commented James O'Neal with a chuckle, "that broad is more fun than Amos and Andy!" We all laughed.

"I wonder where she learned to speak English like that," replied Red Meyers. "And where does she get her records? She's really up to date on that stuff."

"I'll bet you that broad is from San Francisco," answered Custer, who had just walked up to where we were sitting. "In fact, she could have gone to school with any one of us."

"If she's from the States," I replied, "how could she ever end up helping the Japanese?"

"Yeah," shot back Bill. "The bastards sneak attacked us at Pearl Harbor. They're the ones who invaded China, Manchuria, Burma, hell, the whole damn Far East! How could anyone with any intelligence who has seen the way we live in the States possibly support them?"

It was a good question. All of us were of the same mind. Here was an apparently well educated young woman who in all likelihood had grown up in the America. We couldn't understand how she could be blind to the atrocities the Japanese were committing. It was hard to overcome the feelings of honor and fair play that was part of the American heritage.

Custer spoke up again. "My brother was in the Army Air Corps stationed in the Philippines. The Japanese captured him and as near as we know, he was in the Bataan Death March. I watched those newsreels every chance I got. Those men were walking skeletons and the Japanese walked them to their death, beating them—and worse—every step of the way." Custer stopped and sighed. "It's not right for any human to treat another human that way. Not even an animal."

Custer had never acted or said anything like this before. As he continued speaking, his eyes became moist. "Just as sure as what I do helps us to win the war, what she does in just as bad as what those bastards did," he said, nodding his head toward the speaker. "She's a part of them. I hope they hang her along with the bastard who rides the white horse."

Every set of eyes locked on Custer. No one said anything for a while. Tom O'Brian finally spoke up. "I come from the San Joaquin Valley in California. I knew many good and decent Japanese. In fact, half the people I went to school with were Japanese. Those people aren't like the butchers we're fighting. Of course, when the war started we rounded them up and sent them to a camp, because you never know which ones would turn out to be saboteurs and we couldn't take any chances. But, we didn't treat them like they treat their prisoners."

"Did you ever really get to know them though?" I asked.

O'Brian shrugged. "Well, no I guess not. They were always clannish. They're real big on family and usually spoke in Japanese so you couldn't understand them."

"I'll bet if the truth were known, they're all fifth columnists," chimed in O'Neal. "Jeez, I mean they planned Pearl Harbor for years and I heard they contacted every Japanese in America to ask for help. They were just waiting for the right moment. After all, blood is thicker than water."

"You know what I think?" added O'Brian. "There's so many Japanese in Hawaii that they will end up taking that over. In fact, I can't even tell the difference between Japanese and Hawaiians. You just wait and see," he continued. "When they get everything ready, they're going to take over Pearl Harbor. I'll bet that's why they never followed up their attack with an invasion. They don't have to. I'll tell you something else. That Tokyo Rose is right there in Hawaii, broadcasting from a secret radio transmitter."

This logic got a lot of attention. Why not? No wonder the Japs knew so much about our activities. The island was swarming with them and what better place for Tokyo Rose to be than right in the heart of the U.S. command? About that time the music on the radio faded and the voice of Tokyo Rose filled the air:

So, they gave you a few hours of liberty in Honolulu so you can run out and have a few beers with a million other GIs. That's the best they'll ever do for you, Joe. It's a lot different from being home, isn't it? But don't you worry, when we take over Honolulu will be different. We'll get all those submariners out of the Royal Hawaiian and we'll have liberty at night. Oh, it'll be romantic again Joe, like what the recruiting officer promised you. I can still see those moonlit nights on Waikiki, looking at Diamond Head and the white surf. That's not what the brass gave you though, is it?

As her voice fell away, soft Hawaiian music filled our ears. "You know what I think?" asked Doll. "I think she's an American. She doesn't even sound like a Japanese woman. It'll be interesting to see who she really is when this damn war is over."

Tokyo Rose's words actually had the opposite effect of their intent, since most G.I.s got a big laugh from her antics. Here are a few more messages we heard from her: "Well, Joe, how did you like this one? Somebody else is taking my place. Just think, while you are over here packed on a ship with 2,000 soldiers and Marines, your wife is out at the Lake Lodge dancing with Ralph, the attorney. Remember? His dad got him classified 4-F so he wouldn't have to come over here. But, don't you worry Joe, he's doing his part by keeping up the morale of all the wives and girlfriends back home." Then she played the song "Somebody Else is Taking My Place."

Another one of her messages sounded something like: "You men on the *President Jackson*, when are you gonna wise up? While you're steaming up from Guadalcanal to face certain death, your wives and girlfriends are having the time of their lives with all those statesiders stationed nearby who have never been overseas. Get this. We know where you are going and we have a surprise for you. Our fleet is waiting and there won't be a one of you left alive. Here's one for you, *Stonewall Maru*." The next song was "I'll Be Seeing You."

Tokyo Rose used the names of ships, organizations, and campaigns at random. It didn't matter that the message was false and often easily disproved. Her intent was to break the morale of the soldiers and sailors.

Here was another message from her: "You men of Task Force 58. Turn back while you can. Our fleet has finally split Halsey's forces and we have them on the run. Our brave pilots have sunk the battleship *Pennsylvania*, the aircraft carriers *Franklin*, *Enterprise*, and *Shangri-La*, plus the transports *Calloway*, *Monrovia*, *Wood*, *Larkin*, and *Hill*. At least eight destroyers were also sunk. What are you gonna do now, Task Force 58, with all your front lines gone?"

Many times at night I walked to the ship's galley and listened to the radio. To my great surprise, on one occasion Tokyo Rose proudly announced that the *Middleton* was sunk with all hands! We all had a good laugh at that bit of news. As far as we were concerned, it a great honor to be mentioned by name.

The landing at Saipan: This Ken Riley sketch shows the loading of the landing craft on D-Day, June 14, 1944. The LCVP's are loading Marines down the cargo net while a Tank Lighter (LCT) is being lowered by the forward boom.

## Chapter 16

# Saipan: Rattling Tokyo Rose's Cage

Contrary to some of our earlier trips, this time we had a full battle convoy with us in preparation for an invasion. When we learned we were heading for the invasion of Saipan, Doll and I both knew this one was going to be different. Saipan was the northernmost island in the Mariana chain that included Guam, Rota, and Tinian. It was also within bombing range of Japan. Surrounded by a large coral reef, Saipan was about twelve miles long with some very high terrain. The night before we landed, a submarine dropped off frogmen to blow passages through the reef. Our boats had to slip through these narrow passages to reach the beach. An intense study of the beaches began.

Every boat crew memorized each landmark. An old sugar mill, a school house, the mountains, beach characteristics—we memorized everything. Photographs taken by aircraft and submarines were blown-up and passed out for everyone to study. Many lives depended on a Cox'n's memory to get them to the right landing area. It was June 12, 1944.

The Japanese detected our large force moving up around the Marianas and sent out aircraft each day to bomb the convoy. Allied aircraft turned most of these planes back before they reached our transports. Still, a few reached us. The Japanese also had a new weapon to throw at the Americans: suicide pilots known as kamikazes. These pilots flew their airplanes loaded with explosives directly into ships. Kamikaze pilots went through a special ceremony, like their own funeral, before taking off on a mission they knew would be their last. During one of these air raids I witnessed one of the kamikaze's dive into an LSD, (a large Landing Ship Dock). The sky was full of black bursts of anti-aircraft fire, but the plane (it appeared to be a Japanese Zero), rolled over above the LSD and began diving straight down toward it. Instead of hitting the ship directly amidships, the aircraft nearly missed and instead struck one of the forward gun turrets on the port side. The result, thankfully, was that most of the explosion was outside the ship, so the damage was much less than it otherwise would have been. The amazing thing to me was how that pilot managed to fly through what looked like a solid wall of flak.

During the night of June 12, the task force pulled up about twelve miles from Saipan. At dawn we could make out both Saipan and Tinian. The boats and the Marines on the *Middleton* were part of a diversionary force. The ships involved moved into position a few miles off the shore and in full view of the Japanese. We lowered the boats and the operation began. At least, we hoped it looked that way to the Japanese. As each boat pulled alongside the ship, troops appeared to be loading down the cargo nets. Once the first four reached the boats, another four started down. But the ones in the boat climbed back up! This went on for a while for each boat until it appeared every boat was fully loaded. Actually, all the boats were empty except for three Marine officers and some radio gear in my boat. All of the boats, however, rendezvoused and spread out into assault waves. We were much closer to the shore than usual. I was in the first wave.

At the same time all this was happening, our navy fired smoke bombs toward the center of the island. Soon, the lower end Saipan was completely obscured. As my wave approached the shore, the officers with the radio picked up radio messages from the island. Our diversion was a huge success. The Japanese rushed troops to the middle of the island to repel our landing force. One of the officers aboard my boat with binoculars said some of the enemy soldiers were on bicycles. As we drew within mortar fire range, the boats turned around and headed back to the ships. According to Japanese radio, the Japs repelled the American invasion force. In reality, the real landing force quietly slipped ashore under the smoke screen at the lower end of the island.

Once back at the ship, the boats from *Middleton* loaded the 2nd Marines and sped off to land on the southern end behind the first waves that had established a sizeable beachhead. Although the landing went well, Saipan was not a one or two day battle. The 30,000 Japanese on the island put up a terrific resistance. Attacks and counterattacks moved the front lines back and forth many times.

As noted above, the path our boats took to get to the beach was through the passage blown in the coral by the frogmen. The reef was about 100 to 150 yards offshore. The Japanese rolled a large 5-inch gun out of a cave high in the mountains, fired it at the boats slipping through the passage, and rolled it back inside when American destroyers and battleships leveled a heavy bombardment against it. When the barrage tapered off, the Japs rolled the gun out again and opened fire. This process repeated itself over and over until we silenced the artillery piece.

Once through the passageway we ran parallel to the shoreline. Japanese snipers loved to shoot at these "sitting ducks" traveling up and down the beach inside the reef. We learned through hard experience to keep our heads down as much as possible. The ring of rifle bullets hitting the steel plates on the side of the boat and the little splashes of water when they missed kept us well informed.

On the second or third day of the operation, I was waiting to be unloaded on a beach in front of the old Sugar Mill. I had beached my boat and since the reef broke the waves, it could just sit there for hours. I knew it would be awhile before they unloaded us, so I relaxed a bit and struck up a conversation with Jim, a friend of mine and a member of the beach party.

"You should have been here last night," said Jim. "They secured this beach about sunset and we had snipers popping at us all night long. Once a group of Japs tried to penetrate our lines with a bonsai attack, but they were beaten back."

"Boy, that Sugar Mill is a mess," I replied, taking in the devastation.

"Yeah, the Marines had to use bazookas and mortars to get them out," Jim answered. "Come on. Want to look around?"

"Sure!"

I left Bill with the boat and Jim and I jumped out and walked up to the Sugar Mill. The structure was about 200 yards off the beach. It was a crumbled ruin with only some bare walls left standing. I picked up what appeared to be a Japanese newspaper and put it in my pocket. Probing around the rubble, I found a bottle of Saki and also put that in my pocket. I then saw something red and began scraping away at the rubble with three Marines, who had also seen it. It was a Japanese flag. Everyone wanted part of it, so I took out my Ka-Bar knife and cut it into four pieces, giving one to each of the group. I returned to my boat with the souvenirs.

Each time a boat from the *Middleton* left the beach, it carried wounded back to the ship because the *Middleton* had a large hospital on board. Each boat Cox'n was supplied with first aid kits, which included morphine in small dosage tubes. Among the wounded put on my boat was a small boy around eight years old. He had been shot in the leg. The little boy was crying and we later learned his parents had been killed in the fighting. He was clinging to a small dog. There were several hundred 'civilians' on the island taken prisoners. The doctors aboard the *Middleton* quickly fixed the boy's leg. Within a short time he was adopted by the whole crew. We dubbed him "little Tojo." The ship's carpenters built him a red wagon and printed "Tokyo Express" on the side of it. A photographer took his picture and wrote a story about him that made national news. After a few days he was returned to the island.

During one of these operations, the boat crews normally lived in their boats until the operation ended. During the Saipan operation, the U.S. Navy finally engaged the Japanese fleet. Most of the fighting ships deployed north of the Mariana islands. Although they were not able to come to direct grips with the Japanese surface ships, one of the most bitter air wars since the Coral Sea and Midway broke out. This engagement, referred to as the Mariana's Turkey Shoot, dealt a severe blow to the Japanese war effort.

Air raids were a daily occurrence during our journey to the Mariana islands. On the third day of the operation I was pulling alongside my ship when General Quarters sounded and anti-aircraft bursts peppered the sky overhead. Our aircraft tried to engage the Japanese planes before they could reach the large convoy anchored

Author Ken Wiley (right) at 17 years old, just before joining the Coast Guard. *Author's Collection*

My brother Joe Wiley (below), seen here with girlfriend Judy Fuller and our favorite aunt, Grace Wiley, in happier days before the war. Joe was killed over Germany in 1944. *Author's Collection*

My younger brother Bill (left) was temporarily left behind while his older brothers served. Next to Bill are Troy and Dora Wiley and the author. *Author's Collection*

The author (left) with his older brother Joe and Cousin Sue a short time before Pearl Harbor. *Author's Collection*

Ken Wiley with his own car at 16 year old. Every boy's dream was to have his own car. My first was a Model T. After I graduated from High School I bought this 1928 Model A Coupe with a rumble seat. *Author's Collection*

The 1941 Itasca (Texas) High School football team. Top row (left to right): Bill Blair, Bill Thompson, Emmet Dickinson, Shorty Johnson, Roland Knapps, Durwood Kemp, Harold Haroer, Billy Jack Dotson. Middle row (left to right): Benny Alley, Roy Michaels, Lon Mitchell, Ed Morrison, Bill Hooks, Ken Wiley. Bottom row (left to right): Buddy Upchurch, Ernest Whitfield, Dewey Meyers, Christine Briley (the team sweetheart), Grady Arthur, Charles Woods, Gene Strickland, and Bud Meyers. All 21 boys on the team served during the war. My best friend Durwood Kemp (#59) was one of four boys from our class of 45 students killed at Normandy. *Author's Collection*

The girl next door. Jean Young, the sweetie next door and my teenage crush. Living our teenage years apart took us in different directions, but I named my boat #13 for her and we corresponded now and again. Her letters and my memories of her flowing red hair and freckled face shortened the days and lengthened the lonely nights at sea. I only saw Jean on one occasion after the war. *Author's Collection*

Author Ken Wiley is shown here with his sister Ailene (Wiley) Gilmore. Ailene was the only girl in a family of six children. *Author's Collection*

Wiley brothers separated by war meet in a foreign country. M/Sgt Victor D. Wiley (right) and M/Sgt Troy Wiley (right), meet in Central America during WWII. *Author's Collection*

Author Ken Wiley is seen here steering *Lucky 13* during the bloody campaign in the Marshall Islands. Note his helmet, life jacket, and cramped surroundings.
*Author's Collection*

My older brother Troy Wiley in a photo taken after the return from a mission. Troy completed twenty-five combat missions over Europe with the Eighth Air Force, and then volunteered to stay and fly ten more. He flew those ten, and then volunteered to serve his country in the Pacific Theater of operations against the Japanese. *Author's Collection*

Boot Camp, July 1943, in St. Augustine, Florida. The Coast Guard took over the Ponce de Leon Hotel for its East Coast boot camp. This postcard from the hotel is adorned with signatures of some of my friends you will read about in this book. *Author's Collection*

Liberty at last. Bill Miller (left) and author Ken Wiley. "Boots" get their first six-hour daylight liberty in St. Augustine. Bill and I first met in the recruiting office in Dallas. We were together in boot camp, Landing Craft School, and aboard the USS *Cambria* (APA-36) and the USS *Arthur Middleton* (APA-25). Bill was my Motor Mac on my boat. *Author's Collection*

The "Mighty Middle Maru" was the Japanese name we gave to the *Arthur Middleton*. The *Middleton*, or "Mad M" as I printed on this photo taken by the ship's photographer in 1944, was my home away from home. The picture shows the davits with LCVPs ready to launch, the six booms, the 3-inch guns fore and aft, the 40m and 20mm anti-aircraft guns and the unique smoke stack. The smokestack on the *Middleton* was the only one of its kind in the Pacific until its two sister ships, *Chase* and *Climber*, returned from Europe and joined us for Okinawa. A single stack was a great help when we were out in the boats, because we could recognize our ship during dark nights and even during smoke screens thrown out to protect against air raids. *Author's Collection*

The *African Comet*. This luxury liner belonged to the American South African Lines until she was converted in 1942 to the USS *Arthur Middleton* (APA-25). When the Japanese bombed Pearl Harbor and pushed us out of the Pacific, the United States had no viable way to retaliate across thousand of miles of ocean. Initially, some thirty passenger ships were converted to assist in attacking Japanese islands. These ships were followed by almost 200 new ships. The *Arthur Middleton* was one of the early conversions. *Author's Collection*

D-Day, Enewitok, February 18, 1944. Author Ken Wiley took these four photos (including facing page) with a small Kodak box camera during the approach to Engebi Island during the first wave of the assault against Eniwetok. The quality is not the best, but the action is authentic. Heavy naval shelling destroyed the lush vegetation. The author quit taking pictures when machine gun, rifle, and mortar fire raked his boat. The Japs were there, dug in underground waiting for the Americans to arrive. *Author's Collection*

The approach to Engebi Island, as photographed by author Ken Wiley. The pounding surf made it difficult for him to hold the camera steady. *Author's Collection*

Author Ken Wiley photographed enjoying daylight liberty in Honolulu. The only restriction was that he had to be back on the ship by 6:00 p.m. *Author's Collection*

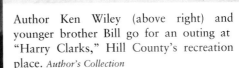

Author Ken Wiley (above right) and younger brother Bill go for an outing at "Harry Clarks," Hill County's recreation place. *Author's Collection*

Charles S. Doll (left), the author's best friend during the war, shared liberty with Ken in Honolulu. *Author's Collection*

# "Over the side"

This remarkable photo of the *Arthur Middleton* (APA-25) was taken by a ship's photographer in the Philippines. Davit and booms are deploying the ship's boats. Breaking into the picture on the left is the author's *Lucky 13*. (Note the number 13, which is visible on the upper right portion of the boat.) Aboard were Cox'n Ken Wiley, Motor Mac Bill Miller, and Bowman Tex Lee. Tank Lighter # 29, commanded by Cox'n Charles S Doll, is being lowered off the *Middleton* by the forward starboard boom. Before we could get the troops loaded, two kamikazes flew in low over the mountains in an attempt to sink the transports. The suicide plane targeting the *Middleton* veered away at the last moment. (Below) Another shot of the *Middleton* while underway off the Philippines. *Author's Collection*

The highest honor. Troy and Dora Wiley are awarded the Purple Heart for the death of their son Joe. Three other Wiley sons (including author Ken Wiley) were still in combat zones (and their youngest son Bill was slated to leave soon) when news of Joe's death reached home. *Author's Collection*

Second Lieutenant Joseph Wade Wiley, co-pilot on a B-17 with the Eighth Air Force operating out of England. Joe was killed on January 30, 1944, the same day Dora Thompson Wiley became a "Gold Star Mother." Joe was killed over Germany on his fifth mission when his plane was shot down by anti-aircraft fire. There were no survivors from his plane. A German family found Joe's remains and buried them, and corresponded with my mother for many years after the war. Joe's remains were eventually moved to a United States Army cemetery in Holland. *Author's Collection*

Ken Wiley and wife Deane (Osborne) Wiley visiting the *Queen Mary* at Long Beach, California. *Author's Collection*

Author Ken Wiley explains his various souvenirs to his youngest granddaughter, five-year-old Scout VanArnam. Scout is holding the hand-cranked siren from Eniwetok while Ken examines the old cane scabbard knife given to him by the grateful liberated Filipinos who rowed out to the *Middleton* in outrigger canoes on D-Day in the Philippines. The placard behind Scout has Ken's discharge, ranking stripe as Cox'n, Amphibious shoulder patch, and various ribbons and medals. The other two framed documents are the Japanese newspaper and the one-quarter Japanese flag taken from the Sugar Mill on Saipan. *Author's Collection*

just off Saipan. Once enemy aircraft penetrated the air screen and reached our ships, the U.S. planes fell back and let the anti-aircraft guns take over.

On this occasion, two Zeros penetrated our air screen. I could see them coming in at about 2,000 feet. The planes separated and one came directly at the *Middleton*. The sky filled with anti-aircraft bursts, but the Zero seemed indestructible. When the plane was almost directly overhead, it rolled to the left and climbed for an instant before completing the roll with a downward spiral. I had seen the exact same maneuver a few days before, when a kamikaze dove into the LSD: roll, spin, and dive. There was no doubt in my mind the *Middleton* was the target.

I screamed at two Marines about to climb down cargo nets to stay aboard the ship, and yelled at Bill and Tex Lee, my seamen, to let go of the cargo net. With a surge of power, I pulled the boat away from the ship to put as much distance as possible between it and my boat. As I pulled away, the Zero pulled up from his dive, rolled gently to the left, and flew lazily off toward Tinian! The "ack ack" bursts, even heavier now and aimed at a much better target, were still missing the aircraft. Once he was out of the ship's perimeter, two F4U Corsairs pounced on him. Their fire quickly found the range and the Zero crashed on Tinian. I never knew why the pilot changed his mind about diving into us. He had started the dive perfectly, only to pull up at the last second. Perhaps he lost his nerve. Whatever the reason, the *Arthur Middleton* escaped unhurt. When the excitement was over, Tex pointed out that my cheek was bleeding. A small piece of shrapnel had grazed it. I was bleeding and did not even know it. As I later found out, about 15 guys on the ship had also suffered shrapnel wounds.

The boats took their personnel and cargo to their designated beach, unloaded, and returned to the ship for another assignment. Sometimes we motored to another ship to help unload men or supplies because many of the Liberty ships and other vessels arrived without boats of their own. There was no time to rest as long as work needed to be done. This went on for nearly a month at Saipan. Sandwiches and coffee were passed down to the boat crew or we were allowed to come aboard the ship long enough to eat. The mess halls on troop ships or Navy cargo ships were all about the same.

We stood in line and someone slopped food onto a tray. The tables were all four to five feet tall and we stood to eat.

On one trip, I ran my boat to a Liberty ship to get a load of cargo to take to the beach. When we pulled alongside, the Officer of the Deck asked us if we wanted to come aboard and eat. These ships were manned by Merchant Marines instead of U.S. Navy personnel. We were ushered into a large dining room with tables for four to six people scattered around. The tables all had white tablecloths on them! They seated us and sent waiters to take our order. We all thought we had died and gone to heaven. We had steaks cooked to order, broiled chicken, real potatoes, green beans, corn-on-the-cob, iced tea, and apple pie with a scoop of ice cream. They even offered us seconds! It was unbelievable. If there had been any way to transfer to the Merchant Marines at that point, they would have had three new recruits.

"How many people do you have in your crew?" I asked one of the sailors.

"About 85," he answered, "counting the naval gunners."

"Do you eat like this all the time?" Bill asked.

"Yeah. We get to plan out our own menus."

"How long have you been aboard?" Bill asked.

"I signed up in 1942 and was in the Atlantic for nearly two years," he replied. "I had two ships sunk under me by U-boats. I've only been aboard here for three months. It's a lot better now, because we can travel with a convoy most of the time. In the Atlantic, the German subs loved to sink cargo ships because we were carrying supplies to England. In the Pacific, the subs are more apt to go for the fighting ships first."

Bill and I thanked him for his hospitality. It was time to head back to our boat. Our time in Heaven had come to an end.

When we stayed in the boats for long periods of time, we used a three-man crew rotation. One person drove the boat while the other two slept. One night, Bill was driving and I was asleep. As the boat approached the reef opening off Saipan, the control boat (a small PT) challenged us to offer the appropriate password. Bill sent the signal with a red flashlight, which could be seen for a long distance. We blinked the password in Morse code. Today's challenge was "GOAT."

The control boat blinked the challenge again. Bill responded a second time. It was at that point the patrol boat let loose with a salvo of 50-caliber machine gun fire right over our heads. That woke me up in a hurry! Bill was yelling as loud as he could and blinking the flashlight like a madman. "What are you people, crazy?" he screamed, clicking the flashlight for all he was worth. It was then he figured out the problem: his flashlight was not working.

"Oh, no! Don't shoot! Don't shoot! I'm B. L. Miller from Fort Worth, Texas. My damn flashlight doesn't work! Don't shoot for God's sake!" he yelled.

"B. L. Miller from Ft. Worth, Texas?" yelled back a voice from the darkness. "You better answer this signal correct or you're never gonna' see Ft. Worth again."

I handed Bill another flashlight and he blinked out a perfect "Beard." As we drew closer, we could see the men on the control boat with their guns trained on us. An officer on the boat took a megaphone and spoke to us. "The Japanese have infiltrated our ships with about a dozen suicide boats. They have been running up to the ships and ramming them with explosives," explained the officer. "We think some are still out there. Be extremely careful. Shoot at anything that does not respond to your challenge. You boys are lucky my men took the time to challenge you again. If B. L. Miller hadn't convinced us about who he was, you'd be dead now. There ain't a Jap alive that could imitate that act you just put on, let alone your Texas drawl."

We later learned the suicide boats had damaged several ships. The action had a reverse effect. When three of the *Monrovia's* boats approached and failed to answer the password challenge, gunners aboard the ship opened fire. Several boats were heavily damaged and several crewmen were injured.

When July 4, 1944, rolled around, the Saipan operation was still underway. We had driven back the Japanese troops to the mountainous end of the island, but they were still very much alive. Dive bombers and surface warships concentrated their fire against this end of the island. On the night of July 4, battleships lobbed 16-inch shells from ten or twelve miles out. The destroyers, closer to shore, fired 3- and 5-inch shells. The L.C.I.s and smaller rocket boats were closer still, firing rockets toward the Japanese positions.

All of these guns fired tracers. It was probably the greatest fireworks display in the history of the world. It lasted all night long, and I watched most of it.

By this time the work requirements for the boats were less demanding than it had been during the early days of the operation. If you had a load and the beach wasn't ready for it, you had to stay nearby. The boats tied abreast of one another and dropped their anchors. This way, the crews could relax and leave only one person on watch. Of course, a line of fifty or sixty boats tied abreast made an excellent target for "Midnight Charlie," the lone Japanese plane that invariably slipped in every night to bomb and strafe the beach.

On one particular night when general quarters sounded, Bill, Tex, and I heard the Japanese plane flying overhead and watched as anti-aircraft fire began lighting up the sky. Charlie spotted the long line of boats and headed in our direction. We laid down in the bottom of the boat and listened as the engine roared and the aircraft picked up speed. He was beginning his diving run. A few seconds later we heard the rat-a-tat-tat of the machine guns as he strafed the boats. Tex Lee was doing his best to crawl beneath Bill and I on the flat floor of the boat. I didn't have to see the plane to know he was pulling up a few hundred feet overhead. The roar of the engine combined with the screaming of the wind sounded exactly like it had in the movies "The Black Ace" and "9 G's." It was all too familiar to me. Now it was real. Several of the boats were hit by the machine gun fire. Miraculously, no one was injured and not one of the boats sank. Several started their engines so their bilge pumps would work and empty out the water flooding in through the bullet holes.

We slowly stood. Tex looked at me and said through chattering teeth, "I was scared. I don't like this."

"Me, too," I admitted.

Bill, who always seemed to have a funny joke to add to everything, added, "Let's get the hell out of here. This tying up abreast is for the birds. I'd rather drive around in circles all night. That S.O.B. nearly killed us!"

The next morning my crew and I were anchored off the beach, loaded and waiting, when Sunrise Charlie made his morning appearance. This time the plane was a twin engine "Betty." The Jap made one strafing run along the beach, banked, and came back for a second run. One of the small landing craft just off shore began firing at him with a 30-caliber machine gun. It was like a chicken pecking away at a rock. The Jap made his beach run but annoyed at the small boat firing at away, turned and headed directly for it. This time the enemy opened with heavier nose cannons and practically cut the boat in two. As the shells exploded, the boat began sinking. The crew dove overboard as the boat sank out of sight. Another boat picked up the survivors. The message was very clear. Thirty caliber machine guns are no match for the heavier artillery of an aircraft in either range or fire power.

Each day, the MPs guarding civilian prisoners brought them down to a particular beach with an inlet that made a perfect bathing pool. The men and women bathed together with no regard for modesty. This became quite a sight for the battle-weary Marines and sailors who thronged to the area to see the show. One day I motored to the scene to pick up some of the prisoners. Two women, one man, and three children climbed aboard my boat with two armed guards from the ship. As soon as the prisoners were loaded, my boat was hoisted aboard and within an hour the ship set sail. Not all the boats had returned, so they were left behind to catch a ride later. Sometimes it took weeks (and in some cases, months) to catch up with your ship.

The Mariana's Turkey Shoot did not draw out the main force of Japanese carriers and warships. The rumor circulating at that time was that the Japanese were planning a counterattack on Saipan, and that the major naval battle might take place right there. All non-fighting ships that could move away from Saipan did so. The convoy the *Middleton* was in ran a zigzag course to a rendezvous many miles away from the suspected battle area. Our orders were to stay there until it was safe to go back to Saipan. Other than a few destroyers, the convoy was unsupported. We were sitting ducks during that time, waiting for a submarine to sink us, or a recognizance plane to spot us.

The sea burials began on the first day out of Saipan. Wounded men who had died after the ship got underway were prepared for burial and carried on deck. Each body had a flag draped over it. I wondered if I had known any of them. Was one of them a Marine I had talked with the night before D-Day? I looked at the white-wrapped corpses. Maybe one of them was the guy who had given me his good flashlight and told me he didn't expect to come out alive. For the life of me, I could not remember his name. I hoped he had made it. The words of the Chaplain filled my ears as the first body slid off the burial board and plummeted to the sea: "Lord, we commit this soul to you and we commit his boy to the deep."

After the Japanese defeat in the air, the threat of a counter invasion diminished. The *Middleton* and the other transports returned and resumed the massive support operation for the troops on the beach.

Once again the crew lowered Boat 13 over the side and three very tired sailors moved back into what would be their home for the next two weeks. Tinian, Guam, and Rota were waiting. The suicide boats and kamikaze pilots continued.

By this time we had pushed the Japanese up to the northern end of the island. The mountainous terrain ended with sheer cliffs dropping off to the water hundreds of feet below. We heard these cliffs were a favorite place for the Japs to commit suicide. Even the women and children leaped off rather than surrender to the Americans.

The *Middleton* pulled out several times for security reasons. On every occasion but one we were left behind in our boat. After miraculously surviving one of the Japanese strafing runs, Bill, Tex, and I decided to move away from the ships in the harbor and try a sea anchor by ourselves. We decided to stay within site of the Beach Control boat (PT) guarding the reef passage. One of us had to stay awake all the time anyway.

It was shortly after midnight when another PT boat appeared to be heading for us. He blinked out the code "Milk" in Morse with a red flashlight. Tex responded with "Shake." Tex was on his toes because there was a new code every day and it had changed at midnight. "Milkshake" was the correct code.

The PT slowed down and pulled alongside us. An officer stood up and shouted over at us, "Have you guys seen anything suspicious? Has anyone passed by since midnight using yesterday's code?"

We looked at one another and shook our heads.

"Six Japanese suicide boats came out about midnight. They moved one at a time at different passages and gave yesterday's code. Some idiots let them all through except the last one, so five of them are out here somewhere." The officer paused, casting a glance around our boat into the water. "Look out for swimmers, too. They might try to trade boats. Anyone who doesn't answer the right code, don't wait for orders from anyone. Open fire. You could save some ship from getting blown out of the water." With that, he turned and sped off to the next boat bobbing a few hundred yards away.

Bill, who had an answer to everything, spoke out. "Damn Wiley, if we're close enough to challenge and they don't answer correctly, I'm supposed to fire into a boat loaded with explosives with this thirty caliber? Now who's a suicide boat? Us or them?"

I didn't answer because we all three knew the answer. Instead, I began to think about the situation. The constant stream of tracers from the rocket boats, destroyers, cruisers, and battleships never let up. There was a sporadic firing of small arms constantly from locations that were indistinguishable. Then there was the constant firing of weapons and explosives on the island. It was almost impossible to distinguish any new sounds of explosives in the darkened harbor.

About 2:30 a.m. we sighted an LCP approaching our position. We exchanged signals and it pulled up alongside. It was Bill Murray, Custer, and several Marines. "The *Middleton's* back in again," announced Murray. "We're checking all our boats to make sure they got the warning. The *Monroe* (APA-32) shot up a bunch of their own boats coming in that didn't respond to the signal. You guys seen anything?"

"Nothing unusual, I replied. "The Control Boat warned us about 12:45 and we've been watching."

Custer climbed over into my boat. Three Marines, one loaded down with radio gear, also climbed aboard. Custer waived for Murray to go on in the LCP and then turned to me. "Wiley, the Japs are getting desperate. They can't lose Saipan. That's why they're throwing everything that they have against us. The ships were all out because the Jap fleet was heading in and if Halsey can't stop them, we're gonna' be sitting ducks in the middle of the greatest battle this war has ever seen. No one knows where these suicide boats are coming from, but the one they stopped gave us a clue as to what we're up against."

"What do you mean?" I asked.

"These boats are not just some boat they load with explosives and call it a suicide boat. It's a speed boat, built for the purpose with ballast tanks indicating that they could be underwater. We don't know where they are coming from or how many they have, but we have to find out. The ship will go out again tomorrow after they pick up casualties for our hospital. With the ship out, I'm in charge of the boats left behind. We've been asked to post sentries around the island to watch. The PTs and destroyers can patrol off shore and support you, but they can't see the shoreline as well as you can if you're beached. They want LCVP's because they can hide in beach coves. Some will be in areas that are not secure yet, but your advantage will be the boat. If trouble breaks out, you can get out of there fast."

"Where do you want us?" I asked.

"'Us' is right, because I'm going with you," Custer added as he unfolded a map. "We'll go around the northern end of the island and cut through the reef right here," he said, pointing at his map. "There is a large passageway our UDT people have already marked with buoys. It's almost 400 yards to the beach and there is a cove protected by a fifty-foot cliff or embankment. You don't have to worry about being spotted at ground level, but you could be seen from the edge of the cliff. The destroyer will lay a few five-inchers in there before you go in to discourage sightseers. You'll go in while it's dark and have a perfect view of the beaches looking out and should not be visible to the Japs, who have a lot of other problems inland."

It took us more than an hour to go around the end of the island. The Marines blinked a code to the destroyer and it laid down a barrage right over the cove we were going in. We slipped in apparently unnoticed just as the shelling stopped. The cove was just as Custer described it. I beached the boat without trouble and we settled down to a watchful silence. The few scrubby trees growing at the foot of the cliff provided us an umbrella over our heads. Even the sounds of firing and explosions seemed farther away, blocked off by the high cliff that extended almost to the water's edge. Tex and Bill stayed glued to the 30 calibers and two of the Marines sat with guns ready as the third one listened and talked on his radio. For the first time I noticed he was an officer, a lieutenant. Custer and I watched with field glasses. We didn't see anything suspicious and before too long it was dawn.

We stayed there all day. Occasionally, the lieutenant passed on news he received on the radio. "Our fleet caught the Japs in the Philippine Sea and is really creaming them. In fact, they're calling it a turkey shoot. We've knocked down three hundred of their planes and have lost only a few. Wonder what Tokyo Rose will say about that!"

"Probably that they knocked out all of Halsey's fleet and have retaken Saipan," Bill replied.

Once that afternoon we heard voices drifting down from the high cliff. They were definitely Japanese. The lieutenant advised the destroyer patrolling off shore and he laid down another barrage overhead. Thank God for accurate gunnery! We maintained the sentry post throughout the day and into the night.

It was Tex who saw it first. Along the north end of the island, about 100 yards off shore, a small dark object was moving away from shore. With the help of my glasses I made out something like a rubber raft with a person paddling it. After reporting it I kept a close eye on the raft before it disappeared from our view. A few seconds later an object suddenly appeared. None of us had seen it coming. It was a boat, and it had appeared unexpectedly. We heard its engine as it began moving fast toward the harbor full of ships. The Navy didn't wait long. PTs, destroyers, and destroyer escorts opened fire on the small boat, which went up in an explosion big enough to sink a battleship.

"We'll never know where he came from," the lieutenant said. "But we couldn't take a chance with that load he had."

We spent the night on our sentry post without further incident. The news of the big naval battle was all in our favor. We not only turned back the Japanese fleet, but also practically obliterated it. The transports came back in and our sentry duty was over. We went back to unloading ships.

Once we got an order to go to the backside of the island, pick up some troops, and bring them around the northern end of the island.

It was almost dark and on the way back we saw a strange boat moving close to the coastline. The area was still not fully secure, and it was too dangerous to move in closer for a look. The boat disappeared almost as fast as it had appeared. One moment he was between us and the coast, and the next he was gone, as if swallowed up by rocky coastline below the cliffs. We reported the strange sighting.

After several days, the transports were called back to Saipan. There were many ships to unload, and the fighting was still heavy. This is where Bill, Tex, and I discovered the "Elusive Yellow Beach."

Saipan was a long and bloody campaign. The island was not large—only twelve miles long and an average of four or five miles wide—so many thought the fighting would be over in a week. But the determined Japanese counterattacked our every move and fought back with a renewed fanaticism. It was a decisive battle, and the Japanese were determined not to let us establish a base so close to Japan. Control of Saipan meant we would be able to launch bombers against their mainland. The fighting on the island reflected the all-out efforts the Japanese fleet made to stop us. They sent their carriers toward Saipan with the intention of turning the war around and throwing us off the island and out of the Marianas. Instead, what they got was the "Mariana's Turkey Shoot."

The Japanese on Saipan fought like there was no tomorrow. They counterattacked us at every chance with their "Bonsai" attacks in an effort to recapture a few square feet of ground already stained with blood. The Saipan campaign witnessed the first organized kamikaze suicide bombers. The threat of suicide torpedoes (known as Kaitens, or human-guided torpedoes) only added to this terror, as did the suicide boats loaded with TNT or other explosives. The Japs slipped in among our boats to get close to a target. They pretended to be American and sometimes yelled friendly greetings in pretty good English. Once close to a victim, they rammed the ship and set off the explosives, often killing everyone aboard both vessels. The Japanese also used swimmers to swim out to the ships and set explosive charges. On land or at sea, Saipan was a dangerous place to be, regardless of whether you were on ships, in boats, or on the island. On top of this was the stress of knowing the Japanese fleet could appear at any moment for a large-scale battle with our warships.

Bill and I had been in the boat for eighteen straight days hauling troops, supplies, and cargo from the ships to the established beaches. Remembering the close call he had a few days before when his flashlight wasn't working, Bill had grown very cautious about the deadly Japanese. We checked our lights often and kept a close watch on every boat that passed. During air raids, which occurred frequently, the harbor was covered by smoke released by ships to obscure them from Japanese planes. Still, we were woefully unprepared for what was about to happen.

We had orders to take a load of ammunition to Yellow Beach 3, the northernmost of the landing beaches. The control boat checked us through the reef passage and cautioned us not to go beyond the fixed yellow buoys marking the beach. It was almost two o'clock in the morning. As I drove the boat down the beach inside the reef, I watched with growing concern as the tracer shells from our warships, launched five or more miles out to sea, streaked through the sky and onto the island just ahead of us.

"I hope those swabbies got their directions down right," grumbled Bill. "We're getting too close to those things."

Tex Lee spoke up from the bow where he was watching the reef and the beach as we cruised along. "Haven't we already passed Red Beach? Look at that buoy." He shined his light on the red buoy anchored to the reef.

"Red Beach?" I asked. "Yeah, I think we are way past that point."

We could clearly hear the steady fire of machine guns and small arms. The firing was much heavier than we expected it would be. I looked behind me and saw three or four boats strung out behind, all heading the same way we were. It struck me as odd that not a single boat was coming from the other way. We continued cruising along and counted Red Beach 2, 3, and 4, then Yellow Beach One. Everything was in order, but it sure seemed to be a much longer trip than I remembered. Tex was worried, too. He challenged the beach with the password for the day "Tom." Back come the correct answer "Mix." We passed Yellow Beach Two and approached Yellow Beach Three when all hell broke loose.

The Japanese launched a bonsai attack on one of the beaches behind us. We figured it was on Red Beach 2 or 3. What we didn't know was that Japanese swimmers had changed the buoys. The attack was actually on the real Yellow Beach Three. I saw four other boats, all LCVPs, on the beach up ahead at what I still thought was Yellow Beach Three.

"Damn," said Bill. "We're gonna' be in a hell of a shape if those Japs break through back there and take the beach. The only way out is right back by them!"

"Let's get in here and find out what's happening. Maybe we'll just stay here until they throw them back," I shot back as I turned the boat to head into the beach.

"Wait!" Tex shouted as he sent his challenge to the beach. The answer came back "Mix," and I was about to resume speed again when Tex again cautioned me again. "Hold it! Just a minute!" He cupped his hands and yelled toward the beach, "Ahoy the beach! They've changed the password. Who did slinging Sammy Baugh play for?"

After a brief hesitation the answer came back, "Yankees, I think! Maybe Dodgers?"

"Japs!" we all shouted at once. I brought the boat to a complete stop and started backing up to get clear of the beach as fast as possible. Tex began blinking an SOS to the other boats behind us as I spun our boat around and headed back. The Japs on the beach opened on us with a machine gun cut and several rifles, the bullets bouncing off the steel plates of our lucky Boat 13.

"Keep your heads down!" I yelled as I applied full throttle. Bill and Tex had other things in mind, however. We were barely away from the beach before they were climbing into the 30-caliber gun pits. The firing from the beach intensified and new firing was coming at us from what was marked as Green Beach 1, 2, and Red Beach 2 and 3.

"The Japs must have taken the whole damn beach!" I shouted as I sped the boat out as close to the reef as I dared.

I didn't have to explain to the other boats what was happening. All four had turned back when the beach firing began. Now it was like running a gauntlet. About 150 to 200 yards separated us from the beach on one side and 30 to 50 feet from the reef on the other. I saw the Cox'n of one of the boats ahead of us duck down as a star shell exploded over his head, illuminating the entire area. Fortunately for all the boats, as we approached the stretch of beach where the heaviest fighting was taking place, the gunfire trained on us let up. The Japs were too busy with the Marines on shore to overly worry about three or four boats high-tailing it out of the lagoon.

Once we passed the fighting area, a control boat sped toward us and issued a challenge: "Tom."

Bill answered back: "Mix."

The officer on the control boat yelled through a megaphone, "Where you from?"

"Ft. Worth, Texas, sir," answered Bill.

"Well, I'll be damned. If it ain't B. L. Miller! What in the hell are you doing past our last outpost? I told you not to go past Yellow Beach 3. Now the Japs are attacking Yellow Three."

"Yellow Three? Have you checked the buoys lately?"

The control boat threw a powerful search light over to the reef until he finally came to rest on a Red Buoy.

"Well, I'll be damned!" he said. "What's going on here?"

"We followed the buoys all the way down, Red Beach Two, Three, Yellow Beach One, Two, and Three," I answered. "We're not the first ones, either. There are several boats beached between here and there, and we would be too, if it hadn't been for Tex here."

"Yeah," Bill jumped in. "Fortunately for us, we got there about the same time they launched their attack, so they couldn't pay a lot of attention to us. I feel sorry for those poor guys they lured in ahead of us, though. We saw several LCVPs beached back there."

"Those boats will be back out in here loaded with explosives before morning if they've got another passage down there," I added.

"There's only one thing to do," the officer continued. "Call for destroyers and LCI rocket fire to destroy those boats. The poor guys who drove 'em are not in them any more." The officer motioned to me. "Better take your boat out of here. Go back through the passage and rendezvous with the outer control boat. You can deliver the ammo after this bonsai is over. It shouldn't take long."

The other four boats filed out with ours and began circling, waiting on the control boat.

"Well, Tex," I said. "We really owe you one for this. What made you so suspicious, anyway?"

"Well, I guess I've smoked just about every American cigarette made—Camels, Phillip Morris, Chesterfields, even Bull Durham, Prince Albert, and Bugler," Tex replied. "I know 'em all and that whiff of tobacco smoke I got coming off the beach was not American. That was awful, awful smelling stuff."

The control boat directed us to pick up a load of wounded Marines and take them back to the *Middleton's* hospital. I recognized the First Mate from the Liberty ship that we had lunch on. He was badly wounded and kept asking for someone called Lars and saying, "It's here! It's here, just like he said!"

I knelt beside his stretcher and introduced myself. A flicker of recognition crossed his eyes and he tried to grasp my hand. "Yes, You're the one with the boat. We don't need to go to Guam. It's right here on Saipan."

I thought he was delirious and tried to comfort him, but he would not quiet down. He tugged on my arm and pulled my face down close to his. "It's the Mariana's treasure. It's not a myth! Tell Lars, I talked to the old man's son before he died. He said it's in the water." He trailed off and became silent.

I looked at the corpsman who accompanied the wounded. He shrugged his shoulders. "He's been talking like that since we picked him up. He went into Garapan and got caught in a counterattack. Why he even came ashore, I don't know. I doubt he'll make it."

"What's all this about a treasure?" I asked.

"It's an old myth about the Marina's treasure. Smugglers supposedly took all this loot out of the countries before Japan invaded them and hid it somewhere in the Mariana chain. Most people think it was hidden on Guam."

"Oh, yeah, that's right," I answered. "That story is common among merchant seamen." I looked down at the poor fellow. He had risked his life to go ashore in hostile territory to track down an old myth. I was much more intrigued by the origin of the suicide boats. I would never see all the gold and jewels supposedly hidden in the Marianas, but I was certain the suicide boats would remain with us until Tokyo fell.

Chapter 17

# Good Morning Charlie

We were winning the land fighting on Saipan, but the Japanese refused to give up easily. They fought bitterly to the very end. The suicide boats remained a constant threat, and their planes from neighboring islands participated in annoying raids, though with little or no hope of returning to their base. Their schedule was almost predictable, and we soon developed names for them.

"They aren't real effective, but those are real bullets and bombs those bastards are firing," Bill noted early one morning. "If you get in the way of one, you'd be real dead, to."

Bill was commenting on a twin engine "Betty" that flew in low and unexpected around the highest mountain at the eastern end of the island. He had probably taken off from Guam or Rota, perhaps even from Tinian. Flying low just above the water, he slipped in undetected. It was barely daylight, and Bill, Tex, and I were anchored just off the reef in relatively shallow water. The Betty made its strafing run on the beach and turned to come back for a second run. As he approached, anti-aircraft fire from the destroyers and LCIs opened up, as did the installations on the island. The Jap strafed again to no effect but this time dropped his bomb, which detonated harmlessly at the water's edge. He avoided the heavy flak curtain and once again disappeared around the mountainous end of the island. A couple minutes later he appeared again, breaking over the ridge in the middle of the island. The Jap pilot headed straight across it through the increasing anti-aircraft fire. This time he didn't bother with the beach, but headed instead straight out for the ships anchored offshore. He had his target picked out, and it was one of the bobbing transports.

Worried about the effects of friendly fire, the anti-aircraft batteries let up. The plane's engines, however, began sputtering. Flying barely 100 feet off the water, the aircraft lost altitude until it plunged into the sea well short of its target. A loud explosion scattered pieces of the aircraft and human debris across a wide area. We kept our eyes glued on the crash site for some time, but there were no survivors.

"Well, that was close," said Bill. "They must be putting together just about anything that will fly. His own engine got him!"

"Have you noticed that we get one or two of those every morning at the first crack of dawn?" said Tex. "I'll bet they come off some field right here on Saipan, maybe Tinian."

I thought about that. I looked over at Tinian, which was in clear view south of Saipan. Word was the Japanese aircraft and landing strips there had been put out of commission, but someone had missed something somewhere. These planes could not have snuck in without detection. They definitely originated from one of the islands visible around Saipan.

"Hey Wiley," Doll shouted from the approaching tank lighter. "Did that Betty strafe you?"

"Naw," I replied, "he had too many troubles of his own." Doll reversed his engines and brought the tank lighter to a stop alongside Boat 13. "I've got to wash myself off, salt water or no," Doll said as he lowered his ramp, walked forward, and dove into the crystral water. The crewmen on both boats followed his lead and nearly everyone was splashing and laughing in the warm clear water as if they did not have a care in the world. Bill stayed aboard the LCVP and Bob Baker remained on the tank lighter to watch the boats.

I was floating on my back enjoying myself when Bill suddenly yelled, "Get out! Get out! There's a Jap in the water!" Tex, Doll, Milton, and I scrambled back up the boat ramp.

"Where?" Doll asked as Bill trained the 30-caliber gun on something under the stern of the boat. The Jap surfaced just off the port side of the tank lighter after swimming under both boats. Instead of trying to get away though, he raised his hand and said in broken English, "Sullender! "Sullender!"

Bob trained the 50-caliber on him and Bill had the 30-caliber ready to pick him up when he cleared the boat. Doll motioned hard and fast for the enemy soldier to come aboard. He nodded his understanding and cautiously swam to the lowered ramp. His left arm and left leg were bleeding, but he did not appear to be seriously injured.

"You speak English?" Doll asked slowly. When the man did not immediately respond, Doll repeated the question a second time.

"Yes, little bit," he finally replied while nodding.

"Take off your clothes," Doll instructed, knowing the first rule of capturing Japanese prisoners was to strip them for concealed weapons or explosives. The prisoner was apparently a pilot, for he was wearing a flight uniform. In about one minute he was standing before us in nothing but his dirty underwear. Bob tied his hands snugly behind him.

"You the pilot?" I asked.

"Yes, pilot," he responded nodding his heard. "Crash."

"Where did you come from?" asked Doll.

The prisoner looked at him as if he didn't understand and said, "Airplane crash."

"Yeah, I know the airplane crashed," Bill broke in sharply. "But where did the airplane take off from?"

This time he looked as if he understood, but chose not to answer the question. He shook his head and mumbled, "Airplane crash."

"Why did you come to our boat?" I asked as I looked into his frantic eyes, which were darting from man to man as if he expected someone to kill him on the spot.

"You laugh. People who laugh, not bad people. You sailors, you laugh. Me sullender you. Not sullender to mallines. Mallines bad. Kill prisoners. You laugh, you sailors. Not kill," he replied.

"We better take him in," said Doll.

"Yeah," I replied. "Keep him in the bow with your 50s trained on him. I'll follow along behind."

"You take me to ship, yes?" the prisoner almost pleaded. Suddenly an idea hit Bill.

"Nope! Sorry Tojo. We are taking you into the shore to turn you over to the Marines."

His eyes grew large in fright. "No! No! Not Mallines. They kill. Take me to ship," he pleaded.

I saw immediately was Bill was trying to so, so I stepped closer to the prisoner and looked him square in the eyes. "We have to find out where your plane took off from. The Marines will make you speak. So we have to take you to them."

A wild look crossed his eyes. "No, you take me to ship! I tell you!" he said excitedly.

"O.K." I said. "Where did your plane take off from?

The Jap looked defeated and seemed to give up. "Here," he said as he lowered his head and pointed at the island.

"Saipan?" I asked. He nodded his reply.

"We'll check it out and if you are lying, the Marines will get it out of you," said Doll.

"Me not lying," he answered, looking at each of us in turn. "Took off from hidden field on Saipan. My airplane was last one still fly, so no more come from there anyway. Please, take me to ship. Not to Mallines."

"O.K. Charlie, let's head for the ship," I said as we started the engines and moved toward the *Middleton*. When we came alongside and Doll reported that we had a prisoner, two armed guards came down to escort him up the gangplank to the Officer of the day.

Five minutes later Custer came to the quarterdeck with a megaphone and peered down at the two boats. "Well done, men! Well done! Go on back to the beach and report to the control boat. He told us exactly where he took off from, and our troops will check it out to make sure they don't patch together another plane that can get off the ground."

As we headed back to the control boat, Bill broke the silence. "You know, that's one of the nicest Japs I ever met. Can you believe that he came to us to 'sullender' because he heard us laughing and figured we weren't bad like the 'Mallines,'" he laughed, doing his best to mimic the prisoner.

"This war is crazy," Tex jumped in. "He takes off with a bomb loaded airplane, bent on strafing and killing as many of us as he can, then makes a final all-out effort to fly that whole bomb load into one of ships and kill hundreds of us. His bucket of bolts won't quite make it, and when all his chips are gone, he suddenly becomes Mr. Nice Guy and comes to where he thinks he can get the most sympathy. We don't really hate these people we're killing, and they don't really hate us as individuals. We all do what we have to do. Someday, we may even be friends."

I shook my head. "I don't think so. The Japanese are cruel and dishonest. The thrive on treachery. Look at Pearl Harbor, look at Corregador, Singapore, and China. Look at what he just tried to do to us. Americans could never be friends with people who want to hurt and enslave others. This pilot was just trying to con us when he saw that he had no other chance."

I began to wonder what kind of home life they must have in Japan. It was well known the Japanese started training boys in the military at a very young age. Could they love like American families do? Most of them didn't seem to care if they lived or died, and only a few were taken prisoner. Individual life was so insignificant in Japan. How could there be any love between them? I reached down and picked up the prisoner's discarded clothes. We had forgotten to turn them in. I felt a wallet inside and pulled it out.

Inside were several pictures. One was a beautiful Japanese woman. Another was the same woman with two small children. There were also individual pictures of each child and finally a picture of an elderly Japanese couple. Here were photos of his wife, two children, and his parents. Each had Japanese writing on the back. This man shared a deep love for his family, and certainly they all loved him. The whole idea seems contradictory, and it confused me. What if I had been forced to kill this man? I thought about the grieving that American families, including my own, went through when news of a terrible loss hit them. The pictures told me that it might be the same in Japan.

"We better turn these things over to the control boat," I said. "Somebody will want them for something."

It was too complex for a teenage mind to figure out. We were all confused. Would the world ever be tranquil again? Would we still hate each other when this was over? They say the Germans never got over their defeat in World War I, and that was the reason we were fighting again now. Would the Japanese do the same thing—

start another war a couple decades from now after we defeated them? There must be a better way. Maybe, just maybe, some of us who were out here could sit down at a table with the leaders of all countries and make them see how wrong war was.

Chapter 18

# A Little Fun in the Midst of Chaos

We had been in the boats for three weeks. The fighting on Saipan was still going on, with the Japanese slowly but surely driven into a box on the northern end of the island. Sniper fire against the boats as we entered the beach area inside the coral reef was still a threat, but as our Marines occupied more of island, the threat diminished. Weary and wary Cox'n's still crouched as low as possible to avoid a fatal bullet. It was only prudent. If we had cargo the beach wasn't ready to handle, or if our boat was empty and temporarily unassigned, we stayed outside the coral reef and slowly circled aimlessly waiting for a specific order.

On this particular day Bill, Tex, and I were empty and had been circling for almost two hours. I was lying on the stern while Bill kept the boat moving in a slow orbit. My head was sticking out next to the edge of the stern, so I was almost directly over the exhaust. Each time the boat headed a certain direction, the wind brought the diesel fumes right back in my face.

"Dammit, Bill!" I said rather grouchily. "Can't you go another way? This exhaust is about to kill me."

"How in the hell can I make a circle without going this way part of the time?" he shot back. "The man said 'circle and wait,' and that's what I am doing."

"Circle and wait," spat Tex. "That's the story of our lives. We're going nowhere and we're still waiting to start to get there."

"Yeah," I answered, as the exhaust dipped under the surface each time the stern bobbed down like a fishing cork. "Well, if you have to go this way, at least keep the exhaust under the water so the fumes don't get me. I'd hate like hell to have my mother get a telegram saying, 'Sorry, but your son died of carbon monoxide because his motor mac didn't know how to circle and wait.'"

"Fine," replied Bill, "You've heard the story of the camp cook? As of right now, I'm going back to my duties as motor mac and will let the person who's signed on this boat as Cox'n come see if he can circle any better." Bill stepped out of the Cox'n's cockpit and laughed.

In the end it was all good-natured fun, but I also knew that my criticism, fun or not, had cut short my siesta time. Me and my big mouth, I thought. Then I had another idea. "Tex, why don't you show this motor mac how it's done," I suggested.

"I wouldn't touch it with a ten-foot pole right now," he responded.

Accepting the consequences of command, I reached the wheel just in time to keep us from overtaking the boat ahead of us. "Hey! Mac! Watch where the hell you're going!" the other Cox'n yelled. "You trying to sink us?"

"Sorry!" I shouted as I stopped the boat, our bow only a few yards away from the other craft. Tex just happened to have a pail of water in his hands and he threw it with all his might over the ramp and drenched all three of the crew in the other boat. After sputtering and cussing up a storm, they got their own buckets and started throwing water back at us. I reversed the engine and pulled out of the circle. The other boat spun around, followed in close pursuit, and finally threw their water. The "damage" was light and the laughs were loud and genuine.

Tex and Bill each filled a bucket to retaliate. When the other boats saw what was happening, they joined in and dog (or water) fights broke out all over the place. The slow circle of boats was gone, replaced with darting vessels, flying water, and evasion at full throttle.

The "fighting" lasted about twenty minutes until a control boats shot alongside my boat. "What the hell is going on?" screamed a young officer over a megaphone.

No one answered, but the boats slowly regrouped into the slow "circle and wait" maneuver until the patrol boat pulled away.

"All right, class," said Doll from the boat behind us. What did you learn from show and tell today?"

"We threw the water on the wrong boats," replied Tex.

"O.K.," said Doll, "let's all go together."

Doll led with his tank lighter and the rest of us followed. We appeared to be approaching the control boat in an orderly fashion, but just as Doll drew alongside his men threw buckets of water at the young officer, drenching him and nearly everyone else on the boat. Almost immediately thereafter, Tex and Bill threw their water from the other side. A dozen more boats whizzed by and drenched everyone on the deck of the control boat. After this surprise attack, we returned to our slow circle, each boat falling into place.

Surprised by the assault, the officer and crew on the control boat could do little other than duck for cover. Once the attack boats cleared they emerged, yelling, swearing—and filling their own buckets. The young ensign in charge had enough sense to know that it had to end somewhere, so he turned to his crew and ordered them to drop their buckets. He didn't say another word about it and there were no repercussions for our unmilitary behavior. I guess he figured he would have a hard time trying to explain it.

Some of the funniest things occurred in the midst of the most serious occasions.

Chapter 19

# The Suicide LCVP

Our experiences in Boat 13 bonded Bill, Tex, and I into a strong team. I celebrated my 19th birthday during the fifth week of operations around Saipan. Bill and Tex smuggled a can of sliced pineapple and fashioned a small "cake" with K-ration cookies under a slice of the delicious fruit. We thought about tapping into the water keg that Dees (the cook) and Gamble used to store their homemade moonshine. They made their booze from alcohol lifted from the sick bay, sugar, and who knows what else. They used all of the boats' water kegs to hide it, and it remained one of the best kept little secrets of the war. The Exec never discovered it. I tried it once and nearly gagged to death. It tasted awful! Bill or Tex thought so, too. So instead of the homemade hootch, we used water from the "other" water keg to wash down my birthday cake.

We had a long trip back to the ship on my birthday. I was tired and we had another hour to go. We had left early that morning to carry a boatload of airplane parts to the airfield on the eastern side of Saipan. It was easier to transport the heavy parts to the field from the eastern side, where the heavy vehicles were maintained. The result was that we got the pleasure of circling around the northern end of the island—the one the Japs still held—to get to the eastern side. We couldn't go around the southern end of the island because that's where Tinian was, and it wasn't secure yet.

It would not have been so bad if we could have returned in daylight, but we sheared a pin in the screw and couldn't move until we fixed it. We searched for what seemed like an eternity, but could not find another to replace it. Bill finally made do with a substitute by filing one down to fit. By this time it was getting dark and we would had no choice but to make the return journey at night around the hostile end of Saipan. The gunfire was far enough away so that the roar of the engine drowned it out. The white caps on the water were clearly evident as we bounced across a new and stronger current that swirled around the northern end of the island. We were about one mile offshore, trying to stay out of range of small arm's fire. I would have missed the danger if I had not been watching the white caps so intently. My eyes were focused on the boiling white sea when I thought I saw a dark shape in the water about 300 yards away on the beach side of the boat. At first I thought my eyes were playing tricks on me, but the longer I stared at it, the closer it got.

"Hey, Tex," I said, pointing toward the shadow. "Look at that."

Tex turned his head to follow my finger. "I think it's a boat," he replied, narrowing his eyes. "Let's go see."

Our 30-calibers were all we had aboard, so anything more than very light combat was beyond our capability. Bill joined us. "Come on Tex, let's get these 30's activated," he said. Both men climbed in the gun pits as if it were a foregone conclusion we were going after it.

"Alright, let's go," I said with more than a little reluctance. "Be ready, and be careful."

I turned and headed directly toward the object. As we drew closer I could see it was indeed a small boat. In fact, it was one of ours. It was then I remembered how the last Jap I saw vacate a barge had left it. I throttled the engine down and brought the boat to a stop.

"Challenge him," I instructed. Tex blinked out MUD. No response. He repeated it several times without receiving any answer.

"Damn," he muttered, blinking the challenge again. The other boat blinked back HEN.

"That's not the code!" said Bill.

"Challenge him again," I ordered.

The answer was the same: HEN. It was supposed to be PIE, as in MUD PIE. I put the boat in gear and eased toward other boat. With a surge of power the dark boat took off. I was heading straight at him, so I increased power. "Get ready," I told Bill, but he couldn't cut loose because the large ramp was in his line of fire.

We both were heading directly into the island. Even with the engines roaring we could hear rifle fire from the beach. Since it was one of our own boats, I did not think I could close the distance on him. Besides, at any moment we might have to reverse rolls and find ourselves being chased.

And then it dawned on us. This was a trap. Tex was the first to speak, but we both had the same thought. "It was no accident that he was out here! He was waiting on us!" Tex shouted.

We were heading straight for the cove where we had "stood watch" before. It was a perfect place for the Japanese to hide captured boats until they could use them. They wanted to draw us in and capture our boat. I quickly turned Boat 13 sharply to port and spun around 180 degrees. Bill and Tex didn't say a word and we headed for home.

"I'll bet they have more of our boats in there and that's where the suicide boats are coming from," Tex speculated.

"Yeah," said Bill while nodding his head. "And I wonder what happened to the poor guys who were originally on that boat?"

"Let's head for that destroyer escort," I said, tilting my head toward the warship in the distance. We altered course and Tex sent a coded message. The escort answered correctly and I drove the boat alongside and reported what had happened.

"Well done, Cox'n," replied an officer through his megaphone. "Did you get a fix on where he went in? Also did you get a number on the boat?"

"Negative, sir. "It was too dark and we never got close enough to see a number, but it was an LCVP with a diesel engine, like mine, and I know exactly where he went in."

I handed over the island map that Custer had originally given us with the cove marked clearly on it. "O.K. and thanks. We'll put him out of commission. Stand aside. We're off!"

The destroyer escort took off for the area where the boat was last seen. We watched as the warship switched on its powerful searchlights and started cruising up and down the beach. Within a few minutes it locked on the cove. The escort must have drawn small arms fire, because it cut loose with 20-calibers against an unseen enemy. Before long the ship opened with larger guns and a terrific explosion followed. We decided it was time to get on around the island and into our own anchorage.

We knew about where the *Middleton* was anchored and I slowed down as we searched the horizon for her silhouette. Two boats crossed our bow in the distance. Tex sent the challenge: MUD. No answer was forthcoming. Tex challenged again. No answer was blinked back from either boat.

"O.K., Bill, here's your chance to get even. Give 'em a blast," I urged.

Bill triggered a few rounds over their head and within seconds, six guys were yelling at once. There was little doubt they were Americans.

"Answer my challenge!" I yelled as Tex blinked it out a third time.

This time they both came back with PIE, accompanied with retorts like "G.I. bastards, you're going to kill somebody with those guns! Can't you even tell an American boat when you see one?"

"Well, we just saw one around the end of the island that was an American boat!" Tex shouted back. "Guess what? It had nothing but Japs in it! You better wake up and start paying attention to the signal!"

"What? Japs in one of our boats? Aw, you're full of shit!"

No sooner were the words out of his mouth than a loud explosion rocked the anchorage. It was one of the baby flattops. Something had hit it directly amidships. We could all see fire raging as the large ship rocked under the impact.

"That one must have got through before we came around," Tex said. "Come on, let's go!"

I slipped the boat into gear and took off for the damaged flattop. The other two boats quickly followed. Several other boats had already come in to help and the ship's crew had the fire under control. I circled off the stern. "What happened?" I yelled up to one of the seamen working on deck.

"One of our barges, just like yours, came at us from the starboard side and rammed us! The damn thing must have been loaded with TNT. The damn fool rammed it right into the side of the ship and it exploded."

"Did you challenge him with the password?" I asked.

"Sure! But hell, we could see it was one of our boats, so we didn't bother that he got the code wrong."

"How did he answer?" I asked.

"Well, I don't know what the password is, but I heard our signalman say the boat answered 'HEN,' and that was wrong."

Boy, that sounds familiar," I responded. It was so easy to get complacent.

We had a good feeling we were winning the war, and just didn't expect anything about that course to change. We had to always keep in mind that there were thousands of Japanese fanatics on Saipan and the surrounding islands, each desperate enough to try anything to kill Americans.

Chapter 20

# The South Pacific

In the 1930s, the popular movies were about the South Pacific and the tropics. The beautiful islands, sandy beaches, and blue water shimmering under a brilliant tropical sun helped the new technicolor films sweep the entertainment world. Movie stars like Dorothy Lamour, Lucille Ball, Rita Hayworth, and others let everyone live their fantasy—for the price of a movie. With the exception of the girls in their sarongs, the real South Pacific was everything the movies pictured. This was the tropical paradise we dreamed of as kids. Quite frankly, I loved every minute of it.

Convoys of ships were constantly on the move. We moved troops and equipment from island to island, wherever needed. We passed by islands with mountains and volcanoes. We saw the most beautiful beaches in the world and we swam in water as clear as the air. The multi-colored coral beneath our feet looked to be within reach, but was really 20 or 30 feet under the surface.

We gathered fancy sea shells from the beach, and coconuts and bananas from the foliage. We traveled to places and saw things tourists will never see. We vowed to come back some day in a different setting and bring someone with us to share in the pure beauty of the place.

Moonlit nights at sea are indescribably lovely. It was lonely in way, but I always looked forward to the evening because it gave me an opportunity to reflect life and dream about the future. Our thoughts were always of home, girls, and life after this war was over. Our dreams were about the life we had not been able to live before we were pulled into the service.

I was corresponding with several girls at this time, but I knew little about them. I looked at the name on my boat and thought of Jean. Would we ever get to a place to share the things that were important to both of us? Would she see this beauty the same way I did? My thoughts shifted to the girl of my dreams. I didn't know her name, but she was petite (to offset my gawky height and brunette (to offset my blonde crew cut). In my mind's eye, her lips were full, and her cheeks creased with a dimple when she smiled that sparked an impish look in large brown eyes. Might as well dream high, right?

Sometimes we were given daylight liberty to go ashore on islands we controlled. It was like a picnic. We played softball, football, and volleyball, swam, ate hamburgers and hot dogs, and drank beer and soft drinks.

After leaving Saipan, we hoped we would get back to Honolulu. Instead, we were taken directly to Moritai Island. Bill, and I were lying on the beach after eating hot dogs and struggling with the Greasidick 3.2 beer. We had just watched the *Middleton's* chief surgeon lacerate his hands trying to open a coconut. Two corpsmen were trying to stop the bleeding and bandage the hands.

"Damn, what a ship," observed Bill. "We have a crazy man for an Exec, a foreigner who can't speak English for a captain, a drunken catholic protestant-hater for a chaplain, and a damn butcher who can't even open a pocket knife for a chief surgeon. Who needs Japs for enemies? We haven't got a chance."

As the latest episode of how not to open a coconut settled down, Doll broke the silence. "How old do you think we'll be when and if we ever get home, Wiley?"

I sighed and shook my head. "We both know it will only get harder each time. The Japs won't ever give up. We'll have to take back all of the Philippines, Truk, and every other island between here and Japan. Then we'll have to retake Singapore and maybe even China. And when that's done, which will take maybe ten years, we will have to take the Japanese home islands. McKay will never let us go. You know that. The more experience we get, the more we nail ourselves to this ship." I shook my head. "Yep, Charlie. We're on a one-way street. If we live through all that, then we get to invade Japan, which is just another bunch of islands and you know what that will be like. "

Doll let my answer soak in. "I'll be thirty-four when we hit Japan. By the time I get out, I'll be twice the age I was when I joined up! I wouldn't mind so much if we got a break and spent some time at home. Margaret said that she was dating some officer. Hell, she won't wait till then."

"Well, just think about all this beautiful traveling you are getting to do at no cost!" I joked in return. "You need to let her know that you're also having fun. Tell her what she's missing and when you tell her about these native women, you don't have to describe them. Just say there's a resemblance to Dorothy Lamour and tell her you're getting her one of those sarong things. Bet she couldn't get that officer to give her anything like that or bring her to anything this beautiful. After all, this is the South Pacific that Hollywood says is crawling with beautiful native girls, romance, and pineapple-rum drinks."

"Yeah, I almost forgot how much fun I'm having," replied a recharged Doll.

Shortly after we secured an island, it was turned into a port for the ships and a landing field for our planes. In this way, we quickly gained air and naval superiority in the area even though the surrounding area contained islands with Japanese garrisons. Not all the islands we visited were completely secured. We protected the port and base, but it was not unusual for the Japanese to rule the hills and jungles.

"Scuttlebutt" was the ship's paper, and I saved every issue. This one honors Commander Robert "Red" Hoyle, the *Middleton's* Beach Master. The cartoon jokingly shows Hoyle on the side gun'l of *Lucky 13* with "Red's Raiders" yelling, "We're going in boys!" On the right is Hoyle and a story about his Silver Star awarded for bravery during the Eniwetok invasion.

Chapter 21

# *Lucky 13* Gets Her Name

After Moritai, we shipped to Manus Island, where anyone who wanted it could get liberty every other day to go ashore for swimming, sports, beer, and food. I normally gave my two cans of beer to someone else. Although, I still did not like to admit it, I had not learned to drink anything, not even beer. Usually I spent my time playing touch football, swimming a little, or gathering shells and coconuts. After a week or so at Manus we left and headed for Pearl Harbor.

"At least, we can see some girls!" exclaimed Doll when he learned the news.

"Yeah, and if you want to stand in line, you can do more than see them," quipped Bill. He was referring to the long lines of servicemen that stretched out of the cat houses and wrapped completely around the block.

"Three minutes for three dollars," I said, repeating the famous slogan reportedly stipulated to by the leading cat houses of Honolulu.

"Let's try to meet some nice girls this trip," said Doll. "There must be some here somewhere."

"And one million servicemen for every one of them," I added, even though I thought Doll's suggestion was a good idea.

On our first liberty Tex and I went into Honolulu. The girls we saw in bars were hard cases, cluttered with servicemen. We ran into a few girls who looked decent in the downtown area, but we couldn't get to first base with them. They were either married, engaged, or just completely turned off by servicemen. We spied a couple nice prospects at the Royal Hawaiian Hotel. They were American girls and seemed to be having some kind of trouble getting their car door open. The car, a 1937 Buick, was locked with the keys inside it. It took me a second to realize I recognized one of the girls. She was one of the nurses who took care of me when I was in the hospital at Pearl Harbor.

"Lori?" I asked.

She shot me a quizzical look. "Yes?"

"Can we help?" I asked.

She narrowed her eyes and shot me a wary glance. "Well, I guess so. Our keys are locked inside." She paused. "How do you know my name?"

I offered a warm smile. "I was in the hospital last spring. Remember the *Middleton*?" I asked, hoping she would remember me. Of course, I was just one of 50 guys in the dormitory at the time.

"Yes, I remember," she answered slowly. You're . . . ?"

"Ken Wiley. This is Tex Lee."

"Sure, that's right, Ken. This is my roommate Helen," answered Lori. "We were just leaving and found out I locked the stupid keys inside."

"It shouldn't be too hard," I replied as we looked in the driver's window. "Do you have a nail file?" Helen fished around in her purse and pulled on out. "That's great, thanks."

I worked the file in between the door and the post until it tripped the lock. I opened the door and handed the file back to Helen. The girls expressed their gratitude and prepared to leave.

"How about having a drink before you go?" asked Tex.

"We've been in there for a couple of hours," Helen answered. "We really must leave now."

I was about to say something when Lori interrupted. "Look, why don't you guys let us drive you back to Pearl Harbor. It's the least we can do."

We agreed. Tex climbed into the front beside Helen and I slipped into the back next to Lori. Liberty in Honolulu was daylight only. We had to be back by 6:00 p.m. It was almost 2:00 p.m. now.

There just wasn't much time. It seemed like there was never enough time.

"When I saw you last," Lori said, "you were just back from Eniwetok. I'll bet you've been lots of places since then."

"We've been pretty busy," I answered with a nod.

"Are you still on the *Middleton*?" she asked.

"Yes, probably for the duration and six. Our executive officer says you have to have a complete clean slate for two years before he will even consider letting anyone off."

"Well, I can imagine where you have been then," she answered. "Let me guess: Saipan, Tinian, and the Philippines?" Before I could answer Lori looked hard at me. "Oh my, I remember you now! You were the quiet boy from Texas! I didn't think you knew I existed. I was just another nurse to you."

"How wrong you are!" I answered with a laugh. "All fifty of the guys in that dorm used to wait until you came in and watch every move you made. I'd say you were the best tonic we had during our stay there."

Lori smiled coyly. "It was real hard to leave that dorm sometimes."

I blushed slightly, remembering how Lori used to walk in during the afternoon. At the west end of the dorm was a large screen door. The first time she left the dorm, the bright afternoon sun outlined her figure perfectly, the brilliant rays of sunshine penetrating her dress. It gave the lovely impression that her clothing was transparent. Fifty pairs of eyes locked on that vision. The scheming minds of young woman-hungry sailors put together a plan. Each day, one or two of the guys would ask her a question just as she reached the door, or the "spotlight," as we nicknamed the door. The goal was to keep her in front of the door engaged in long conversations. She had the habit of pressing her body against the door, which brought out a clear definition of her panties and bra. Lori had a very sexy figure. For several weeks she ranked No. 1 in everyone's mind—above movies, letters from home, and even good food.

Hard to leave? My mouth fell open. "You knew?"

"From the very first day," she answered with genuine laughter. "I will say that you guys were original in some of the conversations you came up with." She could see I had a question on the tip of my tongue, but beat me to the punch. "You want to know why I did it, right?" I nodded, barely able to believe I was having this conversation. Lori shrugged. "I enjoyed it and I know you guys did, too. I was glad I could add a little joy to your lives. What's the harm, really? You guys go through hell out there for so long, and then you're in here for a little while and back out there again. I may be the only girl a lot of you even come into contact with, right? Do you understand?" she asked.

"Yeah," I said. "I do understand. And believe me, you sure soothed a lot of eyes. Several of the guys called you for a date after we got out. I remember Jim Farmer said he had been drinking and really got shot down." I hesitated. "Do you have a steady boyfriend?"

"I'm not tied down to anyone, if that's what you mean," she answered slowly. "I'm careful about who I date. Tell me something about yourself."

It was at that moment that Helen pulled the car off the road into a viewing area that overlooked the ocean. We were several hundred feet up looking out over a cliff at the sea. It was breathtaking.

Tex turned around and leaned over the seat. "Helen said that as long as we had a little time before we went back, she'd show us some of the island." He smiled.

Tex and I had spent long hours during the past year looking at all types of seas and islands, but nothing approached the feeling we had now. Sitting on a cliff overlooking the ocean with a couple of pretty girls was like dying and going to heaven. The four of us talked for awhile as the breakers broke over the rocks on the beach far below. I told Lori about Itasca, Texas, about boot camp, about life on the ship, and working in the landing boats. I told her about the native islanders, the jungle river in Guadalcanal, the beaches at Moritai, Manus, and Makin islands. She told me about growing up in Ohio. Her story included her education to become a nurse, and her enlistment in the Navy. She had a short stay in San Diego and volunteered to come to Hawaii. She dated some, but preferred to go stag with Helen to dances and military clubs.

All too son it was time to go. The girls drove us back to the pier at Pearl Harbor, where we could catch our liberty boat.

"Ken, what's your boat number?" she asked me.

"Thirteen, same as today," I answered. "It's my lucky number, I guess."

"Thirteen! The Lucky Thirteen." She smiled and hugged me. A quick kiss, a wave goodbye, and we were back in the real world again with hundreds of sailors waiting for their boats to take them back to their home aboard one of the many ships at anchor in Pearl Harbor.

"Damn," I sighed. "Every time I meet some decent girl, I run out of time!"

Chapter 22

# In the Burst

Germany and Italy began building up their armed forces in the early 1930s. Japan did so earlier than that. America entered the war on such short notice that there was no way we could put huge numbers of seasoned veterans in the field so quickly. American ingenuity came up with adequate basic training schools, but the bulk of training was the on-the-job variety. We learned as we went, and the training never stopped. Our Executive Officer foresaw a time when each of us might have to fill a job about which we knew little or nothing. He was determined to field an adequate crew for any situation.

When General Quarters sounded, specially trained gunners' mates and seamen took over the ship's guns. The best qualified personnel held the key battle positions. Boat crews and Beach Party members did not serve in these positions because they might not be on the ship during an invasion. Under normal conditions, however, all of us stood gun watches. The Exec knew where the crews on watch would have to respond. Later, when we were in situations that required round the clock alertness, we realized his wisdom.

When the ships were underway outside the combat area, a plane pulling a canvas sleeve would fly overhead and provide target practice for the ships in the convoy. One day I was on an antiaircraft training session, doing watch on the forward 3-inch gun. There were four of us on watch. I liked this watch because it was high on the bow of the ship and the view of the ocean was better there than on any other part on the ship. On that day the sea was just rough enough for the spray from the bow cutting through the waves to spray us lightly each time the bow dropped down. The water was almost green. The convoy was traveling on a zigzag course. When it turned a certain way, our ship was among the leading ships of the convoy, with nothing but empty ocean stretching out before us. I remember watching flying fish working overtime to keep up with the *Middleton*. They shot horizontally out of a large swell in the water, flew along for ten or twenty feet, and then smashed into another wave. I looked aft and a lone albatross were flying just off the stern. We were five days out of Honolulu, and this was the farthest I had ever seen a bird stay with us. Usually we picked up several gulls and albatrosses when we left port. They would follow us and dive after the fish the ship's screws turned up. The gulls turned back first, usually on the first day. The albatrosses lasted longer, sometimes as long as several days. This one had been flying behind us for five days. I wondered whether he flew all the time or rested somewhere on the ship at night when no one was looking.

I loved the ocean. I finally understood now what authors meant when they explained that the sea gets into your blood. It has a tranquil effect on the human spirit. I knew I would not live on the sea for the rest of my life, but I also knew I would have always felt empty inside if I had not satisfied this yearning inside me to see and experience it. I was very comfortable on the water. I never experienced seasickness, and had little or no fear of the ocean depths.

I was on the four to eight watch, and during that time witnessed the most beautiful sunrise I had ever seen. It was now almost eight o'clock and the watch was nearly over. The starboard bridge 20mm. lookout reported it first. "Bridge! Object afloat at two o'clock! Looks like it's about a mile. Bobbing with the waves!"

Immediately, every man on watch swung his binoculars to the area described. Sure enough, I could see something. At that distance it was impossible to identify. The thought ran through my mind that the convoy would be heading straight for it when we turned back to the right in our zigzag pattern of travel.

"Now hear this!" announced the Officer of the Day from the bridge. "Unidentified object sighted at two o'clock. Range about

2,000 yards. Looks like it might be a mine. All hands on watch. Scan your area carefully. Report any new sightings immediately."

"A mine was bobbing out here in the middle of the ocean?" I thought. "It must be a stray."

Sure enough as the convoy drew closer I could see the round shape of the object. It was indeed a mine.

"Now hear this!" announced the voice over the loudspeaker. "Gun crews stand by to fire. The flag wants us to detonate the mine."

I was the pointer on the 3-inch forward gun. Bob Baker was the trainer. I quickly swung the gun around and Bob trained it at the same time. We had it zeroed in perfectly and were moving the gun with each roll of the ship. The mine, in clear view now with its dangerous spikes sticking out in every direction, was bobbing in opposition to the ships roll. The range was about 1,200 yards.

"Forward number three gun, stand by to fire. Fire!"

I knew before the mine exploded that I hit it. The explosive device detonated when the 3-inch shell scored a direct hit. The result was a mushroom cloud several hundred feet high.

"By God, Number Three! That's damned good shooting. Well Done! Well Done!" exclaimed the Officer of the Day.

The cheers of everyone on deck drowned him out. The escort destroyer running close by to let the *Middleton* enjoy the target practice blinked a "Well Done!" The official message came from the *Monroe*, the convoy's flagship. "Well done, Captain Olsen. Your conservation of ammunition is commendable. Let's test your other gunners, too. I'll ask *Jackleg* to put up a burst for a target and you have your gunners try to hit it."

It was a little good-humored service jealousy. The Navy had not expected the less experienced gunners on the *Middleton* to hit the mine so easily, nor did they expect such luck with the first shot. Frankly, the Navy guys were looking forward to the event, believing we would miss the mine entirely and humiliate the Coast Guard by doing so.

"Now hear this!" said Cdr. McKay, the ship's Executive Officer. "It seems our Navy brothers have a little difficulty in accepting what our Number Three gun crew just showed them. The Admiral has ordered a little more target practice for us. The *Jackleg* will put up a burst. He wants us to use all of our guns to see if we can hit it. I don't think we need all of our guns, though. How about it, Number Three? Can you take 'em again or are you going to let them call us hooligans the next time we're in Honolulu?"

"We're ready sir!" answered Bob. All of us knew the risk the Exec was taking. We had seen hundreds of anti-aircraft guns filling the sky with flak the Jap planes seemed to fly through without much trouble. Now every shot we fired would be on display because of the burst it would make in the sky, and the whole fleet would be able to measure its effectiveness. I swallowed hard. The Coast Guard was on the line. Why was the Exec leaving the regular watch on? Why didn't he put the real gun crew in here?

"O.K. Baker, Wiley, and crew. Make every shot count. When the burst appears, fire at will."

The *Jackleg* fired forward and out. The burst came at about 10:30 high and 20 degrees off starboard. I swung the gun. Bob was perfect and we came to rest simultaneously directly on target.

"FIRE!" I yelled, waited a few seconds, and yelled it again. "FIRE!"

All eyes were on the burst of the *Jackleg* shell in the sky. Suddenly, the burst itself seemed to explode outward. Our first shot was a direct hit! A few seconds later, the second shell exploded right inside it and the burst widened. A roar rose from the *Middleton* as all hands joined in. Cdr. McKay sent a message to the flagship: "Sir, we apologize for wasting that one shell that wasn't needed. May I suggest that the next time we have target practice, the *Jackleg* put up a separate burst for each of our guns, so they can all get practice?"

The message blinked back from the flag a few moments later was direct and to the point.

"*Acrobat*, now you will put up a burst for *Jackleg*. Let's see how well the Navy responds. Put up a burst over and forward."

"O.K., so now the Navy wanted to have its chance. At least, the best they could do is tie," I thought, knowing how lucky Bob and I had been on all three shots.

"Well, Number Three," said the Exec as he came back on the P.A. system. "You do the honors. Fire one burst when ready."

This time we placed a burst over *Jackleg* and in front to give them a ten o'clock high, 40 degrees off the starboard bow. The destroyer tried its five-inch guns. The first burst was way off target; the second was closer, and the third overshot it by a hundred feet. Next, the sailors opened up with their 40mm (pom pom's) and 20mm. Another five-incher exploded adjacent to the burst and the firing ceased with an apparent hit.

After what seemed like hours, but was only a few moments, the message came back: "Well done, *Acrobat*! I'm damn glad the Navy has you on its team!"

Chapter 23

# Special Mission

The words "special mission" quickly became anything but special. Every time some field commander wanted to change the battle plan, he assigned some group a "special mission."

"The big invasions are a snap. It's these special missions that are gonna' get us," complained Bill one afternoon while he and I worked on our boat while the ship was underway heading from Tulagi to Manus Island. "At least on an invasion, the brass gets together and plans it for months, then sends in the whole fleet and all the carrier planes to pulverize the Japs for days before we land." He paused and shook his head. "On these so-called 'special missions,'" he continued, "some commander or even a lieutenant decides to sneak into a Jap-infested island to rescue someone, or gather gooseberries for the Admiral, and it has to be done right away—without much planning! Right out of the blue!" Bill stood and impersonated an officer: "Boat Thirteen, you take this slingshot here and go on that island over there and wave a handkerchief back to me. We want to see if there are any Japs left on it. Hell Fire! You don't have to have five thousand Japs to get killed. One sniper with a rifle can do it just as well."

Proud of his speech, Bill smirked and fell silent waiting on Tex or me to comment. I didn't think I could top it, so I answered simply, "I think you have it right!"

Tex, however, always had an answer for everything. "Where would the excitement come from if the big shots planned everything out?"

"Well, planned or not," I replied, "plans go wrong, too. How about Eniwetok? I hope that I never go through another invasion like that one. Anyway, every special mission we've done has been something that needed to be done at that time, I suppose. Beside, how would we ever have gotten all those 'Well Done' commendations?"

"You mean, 'Vell Done!'" piped in Bill. "'Viley, Vell Done!'" he said, mimicking the Captain. "'Now men, you come breakfast, ve have shit on shingle, your favorite!'"

None of us had noticed Cdr. McKay standing on the deck rail walk listening to us until I looked up and locked eyes with him. Bill, who was on a roll with his mimicking, rattled on: "'Ve got another special mission for you today, Boat Thirteen. Ve drop you from davits vile ship going 18 knots. Go mop up those Jap islands and come back. Catch up ship and ve try to take you back aboard at 18 knots!'"

While Tex was laughing, I was frantically trying to let Bill know the Exec was standing just a few feet away. McKay dropped a large water keg he was struggling to hold onto. The noise spooked Bill, who looked up and almost lost his wits when he saw the commander.

"What, ah, . . .Well, I mean . . . Cdr. McKay!" We jumped to attention. The commander looked at Bill without cracking a smile. After several seconds of awkward silence he burst out, "Vell Done!" and turned and walked away.

"Oh, man," Bill mumbled, slumping down on the deck. "I'll bet I know who's gonna' get the next shit detail."

We did not have long to wait. At Manus Island, Cdr. McKay wanted a boat to go ashore for a "special mission." He requested Boat Thirteen. Tex, Bill, and I sheepishly pulled alongside the gangplank and Cdr. McKay climbed in. "Cox'n," he said looking at me. "I want to go over to Hyushu Island. It's about twenty miles away on course 233°."

He saluted and I responding to the salute, saying, "Aye, sir."

Bill was trying to crawl under the engine hatch while Tex coiled and re-coiled the bowline. "You men don't mind special missions, do you?" asked McKay.

"Oh, no sir!" I responded. "No sir, not at all."

"Well, that's good," he continued. "I like for my men to be volunteers, but the word around the ship is that Boat Thirteen loves special missions. Now isn't that right, motor mac?" McKay turned and glared at Bill.

"Why, yes sir! That is really right. You can always count on us, sir," Bill replied, followed with a hard swallow.

McKay turned and looked at me. "I also heard that you and your crew are experienced river men, especially in jungle rivers. Is that right, Cox'n?"

That little observation caught me completely off guard. How did he know about our jungle river excursion at Tulagi?

"Well, sir," I stuttered, searching for an answer. "We did stick the bow of our boat up a jungle river by mistake, but we got right out of there when we realized where we were."

"I see," said Cdr. McKay. "And about how far did you stick the nose of the boat in before you realized that it wasn't just a beach?"

"Oh, not very far at all, sir. You know just till the forward motion stopped," I replied squirming.

"And the natives helped you guys turn the boat around?" he pressed.

"Uh, yes sir." I wanted nothing more than for this line of questioning to cease.

"Now, motor mac, since you and the natives turned the boat around, just how far do you think the boat went up that river?" he asked Bill. "I heard that the only place wide enough to turn a boat around was at a native village. Is that right?"

When Bill did not immediately answer, McKay turned to face Tex. "Bowman, how far do you think that native village was up the river?"

Tex knew McKay already had the answer. "I would estimate maybe two miles, sir."

"I see," the commander replied. "Now, I'm really just checking credentials. Two miles. Yes sir, I think that does indeed make you men experienced river sailors. Just what I'm looking for!"

When we approached the island, McKay asked me move in close and run parallel to the shore. When he spotted the small opening of the jungle river he was looking for, he ordered. "In there Cox'n," pointing his finger toward the opening. I eased the boat through the inlet and into the narrow river.

We moved slowly. The river was just wide enough for the boat, and a thick canopy of trees blotted out the sky. We went up the river about three miles and finally came to a native village with a small pier. Several outrigger canoes littered the bank. I put the boat alongside the pier and Tex and Bill tied it up. Before we would get out, a Seabee came out of one of the huts and greeted Cdr. McKay. "I was afraid you couldn't find it," he said.

"Oh, no! I had an experienced river boat crew bringing me in," he replied. "How about helping load a canoe aboard, men?" he asked Bill, Tex, and I.

The three of us quickly obliged and followed the Seabee to a dismantled outrigger canoe. The canoe fit perfectly and was easily loaded on my boat. The Seabee told Cdr. McKay, "You better be on the alert getting out of here. Occasionally we get a few strays from some other island. Last week a sniper got three Seabees before we found him."

"We'll be on the alert," McKay replied. He turned to Bill. "Well, Mr. Sawyer, if you and Huck Finn can cut us loose, I'll ask our skipper here, Mark Twain, to shove off."

This would be one trip Bill, Tex, and I would never forget. I started the boat slowly back down the river while Tex and Bill set up watch with the machine guns. "So the exec has picked himself up a souvenir, a native outrigger canoe," I fumed to myself. "Where the hell was he going to store this on the ship?"

After traveling about halfway to the coast, the boat jerked to a stop as if a giant hand grabbed it. The engine began to sputter and choke before dying all together. I slipped it into neutral and restarted the engine. It ran fine, but when I put it into gear it choked, sputtered, and died a second time.

"What's the matter, Cox'n?" Cdr. McKay asked.

"We've picked up something in the river that's choking the engine, sir." Bill leaned over the stern and looked down into the water. "It looks like rope or a cargo net, Wiley," he said.

The hair stood up on my neck. I turned to McKay. "Commander, please get down in the boat. This may be a trap. Tex, stay on the gun and keep an eagle eye out. Bill, standby but stay low. I'm gonna' try reversing it and see if I can unwind it. If I can't, you'll have to go down and cut it off."

I shot out the orders as if Cdr. McKay was just another passenger. McKay looked at me in surprise, but did exactly as instructed. I reversed the screw but it choked again and stopped.

"O.K., Bill," I sighed. "Stay low and slide quickly over the side. I don't want anyone unnecessarily exposing themselves. Bill nodded and slipped quickly over the side. Just as he did so, I spotted a puff of smoke from the top of one of the trees and a second later heard the crack of a rifle. A moment later a spray of machine gun fire flooded the puff of smoke in the trees, and it was once again as deathly quiet as it was before the sniper opened. I had no way of knowing whether the sniper hit Bill, so I rolled over the side into the murky water. I breathed a sigh of relief when I saw him slashing and tugging at the cargo net wrapped around the prop. I joined in and together we cleared the screw. We cautiously poked our heads above the surface and looked around. Everything was quiet, so we quickly scrambled aboard, started the engine, and moved forward again.

"Do you think you got him, Tex?" I asked.

"No, but Commander McKay may have," Tex replied.

I looked around in surprise. McKay was crouched with an M-1 rifle in his hands.

"The guy dropped out of the tree and was blind to me for a moment, but the Commander saw him about to throw a grenade and cut loose at him with the M-1," Tex continued.

"I'm sorry I didn't follow your orders, Cox'n," smiled McKay. "I felt it was the thing to do at the time. Now, I don't want to usurp your authority, but there may be another one or two out there. Can I help watch?"

"Yes sir," I answered. "Wow, what an officer!" I thought.

"By the way, Wiley," McKay continued. "I don't want to use this term lightly, but you and your crew deserve a 'Well Done' for the way you responded to this situation."

I nodded my thanks while thinking about that heavy cargo net. It was not in the water when we motored upriver. It would have taken more than one person to haul it here and put it in the river. We moved cautiously, every pair of eyes in the boat glued to the heavy foliage lining each bank. I held my breath each time the boat rounded a bend.

I was beginning to think that we would make the coast without further incident when I thought that I heard the sound of a heavy engine nearby. We rounded a bend in the river and came face to face with an Amtrack. We almost fired on it before we realized it was an American vessel. A man on the bow was frantically waving a U.S. flag at us. I stopped the boat and we drifted up to the Amtrack. There were five men aboard. At first we thought they were soldiers or Marines, but when we pulled aside we saw they were Seabees.

"Did ya'll run into any Japs back there?" one of them asked.

"Yeah," I answered. "They put a heavy cargo net in the river and it fouled our screw. A sniper opened on us, but Commander McKay got him."

"Well, I guess that explains it," answered one of the Seabees. "We caught two of them coming out of the river in an outrigger canoe. They were trying to put another net down about a quarter of a mile farther up. They must have seen you enter the river. This is a new gimmick for them."

"What made you check the river?" I asked.

"We thought we heard a machine gun firing. We help the Navy out and patrol the beach sometimes. Sure enough, when we started up the river, we caught these two Japs trying to hide their canoe. They weren't even dressed like natives. They had on full Japanese uniforms. It was the craziest thing I ever saw, coming here in broad daylight dressed like that. I'll tell you something, you don't know what these guys are going to try next."

"Did you capture them?" asked McKay.

"No sir," replied the Seabee. "Since we have been here, they have killed nine of our men. They put grenades in the latrine, their snipers pick us off one at a time when we get in the chow line—even when we're working on heavy equipment. No one ever asked us to surrender. I suppose you might say we acted in self-defense. If you fool around too long with these little bastards, you're dead."

"Are there are any more in the area?" asked McKay.

"I don't think so, sir," answered the Seabee. "They were in a three-man boat. You saw one and we got two and the boat. We'll check on the one you saw. If he ain't dead, we'll find him." The Seabee's eyes focused on McKay's little trophy. "Heh, you picked yourself up one of them outrigging canoes! Would you like to have another one? Slightly used, that is?"

McKay shook his head. "Thanks anyway, sailor, but I think one canoe is enough for me."

The Amtrack turned around and led the way out of the river. We passed the bullet-riddled canoe and the two dead Japanese and reached the coast. "Don't worry, we'll take car of the bodies," the Seabee said as he waved goodbye to us.

McKay stood with his hands on his hips looking around the boat while nodding his head. "Wiley, you, Miller, and Lee reacted brilliantly under some very trying circumstances. I am proud to have you in my crew. I also want to thank you for helping me obtain this fine souvenir. I've decided to forget about unauthorized river expeditions altogether and I doubt I remember any talk about any officers aboard our ship when you men are working in your boats." He smiled at us. "Everyone deserves some privacy where they can express their true feelings, right? Why don't we just say we took a run over to a friendly island to pick up supplies and threw the canoe in as an added benefit?" The commander had a definite twinkle in his eye.

"Well sir," I said, "That's exactly the way I remember it."

McKay had men on the ship hoist the canoe aboard with a cargo boom and put it on deck amidships in the only open spot available. After securely lashing it down to withstand heavy seas, it remained there until the *Middleton* finally returned to the United States. McKay's souvenir was the envy of not only every man on the *Middleton*, but every man on every ship who moved close enough to see it. Word quickly spread about "McKay's canoe," which in our circles became a legend unto itself.

One of combat artist Ken Riley's illustrations depicting the air raids as we "ran the gauntlet" up the Philippine straits. The Japanese had 7,000 islands in the Philippines from which to launch planes against us. Our planes remained carrier-based until we secured landing strips on Leyte.

# Chapter 24

# Return to the Philippines

We loaded Army troops aboard in Hollandia, New Guinea. It was a time-consuming task, and one that was always more difficult in practice than it might seem to others who simply read about it. Everyone was on edge. We knew wherever we were heading, it was going to be a big operation. Just one glance at the size of the task force put together for the movement made that fact clear.

When we pulled out and after the convoy formed, Cdr. McKay got on the P.A. system and announced:

> Men, this is a historic day. After more than three years of war, the United States is going back to the Philippine Islands. Out landing will be at Letye Gulf, near the town of Tacloban. General Douglas MacArthur sends his best wishes to everyone participating in this operation. We are going to free a nation of people who have been held captive by a cruel and treacherous enemy. We are also going to free our own people, those who are left alive and are being held in enemy concentration camps. I don't have to tell you the dangers we face. Japan cannot and will not give up the Philippines without an all-out fight to the death. We can also expect to see the Japanese fleet that's been hiding from our fleet for nearly two years. They will surely come out now. I know I can depend on you men of the

*Middleton* to do your jobs with the utmost care and nothing short of a "Well Done!" Now, Colonel Hart has a message for you troops.

The P.A. crackled and the Colonel cleared his throat and began speaking. "Men," he began. "We have prepared long and well for this occasion." He continued:

> New Guinea and New Britain were tough campaigns. Many of those who started with us are buried in a strange land. The enemy is devoted to his task of killing, as we all know. He is devious and treacherous, as we have found out through hard experience. You fought bitterly through New Guinea to restore that land to its rightful owners. Now, we're going to take back what was ours. General MacArthur told the Philippine people that we shall return, and by God, now we're are going to do it!

The reaction of the 2,000 men aboard the *Middleton* was never matched by any cheering section of similar size anywhere in the history of the world—of that I am convinced. The screaming men completely drowned out the Chaplain's message. He tried several times to quiet us down, to no avail. He finally gave up.

The invasion force consisted of several large convoys from many different locations. The convoy the *Middleton* was in was the largest I had ever seen. It consisted of transports, LSDs, destroyers, destroyer escorts, both baby and full flattops, and one battleship. Each day the aircraft took off from the carriers and flew missions or practiced carrier takeoffs and landings. Hardly a day passed without a plane crashing, either attempting to land or trying to get off the deck. As the convoy approached the Philippines, Japanese air raids picked up.

One day, the planes from the large carrier were late getting back from a sortie. The carrier had taken a suicide plane during the day and was visibly listing. The scuttlebutt was that its planes had engaged enemy aircraft and had remained over their target longer than originally planned. It was dark when the first planes approached the convoy. It was pitch dark by the time the second plane landed safely. The regulations followed by wartime convoys were stringent and clear: no lights after dark. The skipper of the carrier had some rules of his own, however. Those were his boys up there, and they were running out of fuel. It was hard enough to land on a carrier in daylight. Landing on a carrier with a 15-degree list in the darkness was a feat for the history books. The skipper turned on all the lights on the flight deck. When he did so, everyone in the convoy cheered. One by one, the planes landed on the sloping deck until everyone was safely back home.

During an air raid on the way to the Philippines I saw a Japanese plane come in low over the convoy. I had never seen one like it before, even in classroom instruction. It looked something like a P-47. The plane swept through the convoy, dropped its bombs, and headed out through a wall of anti-aircraft fire. An F4-U dove at him from about 10,000 feet at a steep angle. The pilot should have overtaken the Jap easily, but the enemy plane shot forward and quickly outdistanced the F4-U. An intelligence officer later reported that the enemy plane was one of the new "Tojo" army fighters.

In order to get into Leyte Gulf in the Philippines, ships have to pass by many of the 7,000 Philippine Islands. By now, the Japanese knew our invasion force was heading for the island chain, but they didn't know exactly where we would strike. On board the *Middleton* we watched as island after island passed by. We all knew the Japanese on shore were watching us, too. We finally pulled up to Leyte during the night and each ship took its pre-assigned position. The bombardment of Leyte that followed was even greater than the one against Saipan. When the sun rose over the horizon, the curtain of darkness lifted on a sea of ships stretching as far as I could see in any direction. I had never seen so many ships. Air raids triggered the ships to "make smoke" and hide under the screen, but the landing operation began, smoke and enemy planes be damned.

Our boats were lowered to the water and came alongside the ships, quickly loaded, and headed out to rendezvous for the landing. My boat was in the third wave. There was little or no beach fire, which made the landing much easier. The troops quickly established a beachhead. On my second run in I beached the boat's nose on dry land to unload the troops. There was a big commotion off to my left. Cameras on tripods were being set up on the beach and several cameramen were going out to meet a party of men wading in from a tank lighter that had stopped almost a hundred yards away in the shallow surf and lowered its ramp. I had no idea I was about to witness a memorable slice of history.

The party included General Douglas MacArthur. Apparently, the general decided to wade ashore because all the other boats were landing on dry beach. It was a historic moment. Cameras recorded the event for posterity, but at the time it was nothing more than a fleeting part of the unfolding events transpiring all around me. Only much later did I realize the full significance of McArthur's landing in the Philippines.

On the second day of the operation I was back aboard ship for awhile. Filipinos came out to the ships in outrigger canoes. The ship's crews enjoyed talking to them and giving them food and clothing. In the canoe alongside the *Middleton* was a young girl who spoke pretty good English. A schoolteacher, she answered our questions and explained how they had suffered at the hands of the Japanese. She explained how the girls cut their hair and taped their breasts down to look like boys so they would not attract the attention of the Japanese soldiers, who routinely raped teenage girls and women. Everyone on the *Middleton* went below, got their sheets, pillowcases, and extra clothing, and gave it to the Filipinos. In exchange, they gave us various handmade items. I got a nice knife made from a steel file sheathed in a wooden scabbard.

In spite of the warm feeling almost of us felt for these abused people, there was a guy who demonstrated that he had no feelings at all. He was an obnoxious sailor, and I don't know anyone who liked him. He was crude and uncouth in every situation. When he caught a look at the young school teacher he yelled down, "Hey, Baby! How much for you?"

She looked as if she had been shot. "Sir, we do not sell our virtue," she replied after regaining her composure.

A mob of guys turned and yelled at the smart aleck to shut his mouth and show some class. A couple sailors standing next to the big mouth grabbed him and practically flung him over the rail. The coward squirmed from their grasp and slipped away. Angry comments followed him until he was out of earshot. Several people wanted to go get him and throw him overboard, but the uproar died down after a couple minutes.

Leyte was a tremendous operation. For perhaps half of the time the harbor was filled with a camouflage smoke screen. Navigating my boat was extremely difficult because I could hardly see my hand in front of my face. As I quickly learned, navigating by compass and traveling cautiously were the only way to get around. Once, as I was returning to the ship from the beach, smoke engulfed my boat. An air raid was in progress and it lasted about thirty minutes. When the smoke finally cleared, I heaved a sigh of relief because I was still on course. Over my head zoomed a TBF (U.S. Navy torpedo bomber). The plane was flying over the harbor at a very low altitude of just 200 to 300 feet. With its large torpedo-carrying fuselage, the TBF is one of the most distinguishable Navy aircraft. It would be hard to mistake it for anything else, but the gun crew on an LST did just that. As the plane approached the boat, the LST's 40mm guns opened fire and shot it out of the sky. I never did learn what became of the TBF's crew.

The Philippine operation was massive in every way. We were in the boats twenty-four hours a day, running from various ships to shore, trying to unload all the equipment, men, and supplies necessary to fight the battles on land, all while keeping one eye out for Japanese suicide boats and other nefarious activities. We all moved about with the utmost caution, knowing full well that one mistake could be our last one. Enemy suicide boats were common now, especially once the Japs realized all the havoc they had caused on Saipan. They introduced a new twist at Leyte. Someone was slipping into the harbor and laying mines. We had swept the harbor before the ships came in, and several times since. Somehow they were seeding new mines during the ongoing operation. It quickly became apparent they were doing was during the disruptive air raids, when the ships were obscured under a cloud of smoke. The clever Japanese took advantage of this to slip in somehow and use suicide boats and lay mines. We had to figure exactly how and when.

As I pulled alongside the gangplank one day I eased the gearshift into reverse and gently applied the throttle to the engine. The Gray Marine diesel responded with a surge that brought the boat to a dead stop directly in position for Lt. Wilson to step aboard from the gangplank. As he climbed down into the boat, he turned and nodded to me. Tex Lee, who had grabbed the bow line and was holding the front of the boat in place, let go and I rammed the gear into forward and gave it full throttle. We lurched off and pulled away from the ship. I hadn't asked for a destination because I knew Lt. Wilson would tell me soon enough.

The officer leaned back against the engine hatch and looked me squarely in the face. "Bos'n Custer recommended you guys in Boat Thirteen. How would you like a little missionary work?" he asked.

I shrugged but was unsure exactly what he meant. "Okay by me, sir."

"Head out at 165 degrees. As you go around ships in the anchorage, try to swing back to your course. We're going down to an area designated for seaplane anchorage. When we clear the ships, you'll see some Catalinas in there."

Within ten minutes we could hear General Quarters being sounded on the ships. Smoke generators threw out clouds of man-made smoke. It never ceased to amaze me how fast they could completely blot out everything in the harbor. We heard the anti-aircraft fire and watched the large black bursts in the sky until the smoke hid everything from view. The smoke was so thick I had to lean down to see my compass. If I extended my arm to full length, my hand disappeared from my view. I slowed the boat down to a more prudent speed and carefully felt my way around an anchored baby flattop. Although we could no longer see the bursts of anti-aircraft fire, we could hear its intensity just as plainly as we could hear the drone of the Japanese planes overhead. Once I was around the flattop I knew my course was clear of anchored ships. All I had to worry about was moving ships or boats. In any event, the smoke was thinning a bit now and I caught glimpses of the sky. We moved into an open patch of air.

Tex Lee spotted it first. "Jesus, look!" he shouted, pointing into the distance.

If the visibility had opened up just a few seconds later, we would have missed it completely. As it was, we only caught a fleeting glimpse of it as it disappeared into the smoke. It looked like a Japanese landing barge, and the Cox'n running it saw us at the same time. He ducked out of sight, but there was no mistaking his boat's profile. That was no American landing craft.

"Let's go get 'em!" hollered back Bill.

Lt. Wilson turned to me and asked, "Cox'n, was that one of our boats?"

"No, Sir. That's a Jap boat. Can we go get him, sir?"

Wilson thought about our mission, and weighed it against the ramifications of ignoring the Jap boat and all the implications it introduced to our mission. "Probably a suicide boat, like we encountered on Saipan," he said. "Yeah, let's go—but be careful. If he's loaded, we could go up with him."

I headed toward the Jap boat at an angle that would put us on the trail of the barge and increased our speed. The enemy craft was heading back into the thickest part of the smoke, and the pockets of limited visibility were now few and far between. When we first spotted it, the barge was about 200 yards away. I had no idea whether it would continue on its course or change in an effort to shake us off. I figured that we were approximately a mile away from the last ships in the anchorage. There was no radio on our boat, and the nearest place where we could report the enemy boat was on the baby flattop we passed some time ago. We moved into a couple visibility breaks, but never spotted the Jap barge again. After feeling our way along for awhile, we came upon a destroyer moving slowly and firing its anti-aircraft guns. They answered the challenge and we pulled alongside. Lt. Wilson cupped his hands and yelled to the officer of the deck about what we had seen. The officer agreed to notify the other ships.

We resumed our mission to the seaplane anchorage, which we accomplished without mishap. Lt. Wilson's business was aboard the seaplane tender anchored there. He invited all three of us aboard for lunch.

Wilson addressed us once lunch ended. "Men, the flag wants to know where that Jap boat came from. They believe he was laying mines in our anchorage. These waters were swept clean before we came here, but an LST just rammed one as he was moving toward the beach. It did a lot of damage, too. Same thing happened yesterday to a destroyer. They think this guy comes in during an air raid while everything's under the smoke, lays his mines, then either sneaks out or rams something with his boat and blows it up. The trouble is we can't figure where he's coming from or how many there are."

Bill, Tex, and I were all thinking the same thing. It was Bill who said it first. "Guadalcanal! Remember the jungle river? You couldn't see it until you were right on it. I'll bet there's a river here just like it."

Lt. Wilson had not been aboard at Guadalcanal. "What do you mean?"

I interjected. "We found this river that opened into the gulf. It was hard to see from out to sea because the jungle grew all around the mouth. We followed it about a mile or so inland. It was just big enough for an LCVP to navigate. The Japs probably used it when they were there, at least that's what the natives told us. Once inside, the river had a canopy of trees overhead so aircraft couldn't see I, either. It just looked like a jungle."

Wilson nodded his head. "This could be anywhere along the coast."

"Or even on one of the small islands," said Tex.

"Or perhaps right under our nose," added Bill.

"Tacloban has small piers and boat docks that didn't suffer too much damage, doesn't it?" I asked. "Well, I'll bet we were closer to Tacloban than any other point on land when we spotted that Jap boat."

"Ok," answered Lt. Wilson. "Let's go back and talk to the O.D."

After discussing our suspicions with the Officer of the Deck, the information was relayed to the flagship. Word came back for us to stand by. In about fifteen minutes, an officer from Naval Intelligence came on the radio. "Lt. Wilson, we have to find where that mine layer is coming from. Thank you and your men for their help. We will investigate Tacloban piers and tighten up the coastline patrol with PT boats. In the meantime, tell your men to keep their eyes open and from the Admiral, a hearty 'Well Done!'"

"Well, that's about all we can do," sighed the Lieutenant. You heard the Admiral. Now let's go on about our business." Wilson gestured toward the boat and we filed down the gangway.

Bill shook his head in disgust. "I was hoping we could get in on the search." The truth was that each of us felt a little letdown that we weren't going to be part of it.

Lt. Wilson broke the growing melancholy by announcing, "Incidentally, men, our original mission was to go to Tacloban and pick up three Army officers and take them back to the Flag. They were supposed to be here, but they went ashore earlier." He raised his eyebrows and looked at us as if to ask, "Do you understand what I am getting at?"

Smiles crossed the faces of three anxious sailors. Tacloban was by no means a large city, and it had only been free of the repressive Japanese for a few days. But to three battle-hardened members of the Coast Guard, visions of women and spirits danced in our heads. Any way you sliced it, a visit to Tacloban would be a welcome change from shipboard life.

The smoke was clear now, and the destruction wrought by the bombardment and fighting was clearly visible as we drew near Tacloban. We also carefully examined every pier and waterfront building in the hope one of us might catch some sign of the phantom minelayer's berth. Outrigger canoes and a few larger fishing boats were beached and anchored in no particular order. Most of the canoes had been picked up out of the shallow water and simply hauled onto dry land. I drove our boat up onto the beach because there was no suitable pier for docking. Armed American soldiers were everywhere. We all knew what that meant: the town was far from being fully secure. Lt. Wilson left the boat and walked up to the nearest soldier. They talked for a minute before he turned and shouted, "I'm going up to the command post in the town. Wait here. We should be back in half an hour."

Disappointed that we could not immediately go ashore, Bill, Tex, and I scanned the beachfront for anything inviting. Before long a scattering of young Filipinos gathered to stare at us. Several walked down to the boat jabbering in a language I did not understand. To me, the language sounded vaguely similar to Spanish. The youngsters were crowding around the boat, and I was beginning to wonder if it was going to pose a problem. When a young woman spotted the small mob she left the road and headed directly for us. She spoke to the kids in their native tongue before turning to address us in English. "I am sorry, sirs. They mean you no harm. They are just so happy to see you Americans after living under the Japanese for so long."

It was then I recognized her. She was the young and rather pretty schoolteacher who had come out to the *Middleton* in one of the outrigger canoes.

"Hello," I said. "I was on the APA-25 when you came out to greet us the other day. Come on down and join us. It's okay for all of them to come aboard if they want to."

A faint look of recognition crossed her face. I doubted she actually recognized me since I had been in a crowd of two or three hundred sailors on the deck of the ship. In any event, she walked toward the boat and replied with a smile, "It is good to see you again."

Tex and Bill brought out a case of K-Rations they had stored beneath the gunwale of the boat and began passing the food around to the eight or ten kids brave enough to venture aboard. They immediately dug through the small package until they found the concentrated chocolate bars, which brought an instant grin from ear to ear. Each waved his thanks to us.

The teacher extended her hand, first to me, then to Bill and Tex. "My name is Marcia Rutero," she said.

We introduced ourselves and offered her a package of rations, but she declined. When Bill offered several packages for friends and family, she smiled her thanks and accepted the hospitality. Bill put the care package together and set it on the engine hatch.

"Tell us something about yourself," I asked. "Have you been teaching school for long?"

"Yes, I was born in Tacloban," she replied. "When I was five years old, my father died and my mother sent me to San Francisco to live with my aunt. I went to school there and got my degree at the University of San Francisco. I longed to see my mother and relatives and I wanted to help my people, so I came back to the Philippines to teach. Luckily, I got a job her in Tacloban. I've been here ever since."

Her hair was cut short in a burr haircut, but the natural curl was beginning to announce itself. Her skin was smooth and olive brown. She was really a very pretty girl, in spite of the boyish look she tried hard to display. The first time I saw her I thought she was in her early twenties, but now I could see she was at least in her thirties. "Did you teach while the Japanese were here?" I asked.

"Yes," she answered. "I knew about the Japs before they came, from the English news reports. Those of us who knew what they had done to civilians in China and Manchuria tried to warn the others. Many of our people would not listen. When it became inevitable that the Japs would come, I cut my hair and taped my breasts and became a boy anytime I went out of the house. Most of the other young girls did the same. I kept teaching, but I just changed the way I dressed. The biggest danger for a young girl was to be caught outside by the Japanese soldiers when their superiors weren't around."

"Did anyone complain to their supervisors about being harassed by the soldiers?" I asked.

She shook her head and sighed. "They would not listen to a Filipino. All that did was focus attention on yourself. They would come to your house and get you. They killed many Filipinos this way—and not just the girls. They routinely killed the parents or anyone else who was around."

It was still difficult for me to fathom the barbarity of the Japanese. "Did any of them discover you were a girl?" I asked.

"Almost," she answered. "Once I had stayed late at school and was walking home alone. Two Japanese soldiers who had been drinking saw me and began to follow and harass me, calling me unmentionable names. I tried to hurry away and ignore them, but they wouldn't let me. Then they yelled at me to stop. I knew that if I ran, they would catch me and we were on a lonely street and there was no one to help me. They walked up to me and said in some very foul language that they thought I was a guerillo [resistance troops, similar to guerillas] fighter and they drew their guns and held them on me. Although I can understand Japanese, I didn't answer. They kept asking me questions like, 'Do you have a pretty sister?' or 'Go get your mother and bring her to us. If you give us a woman, we will let you go. If you don't, we will take you to headquarters and tell the officers we caught you trying to kill us. Do you know what the penalty is for trying to kill a Japanese soldier?' This is what they said to me."

"You must have been deathly frightened," I answered, unsure of what else to say.

She nodded. "I was terrified. I thought they were going to kill me for sure. Each time they asked a question, one of the soldiers would hit me, either with his gun or his fist. When I fell down, they kicked me. Then they laughed and commented on how fragile Filipinos were. Of course, they used terribly abusive language. I tried to answer them in my native language each time and they laughed and hit me harder because they didn't understand it. Finally, I fell unconscious to the ground. The last thing I remember was their cursing and kicking. My mother missed me and my uncles went looking for me. They found me and carried me home. I was in and out of consciousness for days and in bed for weeks, but I am one of the lucky ones."

The longer Bill, Tex, and I listened, the more the anger for our enemy intensified. All three of us were Texans. We had grown up where honor was a cherished thing among everyone. If two men had a fight, the fight was over when one went down and didn't get back up. A big man who picked on a smaller man was a bully and despised by everyone, and you only took favors from girls who were willing to give them. This Jap was a different breed. They raped women and little girls, beat up and killed boys and old people, and ravaged countries until their people starved and died. They were every bit as bad as the Germans, and maybe worse. They declared war by sending their envoys to Washington to talk peace, while sneaking up on a surprised Pearl Harbor and killing thousands of people and destroying many of the ships and equipment there. Honor? There was none with these people. I looked at Marcia and could see the sadness in her lovely eyes. What a terrible life she and all of the other Filipino people experienced under the Japanese. I could see that reliving her experiences was painful, so I changed the subject.

"Did the Japanese ever have Filipinos work for them?"

"Oh, yes, all of the time," she replied quickly, thankful for a fresh topic. "They organized work parties and made us work for them—slave labor. They left me out most of the time because I was a teacher, but I was forced to work for them often. I helped build their barracks at the airfield and constructed several of the roads."

"Did you ever work on any of their boat facilities or anything like piers or places to keep or hide boats?" I asked hopefully.

"No, but my cousin was sent to the coast to work. He escaped once and came back to see us. He said they were building canals somewhere in the jungle down the coast. They wouldn't let any of the work party come back home at night and a lot of them were beaten and killed, but he managed to run away."

"Where is he now?"

"He joined the guerillos. That was six months ago. I haven't heard from him since, but I think he is still alive and fighting in the mountains."

"This is very important," I said. "Tell me anything you can about the location where he was working."

"He escaped late one night, and he was at our house before daylight, so it couldn't be that far away. He did say it was down the coastline and that the canal cut through a cliff or hill to get to the shoreline. That's all I know," she replied, turning her palms upside down.

"Thanks, Marcia, that may be a lot of help," I replied. "Would you mind talking to one of our officers about this?"

"No, Of course not, if I can help."

By this time, the younger Filipinos had wandered off the boat and settled on the beach to eat their cans of stew and wafers. I looked up and spotted Lt. Wilson and the Army officers approaching the boat. I waved down the Lieutenant. "Sir, this is Marcie Rutero," I said. "Remember her from the other day when the outrigger canoes came out to the ship?"

"Oh yeah," Lt. Wilson said with a smile and a nod. "How are you?"

"Very good, Lieutenant," she replied, grasping his outstretched hand.

"Well, Wiley, we have to go back to the seaplane anchorage. Are you ready?"

"Yes, sir." I turned to Marcia. "What was your cousin's name?"

"Manuel Rutero."

I turned to face the Lieutenant. "Marcia has a cousin who worked on some secret canals for the Japanese. She's willing to talk to our intelligence officers."

Nodding his head approvingly, Lt. Wilson wrote down her name and contact information. "Someone will check with you soon," he promised. With a wave, she walked away and Tex cranked up the ramp. I never saw her again.

As we drove across the bay and headed down the coast to the seaplane anchorage, I told Lt. Wilson and the Army officers the story about the canals that Marcie's cousin had worked on. One of the Army officers spoke up. "We've made contact with most of the guerrillo groups in the mountains. We can try to locate this Manuel Rutero. When we reach the tender, we can send out a message to try to locate him."

Lt. Wilson remained aboard the tender while Bill, Tex, and I headed back to the *Middleton*. We had no more than gotten started when General Quarters sounded and the ships of the convoy began putting out thick smoke screens above them. I took a good hard look at the course ahead, which I knew would disappear in a moment, and came up with an idea. "Guys, if we follow a straight course we're going to be in the middle of the smoke, but if we cut back toward the beach and follow the coastline, we might miss most of the smoke and catch a glimpse of this phantom mine-laying barge."

"Let's do it!" Answered Bill with enthusiasm. "I want to find out how that bastard gets away so easily." Tex nodded his assent.

I swung the boat 40 degrees to port and headed toward the beach. The smoke was heavy but quickly broke up. We leveled out about a quarter of a mile offshore and followed the coastline. We spotted the Jap boat about halfway to the point where we would turn out to head for the ship. Bill was looking back when he saw him break out of the smoke and head straight into the beach. He was a good one-half mile behind us, and only a quarter of a mile off the beach.

"Do a one-eighty! There he is!" screamed Bill.

Without looking back, I swung the boat around and started after him. There was too much distance between us and I knew we wouldn't catch him before he got to the beach. It was definitely a Japanese barge. The enemy boat turned 90 degrees to port and headed down the coast. We were beginning to close on him when he looked as if he was stopping and sinking at the same time. I continued on, even though the only thing left now was a whirlpool of water.

My first thought was that the Jap had jumped out, but we didn't see anyone in the water. Tex thought the guy had jumped out earlier and scanned the beach with his binoculars. Within seconds he caught glimpse of a lone figure running away from the water and into the thick jungle outgrowth.

"He didn't want to give away his hiding place," said Bill. "He turned the boat, opened up some drain cocks or something to sink it, and jumped out!"

"At least he helped us with the general vicinity," said Tex. "I'll bet if we chart that course he was on when we spotted him, we can find where they are hiding these things."

I maneuvered the boat back to the course we believed the boat was heading when we first spotted him. Once on course, I headed directly into the beach in the same direction the Japanese barge had been heading. The area where he went down was about 100 feet deep. The beach here was a long and open, extending at least a half-mile in either direction. "How could this be a secret entrance to anything? There isn't any brush or cliff or even rocks that can hide boats!" I exclaimed.

Disappointed, I rammed the boat up on the sandy beach. All three of us were thinking the same thing: the phantom had eluded us again.

The beach was a good 100 yards deep at this point. I looked at the jungle growth ahead of us and then right and left. Tex lowered the ramp and Bill and I walked out on the dry sand. In the distance was an army platoon trotting down the beach. A Sergeant challenged us and Bill responded with the password. I explained to the Sergeant our mission.

"We were on patrol and heard the boats," he answered. "When we got to the beach, we saw you fellas. By the way, why did you go back that way?" he asked, waving his left arm in the direction I had gone to retrace the course of the Japanese barge.

I explained about the Japanese barge and our belief it came from a secret hiding place. Then I told him about the lone figure we had seen running into the jungle.

The Sergeant shook his head. "My troops have been mopping up this stretch of jungle for a couple of days now. There isn't any river dumping into the bay along this beach. I'll tell you what, though," he continued. "I'll alert all the patrols to be on the lookout for this phantom Cox'n. He got out right in the middle of our troops and he's got a good ten miles to go to get back to his lines."

"I don't think he is trying to reach his lines," Bill interjected. "He's got a hiding place around here somewhere."

When we returned to the *Middleton*, Custer was waiting for us. We went over the events carefully, down to the finest detail. Custer listened intently. Finally he asked, "Was the barge heading for the beach when you first saw him?"

"Yes," I began slowly. "He was heading into it at about 40 degrees."

"And you're sure that he saw you?" continued Custer.

"Yeah," said Tex. "When we did a one-eighty, he immediately picked up speed.

"But then he changed course and headed down about 60 degrees away from the beach," replied Custer. "Right?"

I nodded as the revelation began to dawn on me. "You mean he wanted to be seen, and that little diversion was just to mislead us?"

Custer's head bobbed up and down. "The Japs know we're looking for them. And they have to suspect that we may find their secret hiding place. That boat was loaded with explosives. He should have been going out toward the ships, not going back to the beach with his explosives. I think they wanted us to think they have an entrance down on the beach to keep us from finding the real place." Custer paused and then added, "Let's go and talk to the exec."

Cdr. McKay listened, agreed with Custer, and sent a message to the flagship. A reply was not long in coming. Security was doubled. Every patrol boat was alerted, and the soldiers ashore were notified to begin an intensive search for the Japanese barges. "Inform all your boats to be on double alert," ordered McKay, who added, "A 'Well Done' to the Cox'n and his crew!"

Bill, Tex, and I took advantage of the briefing session aboard ship and went to the chow hall. Midway through the chow line, the

P.A. system announced, "Now hear this! The crews of Boat 13 and Boat 29 will man your boats immediately!"

Oh, shit!" exclaimed Bill. "The first good meal we've almost had in days."

When we got to our boat, Lt. Ward leaned over the quarterdeck and said, "Wiley, there's a Norwegian freighter in the anchorage named *Ole Swanson*. They have a load of supplies to take into Tacloban."

Boat number 29 was Doll's, and he was already circling off the stern waiting on me and my crew.

"No rest for the weary," groaned Bill as we circled around the *Middleton* to Boat 29.

"Well, at least we got to eat solid food before we left," Doll yelled out.

"Ha! Speak for yourself!" spat Tex Lee as he pulled out a box of K-rations.

Bob Baker and Henry Perkins, the bowmen in Doll's tank lighter, added a little fuel to the fire when they realized we had missed chow. "Well, don't worry Tex. I ate enough for both of us. Best steak I've had, too!"

Bill replied by throwing a bucket of sea water at the side of the tank lighter. Everyone laughed.

Before long we were pulling alongside the Norwegian freighter. As Doll was loading the tank lighter with food supplies, we circled slowly off the bow of the ship. I spent the time looking the ship over. It appeared quite different from American ships because of its darker paint. From a distance it looked like a brand new ship with a spotless paint job and array of flying flags.

Up close, however, I could see the rust peeping through and the imperfection of her rigging. The Norwegians were good sailors and they could make an old bucket of bolts look like a new ship. Most of the ships in the anchorage were American, with only a few of foreign origin. It was then the thought struck me. I quickly dismissed it, but the idea lingered. *What if the Japanese barges come from a ship, even one of our own ships?* Could it be possible? It was doubtful any of the American ships in the harbor would be helping the Japanese. But what about the Norwegian, Brazilian, or Dutch vessels?

My teenage mind wandered, but reality told me it was impossible. Military intelligence knew what it was doing, and they would figure out what was happening. My job was to report anything that looked suspicious, not offer opinions or fantasy.

I watched as another foreign ship lifted anchor and got underway. I turned to Bill and Tex and offered my theory. "They come in, often in convoy, unload, and leave, sometimes alone. Who checks them?" I asked. The idea still seemed preposterous to me, even as I tried to explain it to my crew. Neither gave it much credence.

By the time we were loaded it was getting dark. Doll took the lead with his tank lighter as we pulled away. I followed in our smaller LCVP. We carried the cargo into Tacloban and this time pulled alongside the patched-up pier to unload. I took the opportunity to discuss my new theory about the origin of the Jap barges with Doll.

Doll shook his head. "Those barges would have to be hoisted over the side by the cargo booms if they came from a foreign merchant ship, and they would be visible on the deck of the ships."

I shook my own head. What an obvious answer. "Yeah, that's right," I agreed. "Well, where are they coming from?"

Before Doll could answer, the sky over the anchorage exploded in a brilliant blast of white and red light. After a couple seconds, we heard a loud ka-boom!

"Damn!" exclaimed Tex. "That was a big one. Look at the fire! That ship was really hit hard!"

As we later learned, a suicide boat had rammed a baby flattop. The explosion triggered a fire and within minutes she was burning fiercely and listing. The crew abandoned ship and calls went out for boats to help survivors. Doll and I sped back, but other vessels arrived before us to fish the men out of the water.

"That boat had to come from one of the ships," said Bill through clenched teeth. "We would have seen him if he came out of here, and there wasn't any smokescreen hiding him this time, either."

We learned the Japanese boat was mistaken in the semi-darkness for an American vessel as it approached the aircraft carrier. The carrier challenged the boat, but the answer was confusing. By the time the carrier challenged again, it was too late. The barge rammed into the carrier and exploded. The napalm carried by the enemy boat quickly spread the fire.

Custer was waiting on the gangplank with both arms full of radio gear when we got back to the *Middleton*. He jumped into my boat and motioned for Doll to follow us as he directed me to shove off in the direction of the seaplane anchorage. "Shortly before the explosion," he explained, "one of the *Cambria's* boats coming back from a trip spotted the Japanese barge coming out of the anchorage area. Something's screwy about all this, and the exec wants us to keep a watch on the area."

Custer set the radio up and checked it out with the *Middleton*. "Acrobat One, this is Acrobat Two, over."

A voice full of static replied, "O.K. Acrobat Two, this is Acrobat One. Proceed to target area and check back with me when you arrive." It was Doll's voice.

"Intelligence figured it out," Custer said to the three men gathered around him yearning for some explanation. "If you look at all of the sightings and figure their time and courses, they have to come from this general area," he said, pointing to a patch of sea between the seaplane anchorage and us. "The only problem is that there isn't anything there except open water. The PTs and patrol boats will soon be crisscrossing the area, and we are under orders to anchor every quarter-mile until further notice. There are ten other boats doing the same thing, each assigned to different anchorages."

When we reached the right area, Tex lowered the boat's anchor until it touched the bottom. It was fifty feet deep.

"Tex," directed Custer. "Pull up the anchor about four or five feet off the bottom. Wiley, you start working the area. We're going to do a little trolling."

I slipped the boat into gear and move slowly forward. Custer kept one hand on the anchor rope. I worked out a matrix and began the "trolling." I could see the other boats doing the same thing. We worked for almost two hours before one of the boats began blinking a pre-arranged signal. The radio crackled sharply a few seconds later: "Attention all trolling boats, this is Fandango Three. We've got a bingo, I think."

"Roger," replied Custer. "This is Acrobat One. Acrobat One and Two, proceed to the target area with the blinking red light. This is Patrol 32."

Custer motioned for Tex to haul in the anchor while Doll did the same thing. When we arrived, Custer tested the taut line of Fandango Three's anchor. It was caught on something on or near the bottom, which according to all reports was supposed to be smooth and sandy. Custer took the other anchor and lowered it until it hit something solid. Doll lowered several anchors with buoys attached to mark the area. It was then I noticed for the first time that two frogmen were sitting in Doll's boat dressed in full gear, including scuba tanks. They fell backward off the lowered ramp and disappeared into the water. They surfaced fifteen minutes later and climbed back aboard the tank lighter.

"It's a Jap barge, all right!" explained one of the divers. "It's anchored and tied down to the bottom! It's also loaded with mines and explosives. It has a lot of extra buoyancy built into it, so that when the lines holding it down are released, it will shoot to the surface."

The other diver spoke up. "We couldn't really tell because we were afraid we might detonate the mines, but I'll bet the engine compartment has been waterproofed."

"Can you cut the lines, and see if she'll float?" asked Custer.

"I think so," said the first frogman, but you better clear the area. That thing will probably shoot up like a bullet."

"Yeah, and if it bumps any of you guys, it might explode," added the other.

"O.K.," said Custer. "We'll move out about 150 feet. We've got the area pretty well marked anyway. We'll be out of the way by the time you get back down there."

The two divers eased back into the water. Doll and I moved our boats out and waited. We didn't have long to wait. Ten minutes later the water begin to bubble and churn, and a few seconds later a barge popped up in perfect orientation and settled back down on the surface. Custer motioned us to close, but cautioned me not to risk bumping it. He didn't have to tell me that twice.

When I eased my boat alongside, Custer jumped onto the barge and looked it over. Instead of the open passenger-troop area, the top of the barge was sealed. The diver was right: it looked as if it had been waterproofed to utilize the space for buoyancy. Custer tied a towline on the barge and threw the other end to Doll in his tank lighter. When it was secure, he yelled, "O.K. Cox'n shove off! Head for the seaplane anchorage, and when you get into the shallow water just off the point, we'll anchor this baby and let intelligence go to work."

I followed along behind. Several PT and patrol boats joined us before we reached the anchorage. Once there, we anchored the Jap barge and let demolition and intelligence have at it. Custer climbed back aboard my boat and we headed for the *Middleton*.

"It was the only answer," he explained. "They've got these babies anchored down out there in about fifty feet of water. They send a swimmer out to cut them loose, then he climbs aboard and uses it to do his job. We're going to sweep the whole damn harbor tomorrow and get them all."

"Cunning people, these Japanese," I answered. "They must have planned this long ago." The phantom barge mystery was finally solved. "I wonder what they will come up with next?"

As it was with so many other things, once our participation ended we never learned anything more about it. The good news was that we did not see or hear of anymore suicide incidents at Leyte. I was proud we had played a small role in stopping them.

As we made our way back to the *Middleton*, I thought about Marcia. She was pretty, intelligent, and at least six or seven years older than me, but each of us had accepted the other on our own level. Had I finally arrived at that envied position of being accepted as a man instead of a boy? My mind wandered to the nurse on the train when we were riding to boot camp. She had referred to us as "boys." She was about Marcia's age. I thought about the difficult life Marcia endured and wanted so much to help her. But I was moving away from the pier and away from Marcia's life. This damn war!

# Chapter 25

# Mail Call

We spotted the Catalina coming in from the east. It came straight in, without the normal lazy circle. When I first saw it, it was only about 500 feet up and probably two miles out. There was no mistaking the awkward, gull-like Catalina. It reminded me of the pictures I had seen of the China Clipper, famed for its USA to Hong Kong flights in the mid-to-late 1930s. The Catalina was a Navy version of an amphibious airplane. But that was not why I was so interested in this particular plane. What was much more important was that *this* plane was the mail plane, and it had aboard letters and packages for most of the ships in Leyte Gulf! Unlike earlier operations, we started getting mail within a few days after the landing in the Philippines. I drew the duty of picking up the mail for the *Middleton*.

"It's sure different compared to Kwajalein and Eniwetok, where we got no mail at all," Bill observed.

We were told the Catalina would fly in daily to bring mail. Every man in the fleet recognized the plane and waited impatiently each day for it to arrive. The Catalina and its crew ranked high on our list of favorite people.

The plane settled on the surface and smoothly skimmed across it until coming to a complete stop in the shallow water just off the seaplane anchorage. I was third in line. Someone handed me a sack of mail for the *Middleton* and I headed back to the ship. Bill and Tex were digging through the sack looking for their mail before I had even pulled away from the plane.

"Hey, Wiley, you got a letter here. Do you know a Lori in Honolulu?" Bill chided.

"Really? Here, take the wheel so I can read it!"

"Not a chance," he said, holding up a letter of his own. "When I finish, you can move and I will drive!"

When Bill finished his letter he took the wheel and I moved aside to open Lori's letter. I had not yet read a word before Bill opened a new campaign against Army fly boys. "Damn show off! That Lindsay has been in the Army Air Corps two years and the farthest away he's been is San Antonio. Rita says she just loves his new convertible. It matches his uniform. Can you believe it?" he complained, waving the letter around while his face turned red with anger. "She says that she only goes out with him because he's my friend. Some friend, huh? I'd be better off with Adolf Hitler as a pal."

I smiled as I opened the letter from Lori. It was a surprise to receive anything from her. I considered Lori one of my "unwritten novels"—our brief time together in Honolulu had ended so quickly I never had the opportunity to see her again. I scoured the letter in record time:

> Dear Ken, I know you'll be surprised to hear from me, but I've thought about writing you for several weeks. In listening to the news accounts of the Pacific, I can imagine where you must have been and probably where you are when you get this letter. I won't cheapen this letter by saying things you wouldn't believe anyway. But, I will say that our time together was fun. I really would like to know you better. If you want to, call me when you get back to Honolulu.
>
> As ever, Lori

"Well," I mumbled out loud. "'As ever' beats the hell out of 'Respectfully Yours' or 'Your Friend,' that's for sure."

It took all of five seconds for me to begin daydreaming about Lori. I suddenly felt very old at nineteen and wondered why life was passing me by so fast.

"What did she write?" asked Bill, who had calmed down considerably by this time.

"Damn, but it would be nice to meet a nice girl and have enough time to really get to know her!" I blurted out the observation louder and more forcefully than I intended. Bill shot me a puzzled look. "Bill, have you ever been in love?" I asked.

He looked at me with astonishment. "Yeah, sure, lots of times. Trouble is I don't think any girl has ever been in love with me. I mean, you know, willing to go all the way and wait this war out for me. Every time I think I've got one, one of these leg-spreading fly boys in a convertible comes by and she melts and falls right in his backseat. Now, I'll be damned if I'm gonna' take his seconds!"

"Does that mean no?" asked Tex. Bill shot him a questioning look because he thought he had just answered me in the affirmative. "What do you know about love, Tex?" he demanded.

"Well, I've never been in love, but when I am someday, I won't measure it by whether or not she gets in the backseat with me," drawled Tex. "I'll know her and respect her and she me. I won't worry about fly boys dazzling her, because it won't happen." Tex smiled and nodded smugly. "I'll know for sure when I'm in love." He was holding a pair of letters, and took the opportunity to wave them at Bill before sticking them into his shirt pocket.

By now the Catalina had taken off and was banking low over the water. He flew over the boat and we waved at the pilot. The mail plane was very important to all the men in forward areas, and the flight crew ranked high on the list of the most likable people, even higher than the cooks! As the Catalina climbed, one of the engines began sputtering.

"Oh no," muttered Bill as we watched the great bird soar away until it was a speck in the sky. When it finally disappeared, Bill exhaled loudly. "I sure hope she's alright." Tex and I were thinking the same thing.

It was late evening back at the ship when the call came over the P.A. system: "Cox'n, Boat Thirteen, please report to the quarterdeck."

My boat was tied alongside the ship, waiting on a call to load up and go to the beach. I climbed the gangplank and met Lt. Graves, the duty officer. Custer was standing next to him. "Wiley, we got word the mail plane went down. Did you see him take off?" asked the lieutenant.

My heart fell into the pit of my stomach. "Yes, sir, and it sounded like one engine was missing badly."

"How far did you see him go? Was he climbing out alright?"

"Yes, sir. He was heading almost due east and finally climbed out. We watched him until he disappeared about nine o'clock high."

"Alright Wiley, thank you," Graves saluted. "That's all."

I told Tex and Bill what had happened. Neither said a word. They didn't have to. We felt terrible for the crew, and hoped they were ok. It was also depressing because we regarded the Catalina as an angel of communications. The plane was our link to our own private worlds. We knew how painful it was to go months on end without mail. We had grown accustomed to getting news each day from home or from friends. It was a longing that was hard to explain. The news was like losing a dear friend.

Word quickly spread to every ship and every boat. An air and sea search was launched, but twenty-four hours later there was still nothing new to report. There wasn't a single boat Cox'n who did not want to join in the search. On the second day with no news we began to accept the fact that the plane and crew were missing in action; other events eased aside the news. During a war, it was never hard to come up with new headlines.

We had pushed the Japanese back from the beach and spread out and cut back to encompass the entire shore line thirty miles or more from the original landing beaches. Deliveries of new supplies were made to the beachheads. On one such run, my boat had to go around a point still considered occupied by the Japanese. We landed on a secured beach around the point. Beyond the landing beach was sheer jungle.

We unloaded as quickly as possible and eased off. As we rounded the point, Bill spotted something in the water. He grabbed the glasses and focused on the object about 200 yards offshore. "Look at this, Wiley," he said as he handed the glasses to me and pointed toward the object.

It looked like two shark fins sticking out of the water, but neither moved. "Hmm. That's odd," I answered slowly. "Let's go see what it is." I turned and headed inland.

As we drew nearer I made out the unmistakable shape of twin tail fins sticking out of the water. The hair rose on the back of my neck when I recognized the outline of a Catalina submerged in the shallow water. "Wow! It's the Catalina—the mail plane!" I yelled.

"He must have hit the reef," Tex offered.

I stopped the boat and Tex dove into the water and swam down to the cabin. A moment later he resurfaced shaking his head. "It's in decent shape, but there's no one in there."

I shot a glance at the jungle-infested beach. This part of the island was not yet fully secured, and we were a good five miles from American troops.

Bill spoke first. "Let's go!"

That was all Tex or I needed. I eased the boat forward until it touched the sandy beach. I drove it in good and shut the engine off. A deathly silence hung over everything. The only sound was the lapping surf and miscellaneous jungle noises. The three of us stood quietly and listened for a minute or two until we were satisfied no one had detected our approach. The beach was barely twenty feet deep, and the jungle looked completely impenetrable. If the crew of the Catalina made it out and onto the beach, then they went into the jungle. If so, this was the spot they would likely reemerge—if they were still alive.

"Let's look around," whispered Bill. Tex nodded in agreement.

"Wait a second," I cautioned. "We're in a hostile area, we have no firearms except those 30-calibers mounted on the boat, and it's been two or more days since that plane went in."

"Yeah, and what's your point?" asked Bill. "You know as well as I do that we're going, so let's get on with it."

I shook my head and sighed. "I am just saying we need to be really careful and quiet."

This time Tex shook his head. "Let's think about this. If the crew made it ashore, they would have started back to the southwest to try to get to our lines, right?" We nodded. "I think they would stay close to the beach and they would not have known about the new beachheads. I think that we ought to stay in the boat and travel just offshore. Anyone out there along the beach can hear us. We may pick up a few snipers and maybe a mortar round or two, but I think we will have a better chance of finding the crew if they are still alive."

That made good sense, and Bill and I quickly agreed. I hit the starter. The diesel caught quickly and the roar of the engine split the still air like a bombshell. I backed off and took the boat out about two hundred yards, turned down the beach, and moved cautiously. If we hit the reef, it would seriously cripple us a long way from assistance. All three of us watched the shoreline for the slightest movement as we eased along.

We were not two minutes down the beach when a sniper's bullet whizzed past Tex's head. A second later we heard the crack of the rifle. I saw the puff of smoke from a clump of trees and heard the unmistakable crack of the rifle a second time. Bill reacted quickly, grabbing Tex and pulling him under the protective cover of the starboard gun'ls steel plate. The second bullet creased my kapok life jacket. I rammed the throttle full forward and the boat lifted its nose and picked up speed.

Bill squirmed his way back to the 30-caliber. "Make a circle, Wiley," he yelled. "I'll let him have a dose of this."

As I swung the boat around, Bill raked the area in the trees where the puff of smoke came from. There was no answering fire. Bill kept pouring it on as I made another circle and headed down the beach.

We moved about one mile down the beach and we heard a barrage of gunfire. It was like several rifles and a machine gun. A concentration of fire was taking place in the jungle opposite our position. I turned and was moving away from the beach as fast as the boat would go. Bill once again grabbed the 30-caliber and was ready to return fire, bur there was nothing to shoot at.

Bill spotted an S.O.S. Signal from a point on the land about a quarter of a mile down from the Japanese concentration. It seemed like a trick, but he made out the word "Mail" after the S.O.S.

"Hey! Wiley," he yelled. "It's the Catalina crew off the point!"

I twisted around and looked where Bill pointed, just in time to see the distress call repeated. I turned the boat as fast as I could and headed for the area. As we drew near, the firing picked up again, but this time it was farther away. If the Japs saw us coming in toward the beach, they would be high-tailing it toward us right now.

*Could we get in to the beach and off again before they caught up with us?*

A few moments later we made out three figures waving at us. I headed directly for them. The word "Mail" tacked onto the distress signal had removed any doubts about their authenticity. The moment we hit the beach Bill dropped the ramp. The three were inside in seconds and Bill was cranking up the ramp as I backed the boat off, spun around, and gave it full power. Some sporadic fire opened up farther down the beach. This time I headed the boat directly away from the sand, trying to get out to sea as fast as I could. Finally, after what seemed like an eternity, we were out of range of the small arms fire and heading home, back to the good 'ole *Middie Maru*. Lucky 13, with a few more scars and holes in her, had done it again.

The Catalina pilot explained how engine failure forced him to land the plane. He managed a good water landing, but in trying to get closer to the beach, hit the reef and ripped the bottom out of the Catalina. It sank almost immediately and the three scrambled ashore just in time to miss a Japanese patrol that had seen the plane come down. It had been touch and go ever since. The Japanese figured out they weren't in the plane and had spent the past two days scouring the area to find them. That is, until American soldiers broke through and established a new beachhead. This thrust cut the Japanese off and gave them something else to think about, but it also left the crew right in the middle of a concentrated force of Japanese. The crewmen figured out what was happening when they saw all of the landing craft and ships on the horizon moving into the new area. Since they could not signal anyone at that distance, they wisely did the next best thing: waited until the Americans mopped up the area. The problem was staying alive long enough for help to arrive. When they first saw our boat, they didn't know what to think, but then when the Japanese started shooting at it, they figured it must be one of ours. Adding the word "Mail" to the distress message was a brilliant idea. These guys knew mail was important to everyone, and every American out there would know about the lost mail plane. How right they were.

Word of the rescue spread quickly throughout the Task Force. Once we were back aboard the ship, Tex's near-miss with the sniper bullet was also a topic of hot conversation. Bill offered his two cents by telling Tex that he had missed an excellent opportunity to improve his looks.

Cdr. McKay personally called us into Captain Olsen's cabin, where he delivered his famous "Vell Done!" and shook our hands.

Chapter 26

# The Japanese Strike Back at Leyte

Admiral Halsey's decision to pull his main battle fleet out of Leyte to chase empty enemy carriers allowed the main Japanese fleet the opportunity to sail in and destroy the Leyte beachhead. Some say friction between the Army (General MacArthur) and Navy (Admiral Nimitz) triggered the decision. Others think it was just Bull Halsey's eagerness to destroy the Jap fleet that convinced him to send away his warships. Still others say the Japs were so weak by this time they couldn't mount an effective offensive. Regardless of why the decision was made, it left the American invasion force in the Philippine in a vulnerable position. Only Jap mistakes saved us from a potentially devastating defeat.

And so in Halsey's absence, the mighty Imperial Japanese fleet that we had expected so many times in the past finally made its fateful appearance at Leyte. It arrived from several directions. After fatally crippling the carrier *Gambier Bay* and escort ships from their path, the largest fighting ships in the world turned and ran from our cruisers and PT boats in Leyte Gulf.

My first knowledge that the Japanese fleet was paying us a visit was when I returned to the *Middleton* for another assignment. Custer yelled down to me, "Bring your boat around to the starboard davit! We're bringing you aboard. We're pulling out!"

It only took a few moments to hook the two cables; Custer hoisted us clear of the water. The ship began to move immediately.

Once aboard I heard the story. The Jap fleet had slipped through the straits and was approaching to destroy the concentration of American shipping and troops. All the transports and nonessential ships pulled out. The *Middleton* was already in a state of General Quarters. I resumed my job as helmsman.

We slipped out of Leyte in a small convoy of transports and only one destroyer escort. We were sitting ducks. At one point we passed within fifty miles of the main Jap surface fleet of battleships, cruisers, and destroyers. Word was that the Japanese did not have radar—a rumor we could only hope was true. We did not know it at the time, but our much smaller assemblage fleet of PT boats, destroyer escorts, destroyers, cruisers, and baby flattops had slowed down the approach of the enemy. One lone Japanese surveillance plane flew over us, but we shot it down. We prayed the pilot had not had time to send a message announcing our location. Fortunately, we slipped away unnoticed and headed back to Manus Island.

The Allied navies, which outnumbered the Japanese, fought and won the battle of Leyte Gulf from October 23-26, 1944. It was one of the largest naval battles in history. The cost was high. We lost about 3,500 sailors killed, three carriers of various sizes, a destroyer, and other associated shipping. The Japanese, however, lost 10,000 men killed, more than 600 planes, four aircraft carriers, three battleships, eight cruisers, and a dozen destroyers. The battle crippled Japan's naval power.

As the fighting got underway we picked up troops at Manus and took them back to Leyte. One of the soldiers was Carl Sweeney, a schoolmate from Itasca, Texas. I was stunned. The whole world was at war and 15,000,000 boys from the United States scattered around the globe, and four guys from a little town of 1,728 people crossed paths thousands of miles from home. Carl was the brother of the girl Albert Ellison said he was going home to marry.

The air raids against our ships and beachhead intensified. We made several trips back and forth between Leyte and some of our forward bases to bring supplies and troops. The Philippines was comprised of about 7,000 islands, many of them occupied by the Japanese. We had only one of those islands, and then only part of it. We had to travel within sight of most of them to get to Leyte, something that always made me feel uncomfortable.

The Japanese air raids were bad enough when the enemy task force was moving up through the straits toward Leyte. Now it was worse. The constant raids kept everyone on alert. General Quarters sounded so often that everyone was on duty round the clock. Finally, standing orders were issued that we were to stay in position and man our battle station at all times while on watch. It was the only way anyone could get any sleep or rest. I was so exhausted at one point that I slept through some intense air raids. During one such raid, kamikazes hit some of the ships in our convoy. Their goal was to stop the convoy, and they tried to do so by flying in from every direction. I spent much of the time at the helm of the ship in the bridge, where I heard and saw a lot of the action. The enemy planes often arrived in pairs, flying low and fast toward the ships. When they reached the convoy, they separated to divide anti-aircraft fire. They must have come from one of the many nearby islands, because those that didn't get shot down or dive into ships slipped off to land on one of their strips.

It was good strategy. U.S. carrier planes could not watch or examine every piece of ground. Enemy planes (likely camouflaged while on the ground) took off, formed a beeline for the convoy, did their damage, and slipped off to another secluded strip to land and fuel up, refit, and try again. For our ships, it was like running a deadly gauntlet. The Japs did their best to harass us constantly.

On this day the sky was nearly black with bursting anti-aircraft fire. A kamikaze exploded into an LSD; another targeted a baby flat top. The pilot made his roll and started his fatal dive, coming in at a 45-degree angle. We gave him everything I could, but he flew right through our bursts. In my mind (or perhaps it was out loud) I was shouting, "Hit him! Damn it, hit him! Somebody hit that damn Jap!" At what seemed like the last possible moment, one of the shells scored a direct hit and the plane disintegrated into a thousand pieces. Thankfully, most of the debris missed the ship.

Lt. Stinson gave the command, "Bump it around to 3-2-8. Maintain current speed."

I swung the wheel to port and the ship began turning at the same time all the other ships in the convoy changed course. I measured my override and moved the wheel back to starboard to compensate. The ship steadied out perfectly on course. Now we were directly behind the baby flattop. Damage control consisted of clearing away the debris that had fallen on the deck.

Almost immediately the anti-aircraft crews picked up another Zero slipping in low over the water heading straight for the ship. The *Middleton* gun crews joined in, as did a few other crews from other ships in the convoy. The plane was coming in at 10 o'clock and closing fast. He was so low that only a few of the ships had a clear angle of fire. One of them was a destroyer, whose crews opened with a broadside barrage. The plane began smoking and flying erratically, but his momentum carried him into the side of the flat top. He hit a glancing blow just above the water line, but the ensuing explosion ripped a large hole into the side of the ship. A "Betty" came in from behind, and then a second and a third. They were flying higher than the Zero when they separated to start their run on the convoy. One was shot down over water. The other two made sweeps and dropped their bombs, hitting a transport before speeding off through a curtain of flak unscathed. Once they disappeared, the sky fell silent. We all heaved a heavy sigh of relief, checked our equipment and each other, and waited for the next round of attacks. This was how it was all the way through the straits to Leyte. Hardly an hour passed without spotting an enemy plane or hearing General Quarters.

Before my four-hour watch ended we experienced three air raids. Just as we were changing watch, General Quarters sounded again. My relief, friend John McKim, was also from the boat division. "Is this how it's been?" he asked as he took over the helm.

"Solid," I replied. "At least two ships hit. That flat top took a kamikaze and a transport behind us got a bomb."

Anti-aircraft fire was beginning to show up now off the starboard side. I walked over to the bridge windows and scanned the skies. I couldn't see the planes yet. I looked at the radioman communicating with the gun crews and raised my eyebrows in question. "Where are they?" I asked.

"High this time. Eleven o'clock," he answered. "The report was two Bettys."

I strained my eyes to try to spot the targets of the anti-aircraft fire by identifying the pattern of the bursts. I noticed Doll coming off the 40mm gun watch and quickly went down on the deck to join

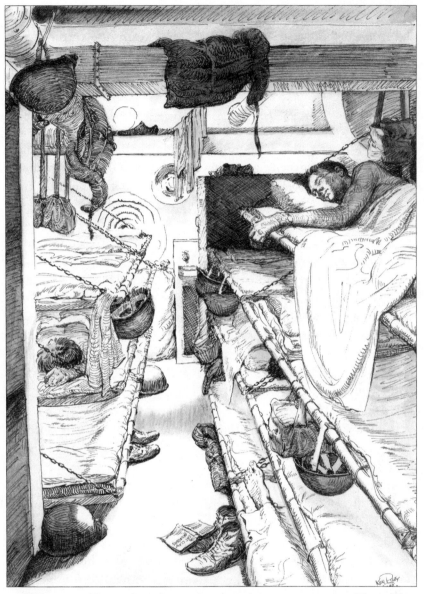

Battle weary Coast Guardsmen try to grab a moment's rest. The raids were so constant the Executive Officer decided crewmen on watch would stay in a state of General Quarters. When we were not on watch we stole any rest we could get. Ironically, we were so exhausted we slept through many air raids, leaving it for others to brief us on what we had missed.

him. We walked into the open passageway leading to the wardroom and stood just inside where we could get a clear view of the action off the starboard side of the ship.

"You know, Wiley," Doll said. "Any one of those things could pick our ship and we could be roasted mincemeat in sixty seconds, but I'm so damned tired that I'm gonna' go down and hit the sack anyway."

"Me too!" I added with more enthusiasm than I felt. Together, we made our way down to our bunks in the 3rd Division. We lay in bed unable to sleep until the all-clear was sounded.

"You know, Charlie," I said. "We can hear and even see most of the planes most of the time. What about a torpedo? We're just about the right level below the water line and all that's between the water and us is one steel plate. How thick is that plate, do you recall?"

Doll reached over and patted the bulkhead, which was actually the side of the ship. "Yup, this is all that's between us and the water," he said with a sigh. Less than an inch from his fingers was the ocean. If a torpedo hit us there, it would happen so fast we would not know what killed us.

"Well, maybe they'll wait till I get to sleep," Doll mumbled before yawning widely. "I'm sure not going to sit up any longer and wait on them."

Bill, who had been listening to the exchange, added sleepily, "No torpedo is gonna' get me. I'll be killed by a jealous husband when I'm 100 years old."

It was important to all of us to appear brave, I thought to myself. "Brave" is a strange word. It has a broad meaning and I wasn't sure I really understood it.

Our ship was never been hit by a bomb or torpedo, though we had many close shaves. We watched others get hit, other ships sink, and other men die. It was like watching a movie from your own deck. I think we figured somehow that it just wouldn't be us.

After almost three years we were landing men on Philippine soil. Tomorrow we would be in Leyte Gulf facing what we had been told was the Japanese Imperial Fleet. There would be no time to watch movies from our deck. I knew I would be in the thick of it.

I drifted off to sleep and dreamed about a girl I had never met, but knew I would someday.

Chapter 27

# Lucky 13

The *Middleton* left Leyte and headed back to Pearl Harbor. We arrived during the night and anchored without incident. Thoughts of liberty danced through our heads until the *Middleton* pulled up anchor and docked at Honolulu to take on troops and supplies. All liberty was canceled.

I was one of several men working on the docks during the loading process. Once the work slacked off, we began tossing a football around. Before long, the ball ended up in the water. Without giving it a second thought, I removed my shoes and jumped in, swam to the ball, picked it up, and threw it back to someone on the dock. The pier was a good ten feet above the water line, and the only way was to climb out was up the posts and structure supporting the pier. Again, without thinking, I swam to the nearest post and began climbing. I felt a sharp tingling in my feet, but didn't think much of it until I was on the dock, where one of the guys yelled, "What the hell happened to your feet?"

I looked down and my mouth dropped open: blood was running all over the pier. Time and the sea had covered the wood with razor-sharp barnacles that had cut the soles of my feet to ribbons. It was only then that I felt the pain and the throbbing. Clenching my teeth, I hobbled up the gangway. A trail of blood marked every step. One of the guys helped usher me into sick bay. The surgeon cleaned and dressed the wounds, which required several dozen stitches. I was off my feet for thirteen days on a hospital bed. My misadventure earned me the new nickname "Buster Crabb," after the movie star and Olympic swimmer for my diving skills.

The number and mixture of ships in the new convoy formed for yet another Pacific operation was larger than ever before. Earlier in the war, the highest number I saw on any attack transport was still below 100. This time I spotted attack transports with numbers as high as APA-225. There were also more LSDs, cruisers, battleships, carriers, and baby flattops. Something really big was in the offing.

"Men," Cdr. McKay announced one afternoon on the ship's P.A. system. "Our next port will bet the island of Luzon in the Philippines. We are going to land our troops on the same beaches the Japanese landed on when they took the Philippines from us. We will be landing about seventy miles from Manila."

"All right!" said Doll. "The capital city! Man, Wiley, this one is going to be big! I'll bet they throw everything at us this time."

We sailed with the convoy out of Hawaii and up through the Philippine straits toward Luzon. One of the worse storms I ever witnessed struck us during our journey up the straits. The mountainous waves were so huge that ships 500 feet long riding the sea just a few hundred yards away fell completely out of sight. One moment you could see the other ships in the convoy, and the next moment the bottom dropped out under your ship and all you could see was walls of water in every direction. Even veteran "salts" got a little seasick. It was the first and only time during the war I felt queasy. Once the storm subsided, the Japanese air raids picked up.

Kamikazes were more numerous now than ever. The Japanese aircraft took off from one of the nearby islands, flew over the convoys, picked out their targets, and either dropped bombs or dove for the kill. Aircraft carriers and large warships were their preferred targets. Suicide raids from the sky were a daily occurrence, and often lasted all day long. It reminded me of running a dangerous gauntlet. We often passed between islands, each of which bristled with enemy troops and aircraft. Enemy submarines lurked in the channels hunting American prey. Mines floated freely in the water. How any of our ships made it through, I will never know. Carrier-based aircraft and anti-aircraft fire worked overtime to protect our convoy from the aggressive Japanese. No one got enough sleep during the operation, which drained every ounce of physical and mental strength from your soul.

Tokyo Rose did her best to sap our morale by talking about "tremendous" Japanese victories on Leyte and the success Japanese aircraft enjoyed against American shipping. She liked to boast about the number of capital ships sent to the bottom. In fact, she often named the individual ships. During our service aboard the *Middleton*, we received accurate news reports several times each day via U.S. Armed Services Radio. Every report she made was either a wild exaggeration of what we had heard, or simply a flat lie, and so her words had little effect on our morale.

Doll and I were sitting in the briefing room examining charts and photographs of our landing beach. All of the *Middleton's* boats were in the fourth, fifth, and sixth waves. Our landing beach was just to the left of an old school building, about 100 yards from the beach. It was a four-story building and offered an easy landmark we could spot from the sea.

"I would have thought this bunch of guys would have been in the first wave," announced Doll, referring to the rugged 1st Cavalry outfit we had on board with us.

"The difference between first and fourth wave is only a few minutes," Tex Lee replied.

"True enough," I answered, nodding my head. "I hear the Japs have 260,000 troops in Luzon. If so, this is where they'll make their final stand."

"Just make sure you learn the passwords each day," cautioned our instructor. "Don't forget the suicide boats at Saipan or the landing control boats." He stopped to clear his throat and then continued. "Lt. Hoyle has a few things to say."

Red Hoyle, the Beach Master, was in charge of the ship's beach party. It was his duty to set up a beachhead with communications and organize the off-loading of the boats so the fighting troops would get the personnel, equipment, and supplies they needed in the proper priority. His efforts at Enewitok earned him a Silver Star. His beach party was nicknamed "Red's Raiders." Lt. Cdr. Hoyle was liked and respected by everyone. When he spoke, everyone listened.

"Men, we have a very special bunch of soldiers on our ship this time. They have been selected for a very special mission. It is important that we land them and all of their supplies in the fourth, fifth, and sixth waves. If there is any trouble that might keep you from getting your personnel or cargo on the beach, you are to notify the wave commander or a landing control boat immediately. We must get these men and their supplies ashore on time. All *Middleton* boats have priority until this is accomplished. My group and I are going in with the first wave to take charge of the beach. We'll be ready to receive you. Any questions?" There were none.

Ensign McHale, the Boat Group Officer, stood up next to give out wave assignments. "Wiley, in Boat Number 13, will be Wave Leader of Wave Four. Colonel Smith and his staff will ride in Wiley's boat."

I could hardly believe it. The colonel was going in with the first wave of his group? No wonder his men liked him so much. Several of the soldiers claimed they would follow him anywhere.

"One more thing," said Ensign McHale. "In all likelihood, we'll be under smoke for the entire operation. You should be use to it now, after Leyte and Saipan. Brush up on your navigation."

Almost all of the ships carried smoke generators, and within a few minutes could put up a cloud of smoke that would completely blot out an entire harbor or fleet of anchored ships. Usually the smoke broke up as we neared the beach.

The massive fleet of many separate convoys came up on Luzon during the early morning hours and by daybreak had secured their respective positions. The heavy bombardment of the beach area was already underway. We were almost ten miles off the beach when the boats were lowered and began to rendezvous. Japanese aircraft tried to penetrate the ring of carrier fighter aircraft guarding the ships, but were turned away or shot down. A few penetrated but were met with anti-aircraft fire from the ships. One of them had dropped down to just a few yards above the water and aimed itself at one of our carriers. Defensive fire broke the plane apart before it could smash into the warship.

I pulled my boat alongside the *Middleton* and Colonel Smith and about twenty soldiers climbed down the cargo nets into the boat. The colonel immediately took up his position, sitting on the engine hatch where he could see everything around him. This, of course, was a real no-no. We Cox'ns were ordered to make all of the troops sit or kneel inside the boat out of sight. This guy was a colonel, though, so I shrugged off my directive and decided he could sit wherever he pleased.

"Well, Cox'n," said the colonel. "Are you going to put us safely on dry land?

"Yes sir!" I answered, moving my boat away for our final rendezvous point.

The colonel busied himself with two of his aides, pouring over charts. One of the aides turned to me and asked, "Cox'n, if the beach fire is too heavy for us to go in on Green 2, can we land directly in front of the schoolhouse?"

I shook my head. That thought had already crossed my mind, and the answer had been bothering me for hours. "Sir, that schoolhouse will probably be full of Jap snipers."

I thought back to Eniwetok, where a young boat wave commander had directed our wave to the left of the planned beach. The decision had driven us right into the main body of Japanese. "I think the best place to land is right where we've already struck the hardest blow," I continued.

The colonel was listening carefully to our exchange and finally spoke up. "What's your name, son?"

"Ken Wiley, sir," I answered.

"You'd make a damn good soldier, Wiley," and he turned back to the aide who had raised the question. "We'll go in on Green 2 as planned."

As the boats took up their positions, heavy smoke spilled over the entire fleet. It was thinner where the boats circled, waiting to make the run to the sand. The colonel's radio and communications unit was in the boat with us, and he was conversing with the other boat wave commanders and the control boat. The first wave of Amtracks (Amphibious Tractors were also called DUCKS) and landing craft hit the beach under light machine gun, sniper, and mortar fire. By the time the third wave hit, we had an established beachhead.

We left the smoke behind us as we motored hard for the shore. Within a short time I spotted the schoolhouse and set my course left of that spot for Green Beach 2. Thankfully, there was no coral reef this time to slow us down and the tide was high. The sea was rough and the breakers coming in were high. It was all I could do to keep the boat straight to keep from broaching. Still, I landed the boat's nose on the sandy beach and Tex lowered the ramp on dry sand. On my right, a navy LCVP with a gasoline engine broached and its crew looked helpless. There was so much noise and gunfire on the beach that I couldn't tell if the enemy was actually directing firing against our boat or not—until I saw splashes of water jumping across the surface on both sides. It was then I noticed puffs of smoke coming from a third-story corner window of the schoolhouse about 200 yards away to the right. Some of the soldiers saw it too, and Colonel Smith directed two men with a bazooka to clear out the room. Dodging sniper bullets, the men ran toward the schoolhouse and took cover almost directly in front of the enemy nest. A few seconds later they fired their bazooka. It was a direct hit. The explosion blew out a complete section of the building.

The entire squadron of the 1st Cavalry scampered ashore in a matter of minutes against only limited resistance. What my shipmates and I didn't know was the real mission of the 1st Cavalry. This lean and mean group of jungle fighters, carrying only light packs and guns, advanced quickly and penetrated the Japanese lines. As we later learned, they traveled seventy miles through Japanese-held territory to free American prisoners held captive in a Japanese concentration camp. The soldiers took the prisoners out of the POW camp and back through Japanese-held territory to U.S. forces holding Lingayen Gulf. The operation was one of the many unheralded heroic acts during the war. The heroism demonstrated by these men was recently depicted in the movie "The Great Raid."

General Douglas MacArthur came ashore late in the day. There was excitement on the beach when he landed in an LCVP. The Filipinos got word he was coming and came out in throngs shouting, singing, and dancing with happiness to welcome their liberator. It was a historic moment when he announced over a loudspeaker from the same spot that the Japanese had landed three years before. The gist of his speech was this: "When I left three years ago, I told the people of the Philippines, I shall return. I have returned."

At Lingayen Gulf, meanwhile, we began the task of unloading the ships while the troops on Luzon pushed farther inland. Air raids provided more of an annoyance than a mortal danger. The great naval battles of the Philippines, beginning with the landing on Leyte, had crippled the Japanese navy and obliterated their supporting aircraft. We whipped them in every aspect. Air losses were 4 to 1 in our favor. Our planes and surface ships sank their battleships, cruisers, and carriers. The Japanese navy was defeated. Kamikazes were now Japan's most potent weapon—and they were a weak substitute for the once mighty Japanese Imperial Fleet. Kamikazes not only flew aircraft, but boats and human torpedoes. The latter were called Katiens, electric torpedoes that carried one or two crewmen to guide the explosive against a target. Their range was much greater than a normal torpedo, which could also not steer itself in any meaningful way. Japanese pilots, soldiers, and sailors vied for these heroic roles to die for their emperor. Those selected attended special schools and were dispatched knowing they would never return.

The results of the kamikazes were visible everywhere: ships with gun ports blown off, superstructures damaged, and listing vessels of all shapes and sizes. The ships we saw in Lingayen Gulf were the lucky ones. The Navy was hit hard in the Philippines—much harder than most people today appreciate. Many American boys still rest somewhere on the seabed in the Philippines, their bodies committed to the deep for eternity. That thought always bothered me.

*At least with a burial on land, there is a traceable part of you. But, if you go down with a ship, there is nothing.*

Going down with a ship or burials at seas was like throwing the body into an abyss. I remembered from my sophomore English the way Webster's defined it. An abyss was like a bottomless pit—the ocean depths. I wanted so badly to reach out and grab bodies, pull them back in, and scream to someone, "No! No! At least tie a buoy to it so that someday, someone can find it. Fighting at sea, to me at least, was an especially terrible place to die. I was glad my brother Joe had not been shot down over the ocean. Someday, I told myself, I would go to Europe and find his grave.

I was so engrossed in my thoughts that I hadn't noticed Custer come up behind me. He seemed to know what I was thinking and remained silent. He just stood there for a long minute before speaking. "I lost a brother, too, at Coral Sea. He's somewhere out there. I was at Pearl when they hit and I lost a lot of friends, but it's different when they're lost at sea with no trace at all. It's so big and lonely down there." I looked up and swore I saw mist in those tough old eyes. Custer cleared his throat and continued. "Well, no rest for the weary. I've got a mission for you."

The mission was this: I was to take troops around two small islands, making sure we stayed well clear of them, and into the natural bay of Conti, where a new beachhead was established. The beachhead was like a small pocket in a large apron with the rest of the apron representing Japanese holdings. The beachhead was reasonably secure and we were pouring troops and equipment into it as fast as we were able to do so. The plan was for these troops to cut across the islands and divide the Japanese garrisons into two groups. The *Middleton* had been involved in the initial landing at Lingayan twenty-five miles away. In order to avoid coastal fire and detection, our orders were to swing well out to sea and cut back into the target beach. The two small islands were on the route, and no one was sure if any Japanese were on them. The trip would take about three hours to complete, and the small flotilla undertaking the mission consisted of approximately thirty boats, including several PT boats.

Getting in did not pose much of a problem, and we landed the troops on the dry white sand beach without incident. "Seems pretty secure right here," I said to one of the members of the beach party.

"Don't let this fool you," he replied. "We landed well enough, but they're really building up in the hills. They've pushed us back several times. That's why you guys are bringing in the reserves. I don't know what's going to happen."

A corpsman trotted up to my boat and asked, "Say, buddy, can you take a load of wounded out to the hospital ship?"

"Sure!" I shouted back. "Bring 'em on."

The corpsman and several of his friends carried twelve wounded men aboard on stretchers. Two of the corpsmen stayed on board with the wounded to tend them on the way out to the ship. It was not a pretty sight. Bloody and field-dressed, the men all looked to be in bad shape. I backed Lucky 13 off the beach and headed for the large white hospital ship anchored eight or ten miles offshore. The rest of the boats headed back the way they had come, some completely empty, and some with ambulatory patients going back to one of the ships.

About two hours later I had unloaded the last of the wounded and was heading back to the *Middleton*. It was early evening and would be dark in another hour or two. I could go back to the beach and pick up the same route we had come in on, but that seemed like a waste of time when we could head almost directly back to Lingayen. The more direct route, however, was around the seaward side of one of the two small islands. It would save a lot of time, but it was also unauthorized.

We debated the issue for a while. "Ah, the hell with it," I finally said. "We are doing it."

"I hope these islands are uninhabited," Tex replied. "We're gonna make a pretty sight for them when we pass between them."

"I think I'll just stay on this 30-caliber," said Bill. "Then just let one of them Saki drinkers show himself!"

The islands were about a mile apart and I was passing right in the middle when "Sunset Charlie" flying a twin-engine Betty made a strafing run on the beach. After strafing and dropping his bombs, he turned and headed directly out to the islands about 100 feet off the surface. He must have spotted Lucky 13 and couldn't resist strafing us. The machine gun fire missed all three of us, but raked the boat from stern to bow. The LCVP has steel plates on each side and a steel ramp in front, but the deck and bottom are all wood. At least a half-dozen shells went all the way through. The Betty pilot made one run against us and continued heading out to sea away from the beach and the islands. He had problems of his own: several Navy Hellcats from the fleet offshore had discovered him and were pouncing in for the kill.

Bill and Tex inspected the serious damage. "Shit, we're taking on more water than the pumps can empty!" announced Bill. "The engine is missing pretty bad, too. I don't think we can make it back."

My decision to take the shortcut was not turning out as well as I had hoped. We could take a chance on the island being uninhabited and beach the boat until we could plug the holes and see what we could do about the engine, or try to make it and probably sink in the open sea. We were one boat alone, and no one knew the route we had taken. It didn't take long to make the decision. "I'm for beaching on the island nearest the main land," I announced.

Tex and Bill both heaved out "Ayes!" at the same time and I turned the bow of the boat for the beach. I increased our speed because we were really taking on water. The engine coughed and wheezed more vehemently with each passing second. We sputtered our way to the nearest point of land, which turned out to be a jagged rock bluff. However, just to its left was a small natural cove with a small white beach. I pulled in behind a big breaker and rammed the boat into the beach as hard as I could. I tried to idle the engine but it sputtered one last time before dying. The island was deathly quiet. It was dusk now. Pitch darkness was only thirty minutes away.

"Tex, you stay on the gun and I'll help Bill try to plug these holes. Let's take our knives and cut some sticks to plug them with."

Bill and I jumped off the boat, ran to some underbrush nearby, and began cutting away at small branches with our Ka-Bar knives. Before long we had a few plugs cut and took them back to the boat, where we yanked up the floor deck plates and drove the sticks into the holes. We finished much faster than anticipated. The problem, however, was that we had so much water in the boat that the stern was nearly submerged and the water level there was above the deck plates. Lucky 13 would have been completely submerged except for the fact that her stern was resting on the bottom. We would have to get the water out before we could float her again. Once we got the engine running, the pumps could eventually get rid of the water—but could get get the engine going again?

Bill was down in the bottom inspecting the plates. "The water is still seeping in around the pegs," he said to no one in particular.

"What about the engine, Bill?" I asked.

He nodded, walked over, and raised the hatch. After digging around a while he announced, "I don't see any damage yet, but one of those bullets sure put a dent in the value cover. Look!" He handed me the cover. It had a crease in it about a half an inch deep, as if someone had sliced a heavy knife across it.

Bill began taking it off. "This may be all the damage. If that crease is deep enough to resist some of the valves, it could explain why the engine is misfiring." As Tex and I nervously scanned our surroundings, Bill offered some good news. "Just as I thought. I can have this baby hammered back out pretty soon and we can get out of here!"

Tex sniffed the air. "I sure smell raw diesel. What about you guys?"

With a sinking feeling, I scrambled back to the stern and looked over the edge. Oily multi-colored designs danced on the surface of the water around the stern. I jumped into the sea and carefully felt around the stern below the water level. I found the hole quickly. A bullet had penetrated at a point where the fuel tanks were right against the stern of the boat.

I told Bill and Tex what I had discovered. "I'll take care of it," I assured them.

Bill, meanwhile, was beating out the valve cover case with a small hammer. "Damn, I wish I had a sledge," he spat through clenched teeth.

"Stop," hissed Tex. Bill and I did exactly as he ordered and the deadly small island silence enveloped us—that is, except for the unmistakable drone of an engine.

"There's a boat coming," Tex commented. "I think its approaching between the islands."

There was good reason for the uncertainty in Tex's assessment because by this time it was nearly pitch dark.

"Come on Bill," I said as I ran back to the undergrowth where we had cut the pegs. "I saw some dead brush around here. Hurry!"

We both tugged at an uprooted small dead tree, courtesy of a recently dropped errant bomb. The tree still had leaves on its branches. With nearly super human effort, we dragged the tree alongside the boat and around to the stern, where we positioned to camouflage Lucky 13 as much as possible. The drone of the engine was much louder now. And then I realized I was hearing more than one engine.

That's no Gray Marine diesel, and that's not a Hall Scott, either," muttered Bill. "In fact, those are not American engines."

From our vantage point, half hidden by the dead brush, we made out the silhouettes of two darkened Japanese landing barges easing past the island about two hundred yards off the beach. Neither displayed any indication that they saw us.

"They have soldiers on those barges," whispered Tex. "Can you see the helmets moving above the gunwales?" Bill and I nodded our answer.

Three very frightened members of the Coast Guard held their breath and waited until the barges disappeared behind the point of the cove in which we had beached. We listened to the sound of the engines fade away, but not entirely. Instead they stopped, suddenly, one by one.

"Damn! They beached, probably no more than half a mile away from us and definitely on this island," I said, shooting a glance at Bill. "How much of that crease did you get out?"

"I'm not sure, but maybe enough," said Bill, "Let me see." He felt the cover and shook his head as he placed it on top of the valves. "Wait just a minute," he added. "I think DeWar gave me three valve cover gaskets the other day." Bill searched around under the stern gun and came out with the three gaskets. "This'll raise it a little." He quickly put the gaskets on the cover and bolted it down. "With their motors off, they're going to hear us," he hissed. "Let's just hope they think its one of their own."

Tex, meanwhile, had been whittling a plug to fit the hole in the fuel tank. He knelt down and inserted it into the hole. It fit perfectly. "Let's hope that sputtering wasn't because of water in the tank. I think old thirteen is going to need everyone of those 226 horses when we leave here."

I nodded in agreement. "I figure we have twenty miles to go to get to the fleet at Lingayen. If we can get past the Japs before they detect us, and get to the open sea, I think we can outrun them until we get within the range of our ships."

"Well, Wiley, hit that ole' starter," replied Tex, crossing his fingers as I met his gaze and smiled.

Let me tell you, on a dark quiet night on a lonely Pacific Island, an engine turning over sounds like one hundred engines. That's especially true when a ruthless enemy who would kill you as soon as look at you is within earshot on the same tiny piece of land. The engine coughed, wheezed, and sputtered, but did not catch on. I hit it again, and it sputtered a few times and quit. I primed it and tried a third time. This time it sputtered and almost quit, but caught on right before it died. I slowly increased the throttle and the RPMs increased, but the engine was not running smoothly. The three of us were living and dying with every firing of the pistons. When it finally seemed all but hopeless, Lucky ole' 13 got her act together and roared up to 2,700 RPMs. It was the sweetest sound any of us had ever heard.

We were backing off the beach, feeling pretty good about ourselves, when Tex exclaimed, "There's another one coming."

I quickly pulled out about the same distance as the enemy boats, turned in the direction they had gone, and increased the throttle. The mystery boat was only about one-quarter of mile behind us. I edged my way out to sea, took a deep breath, and pushed the throttle full open. The engine held and we sped through the darkness muttering prayers for our safe deliverance.

A couple minutes later Bill spotted at least one enemy boat coming out from the shore. They were on to us! We fooled them until we reached their landing point, at which time we should have turned in toward the beach. When we didn't, someone figured out what was going on.

The Japs were angling to intercept us. I turned to starboard, which put them directly behind us. I wasn't worried about the other single boat getting an angle on us. Now it was up to the Gray Marine diesel. A couple minutes later, the Japs opened on us with rifles and automatic weapons, but they were still 200 yards away. The bumpy ride and darkness made it difficult for them to hit us. Other than an occasional whizzing bullet, nothing found its mark. Tex and Bill decided it was time to answer, and began spraying their 30-caliber's back at them.

The running gun battle lasted a lot longer than was comfortable. Lucky 13 slowly edged away from our Japanese pursuers. Thankfully, these Japs were in landing barges instead of patrol boats. I figured I could get close to seventeen or eighteen knots at full speed. My RPMS were maxing out, but the oil and temperature appeared to be under control. The chase went on for about ten miles beyond the islands, at which time it dawned on the Japs that additional pursuit only endangered their own boats. With what must have been great reluctance, they slowed and finally turned back. A minute or two later I gently slowed the engine down to a more comfortable cruising speed.

Before long, we could see the tracers and explosions of the continuing bombardment at Lingayen Gulf. We also spotted the silhouettes of the anchored ships of the task force. I figured they were seven or eight miles out. One of the escort destroyers picked us up on radar and turned in our direction. He blinked a challenge with a red light and Bill answered it perfectly. The destroyer moved within hailing distance.

"We were chased by three Jap barges from a port between the islands!" Bill yelled. "They turned back about five miles back."

"Are you okay?" asked the O.D.

"Yes, go get 'em!" I encouraged.

The O.D. nodded enthusiastically as the destroyer pulled away at full throttle. We turned and headed back to the *Middleton*, tied up, and reported aboard to the Officer of the Deck. We were quickly ushered into to the Executive Officer's wardroom, where we made a full report. Our report was transmitted to Flag, and further information forwarded to the destroyer searching for the barges. The destroyer was two or three times faster than the barges, and caught them just as they were entering the passage between the islands. It sank all three. Lucky 13, meanwhile, was hoisted aboard and given a complete inspection and repair that lasted well into the next day.

Early the next morning, the Captain called Bill, Tex, and I into his quarters. "Ve just receive message from Flag. Vell done, men! Vell done!" he said over and over while shaking our hands.

"Say, Wiley, what the hell is this 'Well done,' or 'Vell done' crap?" asked Bill an hour later while we were standing in the chow hall. "We still have to eat this shit-on-a-shingle and drink muddy coffee for breakfast, while ole' 'Vell Done' gets his eggs over easy and coffee brewed to his liking."

"I tell you ole' buddy, it's a thing called supply and demand backwards," I answered. "The officers demand and we supply!"

I chuckled but Bill just shook his head. "I guess so. I may ship over and become an Admiral just to get it changed."

While we were going through the chow line, I kept thinking about Lori's statement: "Thirteen! Lucky Thirteen!" She had no idea how right she was. We were the lucky ones to have the Chris-Craft LCVP. Somewhere back in the States a company called

Chris-Craft built this remarkable boat with enough foresight to withstand terrible weather, high seas, rugged beaches, and enemy gunfire. The Gray Marine diesel they installed was the most dependable engine I had ever known. Yes, we were lucky, but thank God for APA-25-13—Lucky 13!

Before we could finish eating Custer appeared out of nowhere and announced, "Wiley, Miller, and Lee, get to the Exec's office—now!"

"See, Bill," I said as we left the chow hall and made our way up to the wardroom. "You don't have to eat that S.O.S. after all."

"Once they know your name, the B.S. never stops," Bill shot back.

The Exec and Lt. Hoyle were waiting for us in the wardroom. "Wiley," said Lt. Hoyle. "You may have stumbled on something last night. Intelligence says that Jap barges have been moving troops up and down the beach after dark. We've been looking for their hiding place for the barges for several days. The coast line has been carefully searched and photographed. We're pretty sure it's one of the smaller islands offshore. The Japs last night may have thought you found it, which would explain why they chased you so far. We have destroyers at both ends of the passage and reconnaissance aircraft have carefully studied the island. So far, we don't see anything unusual. Did any of you guys see or hear anything last night that might help?"

It was Bill who came up with an answer. "Well . . . maybe," he began slowly. "When those barges turned and headed into the island, they disappeared from us because of the point of the cove where we had beached. I thought last night that the Japs had entered a much deeper cove than ours because of the length of time it took them to get to where they were going and then shut off their engines. It was a long time. I was surprised when we headed out and around that point and those Japs came off the beach so close to us."

"That's strange," replied Lt. Hoyle, who turned back to face me. "Look, do you think that you can lead some PT boats, LCIs, and a couple of tank lighters full of soldiers back to that point?"

I shrugged. "Sure, I think so."

This time, Bill, Tex, and I were passengers in Doll's tank lighter, along with twenty soldiers. Wymer also took his tank lighter with

Custer and another group of armed soldiers. We picked up two PT boats and two LCIs armed with rockets and personnel and headed for the island. We passed a destroyer patrolling the entrance. Bill, Tex, and I guided the boats back to the area. "There's the point of the cove where we were up ahead, and those barges came off the beach right about there," I announced, pointing to a tall coconut tree I had seen last night. The area wasn't even a beach. Part of it was rocky and in many places trees and underbrush came right down to the water's edge. Lt. Hoyle asked Doll to go in close to the shoreline and edge along slowly.

When we were a scant forty feet offshore when Lt. Hoyle said, "Wait, hold up!" His eyes were scanning a rocky bluff about twelve feet high. "Hold right there," he ordered. "Head in, lower you ramp, but slowly."

He walked out to the end of the ramp as it softly bumped into the rocky bluff. "Back up. Raise the ramp and continue."

Once the ramp was raised, he motioned for Doll to head back to the LCIs and pull alongside. "That's it, the rocky looking bluff!" he announced, pointing toward the shore. Let 'em have a dose of rockets."

The LCI let loose with a broadside blast. What had been a rocky bluff went up in a cloud of dust. Every rocket had found its target. When the smoke and dust settled, a small river about thirty-five feet wide was visible leading back into the island. The trees formed a canopy over it so it was impossible to spot it from the air.

The two LCIs moved in first, followed by the tank lighters. The river, which looked to be largely man-made, wound around under the canopy of trees. Along the way, we passed several Jap landing barges tied to the side. We didn't spot a soldier. Everything seemed deserted. About 1,000 yards inland we came upon a dock and several camouflaged buildings. They, too, appeared deserted. Wymer's tank lighter stopped and the soldiers cautiously disembarked. Doll and one of the LCIs continued up the river until they came to a gate-looking structure.

Lt. Hoyle grunted. "Ahhh . . . . So this was their escape route."

He told Doll to back up and motioned to the LCI, which blew the gate away with a single blast. Hoyle quickly radioed the PT boats and destroyers of the escape hatch. The Japanese barges had passed out here and headed for the Philippine mainland. We found the barges along the beaches. There were fifteen in all. Believing their hiding place had been discovered, the Japs escaped to join in the fight at Lingayen or in other areas. Back at the river port we found barges loaded with TNT tied alongside the dock. The Japs were preparing them for suicide boats. Our discovery had come just in the nick of time.

When we arrived back on the ship late that night, Captain Svenson had left us a message: "Wiley, Doll, Miller, Lee, Custer, and Lt. Hoyle. The captain requests the pleasure of your company at breakfast at 0700 tomorrow morning in his quarters."

"Oh, boy!" Bill exclaimed. "We're going to get to eat a decent meal for a change!"

We were up at the crack of dawn, dressed in clean dungarees and shirts with black low-top shoes. All of us were seated in the Captain's wardroom when he stepped in. "Vell, I gonna' say it again. Vell done! Vell done! Bring coffee!" The mess cooks scurried around till everyone's cup was filled.

"Funny," whispered Bill. "This coffee tastes just like our own—lousy." Tex and I were thinking the same thing.

"Now, ve are going to have a special breakfast. I asked Custer, and he told me your favorite food. Special vite sauce viss ham chips on toast!"

Several mouths dropped open in shock and dismay. "They are feeding us shit-on-a-shingle!" muttered Bill. We all kept a smile glued on our faces as the mess cook slopped our "special breakfast" onto our plates. I shot a glare in Custer's direction. My crewmates did the same thing. Custer was the picture of innocence, smiling, looking about, happy as a clam. Only the gleam in his eye told us he was doing everything he could to keep from bursting with laughter. After what seemed like minutes, he looked at us and managed to sputter, "Yeah men . . . vell done!" before breaking out in a gut-wrenching belly laugh. We had been had.

After two weeks at Lingayen Gulf, the *Middleton* pulled out with a small convoy and headed south. In a few more days we reached Ulithi atoll. Ulithi (also known as Urushi or Mackenzie Island) was a weather station and giant naval base we had secured a month or so earlier. Its natural harbor, one of the largest in the world, provided a halfway house for damaged ships. The *Franklin*, *Saratoga*, *Hancock*, and *Essex* were all anchored there. These four famous U.S. carriers had been roughly handled in the recent fighting. The *Franklin* was listing nearly forty degrees. It had taken a several direct hits from kamikazes, including one or two into its flight deck, where large gaping holes remained. As all of us quickly learned, several hundred men, including pilots, had been sealed inside by the explosions; they were still there. Of the four carriers, the *Franklin* appeared to have suffered the most damage but all four were out of commission. Other damaged ships were also in the harbor. The atoll provided a break from the rough seas. The Navy used it as a staging point to assess the damage before deciding whether or not the ships could make the long voyage back to Pearl Harbor for repairs in dry dock. There was even talk of bringing a floating dry dock all the way to Ulithi.

The *Middleton* was anchored near the inlet where the ships came into the atoll. I drew boat duty our first night. Four boats dropped over the side and tied astern of the ship. We stayed in our boat, old Lucky 13. If needed, we would be ready at a moment's notice to transport equipment or troops from ship to ship or to shore. The sea was unusually heavy that night, and with the *Middleton* anchored near the mouth of the inlet, we caught the fury of the rough seas as the storm mounted.

I saw a landing craft about a quarter of a mile away drifting toward the passageway. An S.O.S. blinked in Morse Code with a red flashlight. Strong currents were pulling the boat out to sea. I called the nearest gun crew on deck and asked for permission to go after the errant landing craft. The response came back immediately: "Secure that stray boat."

I revved up the 226-horsepower Gray Marine diesel and headed for the boat at full throttle. The sea was tossing the boat unmercifully. The men aboard had no control at all without the engine and their engine was dead. The risk of capsizing increased with each passing minute. My boat crew and I were now in the passageway, and we could see two sailors frantically waving their hats and calling for help. I pulled up as close as I dared and we passed a line to them. They tied the line to a cleat on the side of the boat, and when we tried to tow the crippled boat, it pulled at an angle. The sea was really rough out there. The waves were at least ten feet high and growing.

"Let's tie the boats abreast and tow it that way!" Tex yelled above the wind. We tried, but the sea was so rough the boats banged together violently, threatening to tear both of us apart.

"We can't go this way!" I yelled at the other Cox'n. "We're going to have to tow you, but you've got to fix a bridle so that my pull will be in the center!"

I surprised myself with the way I had taken command of the situation, and that everyone else expected me to do so. The other two sailors quickly tied each end of a line to the port and starboard forward cleats before carrying the line to the ramp in front of the boat. I passed my line to them and they secured it to the bridle with a bowline-on-the-bite knot so the line would not tighten on the bridle. This time the towing worked. The rough seas, however, made for a very slow ride back to the sailor's ship. They hailed from the other side of the atoll and had been making a run from their ship to pick up some officers on shore when a huge wave broke over their boat, drowning their gasoline engine. It took us three hours to get them back. Their Officer of the Deck called down his heartfelt thanks for our efforts. Both of the grateful sailors climbed into our boat to shake our hands before going aboard.

The next morning I received an order to go to see the Captain immediately. He and Cdr. McKay were on the bridge when I walked up and saluted. The Captain handed me a brief telegraphic message. It simply read: "Pass on to the Cox'n of boat Number 13, Well Done!" It was signed by the Commodore.

The Captain shook my hand and Cdr. McKay did the same, repeating, "Well Done!" I returned their salutes.

After a few days at Ulithi the *Middleton* headed out again. This time our destination was Manus Island. Once underway we settled down to regular shipboard life. It felt as if we had been on high alert for most of the last two months. I was on duty as the helmsman. The Executive Officer decided to catch up on all of the disciplinary actions filed during the previous weeks. A Captain's Mast is more like a minor J.P. court than it is a regular court for major offenses. One of men up for Captain's Mast was Eugene Cooper, a mess steward who served the Captain. Cdr. McKay read the offense. The beach party had been short-handed and unable to unload some of the LSTs at Lingayen. Lt. Hoyle asked for twenty or thirty additional men from the ship. The posted list of available personnel included Eugene's name. The work party mustered on the quarterdeck, was put into boats, and taken ashore. Eugene was nowhere to be found. He cooked and served Captain Svenson's meals and was essentially his personal valet.

After the Captain listened to Cdr. McKay read the offense, he walked in front of Eugene and looked him square in the eye. "Eugene, vye didn't you go vith the vork party?" It looked as if it pained the Captain to even ask the question.

Eugene might have been slow in mustering for the work party, but he was plenty fast thinking on his feet. "Captain, I didn't know that was a work party. I thought that was a liberty party, and I didn't want to go on no liberty at no Philippine Islands where them Japs was throwing hand grenades and stuff. No sirree, not even for two cans of beer."

The Captain nearly bent double with laughter. Even McKay guffawed so loud that all of the other officers felt free to join in. The Captain shot a look at McKay, shook his head, and walked away. McKay took the hint and dismissed the Captain's Mast. I was laughing so hard I could barely keep the helm steady.

Six of the soldiers in the sick bay died, and a day was set aside to bury them at sea. As usual, the bodies were wrapped tightly with linen and weighed down. As they slid out from under the flag and splashed into the ocean, the words kept coming back to me over and over: "Commit their bodies to the Deep." What wife, mother, or girlfriend was about to read the terrible words . . . "We regret to inform you that your husband, son, father, was killed in action?" They will never know much about what really happened to their loved one, and will always doubt just a little bit as to whether it actually happened at all. I still had dreams about seeing my brother Joe again. Maybe he was a POW. Maybe he . . . . there were just too many possibilities that crossed one's mind when trying to erase the inevitable.

Wartime life aboard ship was filled with humorous incidents. During General Quarters when the ship was under way, the boat crews met in the officer's wardroom. One day we were sitting at the tables while a drill was going on. The door to the officer's galley was open and one of the officer's mess cooks named Bill was preparing a large vat of potato salad. A young Ensign, an obnoxious guy who picked on this particular cook often, sauntered in. When he spotted the black cook without his helmet, the Ensign yelled, "Where the hell is your helmet? You know everyone has to have a helmet on during General Quarters! I am sick and tired of you gold bricks who never do any work anyway, trying to make your own rules!"

The mess cook tried to explain that it was hard to prepare a meal with a helmet on, but the Ensign raved on: "Don't offer me a bunch of excuses and stand at attention when I talk to you! Now by God, if I ever catch you without that helmet again during General Quarters, I am going to put you so far back in the brig, you will never find your way out!"

By this time the cook was steaming mad but he stood at attention and took it all. Racial divisions aside, all of us took his side and watched the affair unfold. After the Ensign walked out and closed the door, the cook's steam erupted. "Damn white son of a bitch!" he muttered. "Take that," he said as he spat into the potato salad. As fast as he could gather spit in his mouth, he shot it into the salad. Bill, Tex, and I watched in disbelief, but did not say a word.

Still not completely satisfied, Bill unbuttoned his pants, flipped out his penis, and cut loose a stream of urine into the potato salad. The whole time he kept mumbling, "Ninety day wonder, bullshit, ninety day blunder, enjoy your potato salad, you white bastard." We could not believe our eyes. As the final gesture, Bill wiped his penis in the potato salad before carefully mixing the salad around to cover up the evidence of his actions.

Not ten seconds after he finished two other officers walked in. When they spotted the fresh potato salad, one of them exclaimed, "Boy, that potato salad looks good. Mind if I taste it?"

"No sir, you go right ahead," Bill answered with a smile. "You all gonna' get it all tonight anyway." We nearly fell on the floor in an effort to remain quiet.

The officer took a large spoonful and said, "Bill, it sure does taste good. Tell me, do you have your own secret recipe for this?"

"Well, sort of," drawled Bill. "I guess a lot of it has to do with the mood I'm in."

When the officers left, Bill, Tex, and I exploded in laughter. We vowed never to be jealous of "officer's chow" again.

Manus Island afforded alternate days liberty for everyone who cared to go ashore for swimming, sports, beer, and food. I gave my two cans of beer to someone else and played touch football, swam a little, and gathered cat's eyes and coconuts. When we left Manus a few days later, word quickly spread that we were heading for Pearl Harbor.

"Let's try to meet some nice girls this trip," said Doll. "There must be some there somewhere."

"And a million servicemen for every one doll, Doll," I laughed, even though I thought his idea a good one.

"At least, we can see some girls," said Doll

"Yeah, and if you want to stand in line, you can do more than see them," added Bill, "I ain't doing nothing that I have to stand in line for."

I remembered well the long lines stretching out of the cat houses and wrapping completely around the block in downtown Honolulu. So did Tex.

"Me neither," Tex replied with a grin. "We'll find some girls somewhere. After all, we're the crew of Lucky 13!"

Chapter 28

# Shove Off, Cox'n

The term "Shove off, Cox'n!" was the command given when an Officer of the Deck dispatched a boat. The term took on a much broader meaning when others used it as slang. Its meaning was clear: get out of here! The phrase was widely used in bars, work parties, street gangs, and dance floors, as well as shipboard decks. In its truest meaning, it applied only to the Cox'n of a landing boat, or barge. It was a command that directed his life like no other. He was to shove off from the ship; shove off from the shore; shove off from the dock or pier; shove off from the beach. In fact, he was to shove off to imitate his every move. It was little wonder then, that I was well familiar with that phrase.

"Shove off, Cox'n," the O.D. ordered as I pulled the boat away from the gangplank.

We were in Pearl Harbor, and my task was to proceed to the main landing strip, pick up supplies, and on the way back stop and pick up one of the crew members released from the hospital. That was the part that had caught my attention. We were in Pearl for a quick provisioning. There would be no liberty. And that, of course, meant I would not be able to see Lori.

I overheard Custer passing out the orders to Red Meyers. I traded trips with Red. Maybe, just maybe, I could sneak away to the hospital and accidentally catch Lori. I knew it was a long shot, but what was so different about that? My whole life was a long shot. I could never "light" anywhere for long. The inevitable "Shove off, Cox'n" seemed to go off regularly like a cuckoo clock.

As luck would have it, the crewman we were to pick up, a guy named Swain, was not on the dock when we arrived. I settled the boat and we waited. I contemplated hitching a ride up to the hospital, but quickly shook the foolish thought from my head. I was lying on the engine hatch with my eyes closed daydreaming of Lori and the light illuminating her figure when the command came. "Shove off, Cox'n." Well, there it was again; the same old command, even when it was a woman's voice.

A woman's voice?

My eyes shot open. When I beheld who was looking at me, I rubbed my eyes and blinked several times. "I must be dreaming," I said out loud.

There was Lori, smiling and standing on the dock with her hands on her hips. I leapt to my feet and stammered, "Lori! I'm running the duty boat, and we just stopped by to pick up one of our crew who had been in the hospital." My mouth felt suddenly dry and I swallowed hard. "What are you doing here?"

Lori laughed and smiled broadly. "I took a chance. I heard the *Middleton* was sending over a boat to pick up Swain, and I was hoping it was number thirteen." Her eyes twinkled. God, she was lovely. In almost one single jump I was out of the boat and on the dock next to her. "I did cheat a little bit," she confessed. "We watched from the hospital with binoculars and when I saw that it was boat thirteen, I got Mary to cover for me and got down here as soon as I could."

I took both of her hands in mine and held her at arm's length. "This can't be true," I said, shaking my head slowly. "Except that you're just as pretty in this dream as you were the last time I saw you."

"Well," she teased, "and you don't even have me backed up against a lighted doorway, either. I think you may even like me for my other qualities." Her laugh was low and sultry, and it spread through her entire body. I could see and feel the melody of that laugh without hearing it. I can still hear it today.

"I was hoping I would have an opportunity to go over to the hospital and look you up. When I heard about this run, I traded with Red Meyers to get it. But I didn't know how I was going to get from here to the hospital, even though it's not far."

"Why Cox'n, don't you know that the Navel Nurses Corps is at your service? Now, we could have just sent Swain down here in the shuttle, but Dr. Lanier had this sedan just sitting there and we thought I should come down and inspect the boat that's going to carry our patient back to his ship. So, here I am."

"And what does your inspector tell you?" I asked.

"Oh, it takes a long time to inspect a boat! Besides I want to inspect the Cox'n first."

I shot a hopeful look at Tex, but before I could say anything he beat me to it. "Don't worry about the boat, Wiley. I'll watch it till you bring the patient back."

"Well, let's go," I said, and we walked over to the car. I opened the door for her and she got in the driver's seat. I went around and got in the other side.

"Are you going to get liberty while you're here?" she asked.

"We've been told that we won't get any," I answered, shaking my head. "This may be a short stopover. How long can you be away right now?"

"One or two hours," she replied. "Look, I know that even if you had liberty it would just be six or seven hours of daylight, right? I also know that you can't tell me when you're leaving, even if you knew. This long damned war. I am so tired of it. It spoils everything about living. I know that I can't take you to the officer's club, but sometimes we girls figure out ways to get around rules when there is someone that we want to be with. We can go to the nurses' lounge. It's not too lively, but it has music, soft drinks, and a relaxing atmosphere."

"Fine by me," I agreed with a wide smile. After what I had been through, it sounded like a big slice of heaven. Anything was better than the crowded dock or one of the open restaurants swarming with GIs.

Lori talked while she drove. "What are you going to do when you get out, Ken?"

"I don't know," I replied. "Well, yes I do, too. I'm going to college and take engineering. I also want to go somewhere where I can play football."

"In Texas?" she asked coyly.

"Yes, I've always wanted to go to Texas A&M. I guess I'll go there." I was surprised it came out so definitively. It was the first time I had actually put it all together, but I knew that was what I wanted to do. "I got out of high school at sixteen," I said, feeling I needed to explain my plans in more detail.

"I understand," Lori answered.

"I was too young for the service, so I worked for a year for the Soil Conservation Service," I continued, trying to explain myself. "The engineer there told me that I should go to A&M and major in agricultural engineering if I liked that kind of work. So, that's what I'm going to do."

Lori nodded slowly and changed the subject. "I noticed the name 'Jean' on your boat. Is that your girl?"

I laughed. "There was a girl named Jean, and I have tried to convince myself she was my girl, if you know what I mean. She was really the girl next door growing up, but I've only seen her once since we were fourteen."

"And that one time was just before you left to go in the service, right?" she replied as that silent laugh of hers permeated her whole body again.

"Yes! How did you know?"

"Oh! I just know about things like that," she said. She was relaxed and seemed satisfied with my answers. "Have you met any pretty girls since I saw you last?"

I thought for a moment before responding. "Not like you think." Then I told her about Marcia Rutero, the schoolteacher in the Philippines who paddled out to the ship in the outrigger canoe. I told about seeing her again on the beach at Leyte and Luzon with all of the school children. When I finished, I put my arm over the back of the seat and turned to face Lori. "Now it's my turn. What about you?"

She mused for a moment and then answered, "I dated a few guys. Mostly just one time, though. Most of them turn out to be married or committed in some way. I just don't like to go out with someone if I feel I'm invading some other girl's property. It's not that I'm looking for a commitment myself, either. I just don't like it. I guess that's the reason I don't date that much."

"What will you do when it's over?" I asked.

She sighed and shrugged. "Go back to Ohio, I guess. Go to college, get married. I would like to finish college first. Maybe it'll work out that way. Who knows?"

By this time we had pulled up in front of a barracks-like building and Lori stopped the car. "All out for the Florence Nightingale Resort," she announced. We both laughed.

We got out of the car and entered the dull drab gray-blue building. Inside was a large lounge with sofas, easy chairs, ping pong tables, and a jukebox on the wall. There were three or four other nurses, one of them with a young soldier. After waving her greetings, Lori led me to a sofa and we sat down.

"Well, it's not much, but it beats main street," she said.

"It's great!" I replied, and I meant it. "You can't imagine how much we miss comfort like this. Just to be away from all those GIs is enough. Being here with you is a real bonus."

We never had the room completely to ourselves, and I knew without asking that this was as far as it could go this time. It was the most wonderful hour I had had spent in almost two years. We passed the time talking, dancing, and just listening. Everything I said seemed to be so important to her, and I relished every word she spoke. I think we both knew a love was being born, but we also instinctively sensed it was not going anywhere. It was just not to be—at least not yet. Lori was everything I dreamed a woman should be, and that's what she was—a woman. When it was time to go, she took a piece of paper and wrote her address and phone number on it.

"When you come back, if you want too, that is, tell your officer you have a place to stay in Honolulu. Sometimes they grant overnight passes to sailors if they have proof of a place to stay. I'll be your cousin if they want to check. I want you to spend the night." Her lingering kiss was like the one Janie Phillips gave me so long ago, only better.

"I could love you, Lori," I finally said.

"I know," she responded with tears in her eyes. "Damn this war anyway. I may never have a chance to love you, but you have set a pattern for me to measure the man I might love someday. Please come back. Let's find out."

The ride from the hospital to the dock was the shortest ride I ever experienced. The boat ride back to the ship was the longest ride I ever had. Back on deck, preparations were underway to pull out.

"Wiley, what the hell took you so long?" asked Custer. "You are way overdue."

"Darn red tape, I guess," I responded.

The next morning we pulled out early for Maui to pick up troops. There was still a war to fight.

# Chapter 29

# New Hebrides Incident

Moritai in the New Hebrides was becoming a primary staging point for task forces moving deeper into the western Pacific, so it was also a popular "Liberty Party" location. The liberty parties consisted of an all-day outing on the beach with swimming, beach combing, baseball, football, volleyball, horseshoes, food, soft drinks, and the famous "Greasidick" 3.2 beers, two bottles per person.

It was after one of these all-day affairs that Bill, Doll, and I were sitting upon the deck of the ship waiting on the nightly run of "Midnight Charlie." Although Moritai was under our control, the Japanese still occupied most of the New Hebrides islands, including Java and Borneo. The topic tonight was which island the Jap planes were coming from. We generally agreed they were flying from bases in Borneo, probably because we remembered the name of Borneo from some long ago geography lesson or a movie, and couldn't pronounce the names of most of the other islands. Only Doll thought otherwise.

"Did you see the movie with Dorothy Lamour when she was wearing her sarong?" asked Doll. "She was a nature princess and Jon Hall was a British explorer? Wasn't that on Borneo?"

"Yeah," I answered, "And there was another girl named Lucille Ball. Wouldn't you love to find something like one of those?"

"What bothers me is why would they have women like Dorothy Lamour or Lucille Ball on Borneo, while a few miles away we've got a cross between Ma Kettle and Tarzan's Cheeta, like we've seen on all these other islands?" replied Bill.

This sobering thought sank home to each of us as we thought about the native women we had seen so far in the South Pacific. Nothing to write home about, that was for sure. "Well, maybe we just ain't been to the right places yet," I theorized. I always heard about the beautiful Polynesian girls. "Maybe that was in the Polynesian islands where Dorothy Lamour was supposed to be."

"Yeah," Doll piped in. "And Borneo is the place where the natives are cannibals and have bones in their noses."

With this bit of geography and history lesson accomplished, the three of us turned our attention back to "Charlie watching." We didn't have to wait long. He came in low and was over the mountains before General Quarters sounded. The anti-aircraft fire quickly began tracking his flight path. Tonight he was lucky, and the batteries set up around the airfield missed him. He made his runs, dropped his bombs, and streaked away across the other side of the field.

"I still say that couldn't have been a Borneo plane," said Doll. "Look at where he came from. Besides, Zeros don't have the range to fly here and return."

"Well, maybe he's taking off from one island and landing on another," I offered.

"But our sorties over these islands every day would spot an active airfield," he countered. "We control the air by day, right?"

No one noticed that Custer had walked up behind us until he spoke. "Wiley, you and Doll are assigned a special mission for in the morning at 0300. You'll need some sleep, but report to the wardroom first for a briefing."

"What's up?" I asked.

"You'll find out soon enough."

Lt. Hoyle and two Marine Captains were in the wardroom when Doll, Bill, Tex, and I entered. "Men," began Lt. Hoyle, "I suppose you all saw Midnight Charlie up topside a few minutes ago. Well, he gave us the last piece of the puzzle we were looking for. We needed to know where he was going, so we purposely missed him with the shore batteries and had two night fighters at altitude track him to his destination. He landed on an island not fifty miles away from us. We think he refuels there, and then takes off back to Borneo or wherever he originated. This way he doubles his range. We've known for some time that they were doing this. See, this way, they can send the planes in from any number of places. The key is the refueling station and of course, they come by night to keep us from discovering where that refueling station is. Tomorrow when our sorties are out, it'll just be a deserted strip. Well, tonight we were able to track him till he landed."

Lt. Hoyle unfolded a large map on the table that showed an expanded view of Moritai and the surrounding islands, including Arutha, which was supposed to be deserted. "We're going to send in a team of Marines with Captain Leonard," he continued, nodding in the Captain's direction. "We'll go in with two boats, Thirteen and Twenty-nine. We'll land right here," he added, pointing to a place on the opposite side of Arutha.

"Won't they spot us, sir?" I asked.

"We have a pretty regular run of patrol boats up this strait, so you won't be out of the ordinary. We'll break off the path here and make a run for the beach. We hope we won't be detected doing that. Now, we don't think the Japs have more than twenty-five or thirty men on the island. Captain Leonard and his men will put them out of commission and capture their facility. If they can do this without the Japs sending back a message, we might be able to welcome personally each of their planes as they land. That's why we don't want to send a massive force in there and announce to Tojo what we're doing."

"How many men will we be taking in?" Doll asked.

"Twenty-two," answered Captain Leonard. "But the reason we need two boats is because we want to carry in enough equipment and supplies for these men to stay awhile. But rather than have them move all of this across the island, we want you to land the men on the far side. You should land them at 0500. After they've unloaded, you will go back around the island to this side, nearest the airfield," he explained, pointing to the map. "Pull in here and wait just offshore. My men should have the airfield secure by 0800. We'll signal you from the beach, right here." He pointed to a small natural cove on the island. "Then you can come in and unload. Don't come in till you get the signal and if you draw any beach fire before we get there, just back off and wait."

We had the boats loaded and lowered by 3:00 a.m. Lt. Hoyle rode with me in Lucky 13. "Well, Cox'n," he commented as he looked at me. "Isn't this more fun than an old liberty party on Moritai?"

"Yes, sir!" I grinned. "Any time!"

We charted a course across open water as much as possible, although land from the islands was visible in all directions as dark blots on the horizon. There was no moon, but the sky was clear. I navigated with my compass although dead reckoning was possible.

Arutha was a hilly, almost mountainous, island covered with dense undergrowth. Most of the islands had some native population, and most were friendly to Americans. Our troops had often made contact with them. There was no record of any native contact on Arutha.

Lt. Hoyle pointed out the way as the boats closed on the island without incident. As we approached the shore, I could see white breakers on the beach. It was a good sign that assured me of a landing beach. We brought the boats in simultaneously, the larger tank lighter stopping first as the lighter LCVP drove higher onto the beach. We lowered the ramps and the Marines crept cautiously out.

When we were assured there was no opposition, Captain Leonard made a few hand signals and the Marines crept away into the jungle. A creepy chill walked its way up my spine once the Marines vanished into the greenery. We waited about ten minutes, as agreed, to give the Marines time to slip away before making any noise. I backed Lucky 13 off the beach and headed back around the island. It took ninety minutes to get all the way around to the cove. We pulled the boats into an area about 500 yards offshore. Rather than anchor, we decided to drift and occasionally correct our position.

We turned the engines off and immediately heard small arms fire coming from deep within the island. The sporadic firing stopped after a few minutes and the island was once again quiet. As we later learned, the Marines had an easier time of it than we imagined. We kept our eyes glued to the beach looking for some sign of activity to indicated the Marines had arrived there. I looked at my watch. It was 19:45 hours (7:45 a.m.). Fifteen more minutes to go.

Bill heard it first. It was an engine. We initially thought it was a boat, but quickly knew it wasn't. It had the unmistakable sound of a Japanese airplane coming in for a landing. All eyes glued themselves to the sky and followed the aircraft by its sound. It was daylight now, so darkness was no longer our ally. Would he spot us? If so, it would give away the whole program. We spotted his exhaust flames as he flew in above the point a few hundred feet in the air and disappeared behind the dense jungle growth. His throttle eased back for landing, and then the sound of his engine faded away. The last sound we heard was the engine turning off. I looked at my watch. It wasn't time to go in yet, and I knew the Marines had to deal with the pilot before they could leave.

In about twenty minutes, which seemed like hours to us, we heard the sound of small arms fire. This time it was much heavier than what we heard before, and was a mixture of rifle, machine gun, and either grenades or mortars. The fighting only lasted perhaps a minute or two. I looked at my watch. It was time to go.

We headed the boats into the cove just to the left of the point where the plane had flown over. I remembered our briefing and found the passageway through the reef with no difficulty. We eased the boats onto the sandy beach. Off to starboard was a Japanese barge, demolished and half submerged, still carrying the covering of tree branches to hide it. I recognized one of the Marines standing behind it and he waved to us.

As we beached the boat and came ashore, he said, "We didn't want any of them to get away, so I got over here and scuttled this baby first thing. They didn't even have a guard!"

As we waited, he told us the story. There were fewer Japanese on the island than they thought. It was indeed a refueling station for their planes, but they only had enough people to re-fuel the planes and not to guard them. They depended on secrecy more than manpower.

"We only encountered two of them at the airstrip," the Marine continued. "We put them down real fast and were looking around for the rest when we heard the plane coming in. We saw them trying to signal the plane, but he didn't see their signal because he landed anyway. When the plane landed and the pilot got out, they tried again to warn him of our presence, but it was daylight and we cut loose on all of them. There were four, and the pilot made five. I'm glad we got their boat too, or you boys might have had a little sea war of your own."

"Lt. Hoyle, my hat is off to you and you men. Please accept a hearty 'well done' from the Marine Corps," offered the grateful Captain Leonard.

The Marines "welcomed" several Japanese aircraft over the course of the next week, each of which landed on the airstrip after a bombing and strafing run. When the *Middleton* pulled out of Moritai the subterfuge was still underway. I never knew the total number of Japanese planes captured or destroyed.

We were on the deck of the *Middleton* sailing away when I asked Doll what he would have done if those Japs had gotten away in their barges and came out to meet us. "It wasn't the Japs I was worried about," shot back Doll. "I was trying to figure out how to stay out of your way! You ought to be careful with that little tub you drive. You're gonna' get run over some day!"

Chapter 30

# The Grass is Always Greener

I spent Valentine's Day 1945 at sea en route to Manus Island, where the initial staging began for the next big invasion. The first reports came to the *Middleton* on the day of the landing on Iwo Jima. We wondered what ships were involved and tried to figure it out by discussing which had been missing for the last month. The reports we received from Iwo Jima were not good. Japanese resistance was fierce and heavier than anticipated. It took several days before a firm beachhead was established.

"Do you think our next one will be Japan?" I asked Bill one day as we were working in our boat.

"We got to do it sooner or later," he answered. "Might as well be now and let's get this thing over with. I want to get back to Ft. Worth." He paused before adding, "Naw, I take that back. There are too many of these Philippine Islands that still have to be mopped up. I'll bet it's Samar or Mindinao first."

"Well ok, but just as long as it's not Truk," I answered with a shake of my head. "You know that place is supposed to be solid concrete."

"You know what I want to do?" asked Bill, changing the subject. "Make an assault landing on Carter Riverside High School. Boy, how I'd love to go back there now, with the knowledge I have. The first thing I would do is screw Wilma Blissett. Remember? She's the one I told you about—the cheerleader."

I nodded quickly, which meant I wanted to hear about Wilma Blissett all over again.

Bill understood and jumped in enthusiastically. "Man, she had knockers the size of her head. When she was out in front of everybody, she sure put on a show. She twirled all the time, just so her little 'ole skirt would fly up around her belly button. Boy was she something," he sighed wistfully.

"Didn't you ever go with her?" I asked.

"One time," replied Bill. "All she could talk about was Howard Spruce and his convertible. He went into the Army Air Corps and came home on leave. He used to brag that his wings were leg spreaders. He was always the richest kid in school and he sure acted like it in that damn convertible."

"What happened when you dated her?"

"We went to the drive-in theater. Spruce was home on leave and we double-dated. Naturally all of the conversation was between them. Wilma was making a play for Spruce. His date fought a losing battle trying to defend her position, and Spruce spent the night acting like the asshole that he was and enjoying it immensely. Every time I would try to get Wilma's attention in the backseat, Spruce cut in with another one of his buzz-boy cliches."

I shrugged and waved my arm in Bill's direction. "Ah, don't sweat it, buddy. Things are gonna' be different next time. When you get home with all your ribbons, battle stars, and a Medal of Honor, you might have little leverage on leg spreading yourself." I winked at him while I coiled a line and stowed it beneath the gunwale.

"Damn right!" Bill shot back. "And I want Spruce to be there, too. He's spent the whole war at Randolf. Then I want to get Wilma by myself. After that, I may go back and clean up on Spruce. He's bigger than me, but I'll do him like I did Horace Taylor."

"Horace who?"

"Taylor," answered Bill. "This big guy was a tackle on the football team and he kept picking on me. One night after a basketball game, he jumped me. We were in the middle of the block and there was this bright street light shining on the corner. I knew if I could keep that light in his eyes, I'd have him. I danced around, trying to keep the light over my shoulder and in his eyes. I kept giving him haymakers until I finally knocked the big ox down. By this time a crowd had gathered and one of the teachers stopped the fight."

I had seen Bill box in boot camp and knew he was a good boxer. He only weighed about 150 pounds, but he had long arms and was real quick.

"Then it will be too bad for Spruce," I replied. "Bill, tell me about some of the girls that you did get. I'll bet there were a lot of them in Ft. Worth."

"Wiley," said Bill, lowering his voice and suddenly becoming serious. "There weren't as many you might think. I'll tell you, but don't tell anyone else—you promise? See, the thing is, I could have had it many times but didn't follow through. How about you? Boy, I'll bet you've got a list long enough to have to fold to get it in your pocket!"

"Once for sure and a few probables I guess. That's about all," I answered without looking him in the eye.

"Well, they better look out when we get back to the States," continued Bill. "That's all I can say. And there won't be any 'probables' with me!"

With troops on board, we were under a strict rationing program as we always were when we moved at sea with troops. That means we had only two meals a day. There was no fresh water in the showers. Our choices were to shower with salt water, which was plentiful, or take a "whore's bath," which consisted of filling your helmet with fresh water from the drinking water dispenser and washing yourself with that. The military had a special soap for the salt water, but it didn't work very well and left you sticky and clammy. Everyone showered down with saltwater and used their helmet with fresh water to bathe. After a week or two of this, a real shower was luxury longed for by everyone.

The shower area on board the *Middleton* was large enough for us to take in our helmet of water and splash it freely without worrying about a messy deck. The showers were a part of the living quarters, which consisted of four or five high bunks similar to hammocks. A steel frame with tightly laced canvas supported our body. There was not a single chair or table in our spartan living quarters. Each of us had a locker about three feet tall, ten inches wide, and a foot deep. Our worldly possessions were kept in the locker or in our bunk. Each bunk had a small mattress and a pillow. Part of our stores included sheets and pillowcases.

Aboard ship, the enlisted men wore dungaree pants and shirts called Chambrays, with either high-top work shoes or black low-top dress shoes. When on liberty, we wore either white or blue uniforms depending on the climate. These uniforms had the rank and ensign on them. Most sailors, including me, carefully laid out our uniforms under our mattresses and pressed them that way until the time came to use them. We kept our dungarees, shirts, hats, socks, and underwear in our locker. In order to tell which clothes belonged to whom, each piece was stenciled except the dress blues, which had to be dry cleaned. Traditionally, sailors stenciled their work shirts and dungarees with peroxide. However, peroxide made our clothes look old and worn. The familiar "old salt" moniker was a name of respect given to those with the most worn looking dungarees and shirts. A dark blue navy "pea coat" was also issued to everyone, as was a foul weather jacket. Mine was a heavy jacket lined with wool. All of these things, plus the famous Navy sea bag, had to go into the locker. As should be obvious by now, it was hard to find space for souvenirs. However, I managed to stash away the Japanese siren, flag, Filipino knife, and some Japanese money, as well as some briefing materials and ship's publications.

While the *Middleton* was at anchor at Manus, we tied fourteen landing craft abreast and then with a long hawser secured them to the stern of the ship. Two men were always on the boats as the "boat watch." On this particular night both were fast asleep. The long hawser fell slack and draped over the ship's screw. Whether in port or at anchor, a ship's screw turns very slowly to keep from freezing up. As the screw turned, it took up the slack in the hawser, which wound around the screw. Within a short time, the hawser tilted each boat and, one by one, they rolled over on their side and sank. The two men were startled awake when they were dumped in the water. A diver cut the hawser and the *Middleton* was fortunate enough to pick up new boats. The two sleeping sailors survived the ordeal, but spent a well deserved week in the brig.

We conducted maneuvers for loading troops for several days. These men had never had the experience of being loaded into a landing craft at sea. Seasoned troops like the 2nd and 22nd Marines and the 1st Cavalry knew how to pack their backpacks with as little weight as absolutely necessary. They wore just enough clothes to be comfortable and carried only essential items. Each soldier left the ship with what he would have to carry for days—and still be able to run, jump, and fight. This particular group of troops was packed to the gills with everything you can imagine, as if each had been tasked to carry supplies for the whole squadron.

Bill, Tex, and I smiled and shot one another knowing glances when we watched the first group of green soldiers climb down the cargo net into our boat. "They'll drop 90% of this stuff the first hour ashore," Bill predicted.

Most of the men were wearing several layers of clothes, fatigue jackets, with a host of things hanging from their belts. They had canteens, ammunition, flashlights, bayonets, gas masks, very full backpacks, and their rifles. The first four reached the bobbing floorboard of the boat and turned loose of the rope net. Two sprawled on the bottom of the boat—hard. Tex Lee, who only weighed 125 pounds, helped them to their feet. When another wave reached the boat a huge swell lifted us so high their feet touched the gunwale. As the swell receded, the boat dropped about six feet and rolled away from the ship. The first soldier missed the boat and hit the water. Weighed down as he was, he headed straight for the bottom.

I was always ready for such an event, and so instantly threw off my helmet and life jacket and dove in after him. I caught him about ten feet down and slowed his momentum, but we were still sinking. Both of us kicked and struggled in the direction of sunlight, but we were getting nowhere fast. I was quickly running out of oxygen and the terrible thought popped into my mind that in a few seconds I would have to let him go or we would both drown. Thankfully, I never had to make that decision because at that moment Bill arrived. He had dived in after me. Together we managed to get the soldier back to the surface, where all three of us coughed and choked our way to the back to safety. It took several people to pull the poor guy back into Lucky 13. If Bill had not jumped in after us, that man would have died.

Cdr. McKay, who didn't miss much that happened on his ship, yelled from the bridge with a megaphone, "Boat No. 13, are you carrying troops or cargo? If you're overloaded with cargo, then send those men back up on the ship!" Far be it for our executive officer to tell Army troops how to pack for battle.

After a wide variety of maneuvers at Manus (and lots of speculation as to our final destination) the *Middleton* headed for Guadalcanal and Tulagi. Once there the task force increased and more extensive maneuvers were conducted.

I remember one particular incident involving a good friend of mine named Red Myers from Arkansas. Red was a Cox'n like myself. One day he went ashore to bring back a load of supplies, which included beer for the next liberty party. Red was a quiet, congenial sort who never gave anyone any trouble. By six o'clock that evening he had not returned, and did not return that night. The next day we discovered that he had picked up his load of supplies on time. Word went out that his boat was missing and everyone was alerted to be on the lookout for it. Red's boat was Number 14. Three days later it was spotted approaching the *Middleton*. Like a ghost from the dead, a grinning Red Myers was in his place driving the boat. He zigged and zagged until he came alongside the runway. By this time, nearly everyone on the ship had heard that Red was back.

Cdr. McKay stood on the quarterdeck and yelled through a megaphone: "Myers! Turn your boat over to the duty boat crew and report to the quarterdeck immediately!"

Still smiling, Red tried to climb the rope gangway but failed repeatedly until two seamen helped him up to the quarterdeck.

"Myers, have you been drinking?" McKay asked.

"Well, I'm not sure what you mean, skipper," Red slurred back.

"My God man, you're drunk! Where did you get that booze?

Red brought the house down with his next answer. "I got mine, sir. You'll have to get your own."

Red went straight to the brig and stayed there for three days until he sobered up. He never told anyone where he had spent his nearly four days away. Food in the brig consisted of only bread and water—officially, that is. Unofficially, friends often smuggled food in with the help of the ship's cooks.

One day I made a run to the supply depot and passed around an anchored Portuguese cargo ship. As we swung around the bow on the port side of the ship, I looked up at the flying bridge and couldn't believe my eyes. Standing out on the bridge waving and smiling at me was a beautiful suntanned blonde in white shorts. The sight of any woman in these surroundings was shocking, but a blonde goddess was devastating. I slowed the boat to get a better look. I didn't have to tell Bill and Tex; they had already seen her. She kept smiling and waving. I let the boat drift down the side of the ship before deciding, "Why not?"

I moved Lucky 13 around the stern and eased up to the boat ramp on the starboard side. The ship's utility longboat was tied to the gangway and several sailors were in it. We came alongside and exchanged greetings. One of the sailors spoke decent English.

"Where did you come from?" I asked.

"Australia. We bring a load from Australia," he answered.

"Who's the girl on the bridge?" asked Tex, getting right to the point.

"Probably Monica. She's on duty up there now."

We could not believe our ears. "On duty?" I asked. "You mean she's part of the crew?"

"Yes. We have twenty-six women sailors aboard."

"Twenty-six women!" Bill replied sharply. "Women sailors?" He still couldn't believe it. "Damn! How many men do you have?"

"Oh, about sixty-five, counting gun crews." The sailors had been down this road before, and the shock clearly on display on three American faces was nothing new to him. "All our ships have men and women crews," he said with a sly smile. "Most European ships do, too. We just don't have enough men to do everything."

"Well, how are they? As sailors, I mean," Bill asked.

"They do good on most things. Some of them are as strong as men." The sailor looked up as a feminine voice spoke to him in Portugese. We spotted another girl on the quarterdeck. She also had shorts on, but she was not as striking as Monica.

"What did she say?" I asked.

"She wants to know if you boys are ready to join the Portugese Merchant Marines?" The sailor broke out in a hearty laugh. The woman laughed too when she realized he had translating her message for us.

Tex was nodding his head as fast as it would bob. "I'll join right now!"

"Me too," added Bill. "And I'll take the dirtiest job on the ship." That translation brought laughs from everyone. We thanked them for their hospitality and shoved off.

"By God, Wiley, did you hear that? These European ships carry their own women! We can't even get a decent movie on the *Middleton*. We joined the wrong Navy or Coast Guard, buddy."

Tex's head was still nodding. "Got that right, Bill. We haven't seen a woman in months. And, if you don't count whores in Honolulu, it's been years. Those guys get to eyeball these girls all day long, probably rub up against them all the time, and I'll bet play musical bunks at night."

When we told the rest of guys on the *Middleton* about what we had seen, most of the men scoffed and called us liars. But we did notice that regardless of where a boat was going, from that day forward each routed itself to glide past the Portuguese ship.

Tulagi Bay was the most beautiful harbor I had ever seen. One side was too shallow for ships, where the water was only five to fifteen feet deep. The floor was solid coral with a brilliance of color only the South Pacific can create. The water was light green and perfectly clear. At every opportunity I sailed my boat over this area, about three or four miles square, and just turned off the engine to drift. The water was so clear it was impossible to tell how deep it was. We sounded the bottom with an anchor and never failed to be amazed. What looked like two or three feet of water was ten or fifteen. It was like scuba diving without going under water. I dreamed of the day I could return to the South Pacific after the war.

Reports from Iwo Jima and Peleliu were bad. We were losing hundreds or thousands of men, depending upon the source. The Japs were fighting harder than ever. I recall Tex's description of the action: "Each time you go into a beach, you got to remember you are going into their backyard and they are there waiting on you."

Resistance at Iwo Jima included everything from machine guns, rifles, mortars, and mines to kamikazes, suicide boats, and kaitens. The closer we got to Japan, the tougher it got. Some day, we knew we would be landing on Japanese soil. We also knew they would meet us at the beach with everything they had.

# Chapter 31

# April Fool's

The *Middleton* took on Army troops again and prepared to depart Honolulu. This time a special entourage came to the ship and boarded just we departed. The entourage was a special group from Coast Guard Public Affairs and included Cdr. Jack Dempsey, the former heavyweight boxing champion of the world. The group brought movies of all of Dempsey's fights, including the famous "late count" fight with Jim Tunney.

To my surprise, Dempsey was friendly and approachable. He answered questions and discussed each fight with us every night. He spent his days interviewing anyone who wanted to be interviewed, and then had the tapes sent to their hometown radio station. The theme was "In the South Pacific with Jack Dempsey."

Dempsey and his group brought a lot of entertainment to the ship. Just watching the movies of his fights with Firpo, Jess Willard, and Tunney made it easy to see why the 'Manassa Mauler' was considered the greatest fighter in the world. He was always the aggressor. He rarely backed up, and he had a special way of putting his whole body into every punch. Dempsey firmly believed he should have won the first Tunney fight. "I was in the right corner and Tunney should have been counted out," he told us. Actually, the referee stopped the count because Dempsey was not back in his corner, but you don't argue with Jack Dempsey! The former boxer spoke with an authority some mistook for arrogance. He had the limelight and he loved it. He was a perfect match for a Coast Guard trying to retain its identity in a time of war when it had been consolidated under the Navy.

I have often wondered why Ken Riley, the artist aboard the *Middleton* whose battle scenes and shipboard drawings have won national acclaim, never did a drawing or painting of Dempsey while he was with us. Perhaps he felt it would have taken something away from his use of common servicemen in real life scenes.

We met some of the stiffest opposition in the Philippines as we faced anywhere. Everyone expected that the war was going to slow down now as we crept closer to Japan. It seems hard to believe today, but back then many of us expected the war would last many more years.

We off-loaded the troops we had carried with us on Guadalcanal, where they were ordered to perform occupation duty. We liked unloading troops because it meant we could have our three meals a day again and use more water. With the holds empty, we also enjoyed a full-size basketball court, where we played endless games whenever we were off duty.

One day we loaded a group of the 1st Marines aboard, complete with their vehicles and tanks. It was time to go again. A small convoy including the *Middleton* sailed to Moritai and rendezvoused there with additional ships. A task force was definitely forming. The next stop was Ulithi, where still more ships joined up.

After leaving Ulithi, the long awaited message came over the P.A. system: "Now hear this! We've made our last stop at a friendly island. The task force is heading for one of the Japan's true strongholds. We are scheduled to land on Okinawa in the Kurile Islands, just below the Japanese mainland. We will do so on the first day of April. Men, this is not an April Fool's joke," Cdr. McKay added with a sort of finality. "This is the largest task force ever assembled in the Pacific. We can expect all-out resistance from the Japanese. Kamikazes, kaitens, and suicide boats of all kinds, and perhaps some things we haven't heard of or seen yet. I know that you men of the *Middleton* will do your jobs well and give our friends, the Marines, every advantage that we can.

A Marine Colonel spoke to the troops next, followed by our new Chaplain (the ship had rotated Chaplains at Pearl Harbor) spoke to everyone. "Lord, may we be worthy of having your help in this task to restore a free world. Will you bless every single man on this ship so that we may look to you and say, 'I have fought a good fight, I have kept the faith.' Now protect me if it be Your will, and guide me safely through this ordeal. Lord, this war has already cost this world millions of people. Thousands of our comrades lie buried on foreign soil. Thousands more lie at the bottom of this very ocean, committed to a lonely, watery grave. We do what we do to put a stop to all this senseless war. Will You help us stop it soon? Amen."

The Chaplain's prayer was better than anything any of us could have come up with. It reminded us of why we were here and it also opened up that yearning within everyone to end this war and go back home. The excitement of my early days in the service and the battles was dimming within me. Okinawa would be my seventh invasion. I just wanted to go home. Everyone did. It had been too long already. I was nineteen years old, but I felt twenty years older. I had already experienced a lifetime's worth of adventure in just the two years since leaving Texas.

Although we did not know it at the time, Okinawa—the doorstep of Japan—would be the last campaign of the war. It was ironic that D-Day was April Fool's Day—April 1, 1945. Even the lowest ranking among us had a map of the Western Pacific indelibly stamped in his mind. We knew we were finally going to be fighting the Japs on their own land. Okinawa was the outer edge of Japan. The Japanese would see the invasion as their last opportunity to stop us before reaching the main islands. That's why they would throw everything into it.

Doll and I went up to his boat. "Well, Wiley," Doll began in his heavy Southern drawl. "The good Lord has certainly been with us so far. I don't think he's gonna' desert us now."

"You know, Doll, we are really the lucky ones. Every time I put my boat on a beach and watch those guys run out the end straight into that fire, I thank God that I can back the boat off the beach and go back to the ship." I stopped and shook my head. "I'd hate to have to run out the front end on to that beach."

"We have to turn right around and bring another load right in there," Doll replied. "What about mortar fire, machine gun fire, and snipers? What about air raids? What about the torpedoes and mines? What about the suicide boats?" He shrugged. "It all evens out. Besides, I thought that I wanted to stay in Florida in some Captain of the Port detail, but I'm glad that I got into Amphibs. I'll tell you something else. When they took our boats away from us when we first came on the *Middleton*, Cdr. McKay was right. We weren't experienced enough at that time, but now I feel important. I'm good at what I do, too."

"All true," I agreed. "But I'm glad I don't have to run onto those islands and crawl from foxhole to foxhole. I'm glad I do what I do."

We both agreed that as long as we had to be there, we were in the spot we wanted to be.

The air raids began as the convoys entered the Philippine seas. The ships were on constant General Quarters again. We watched much of the action from the wardroom. The kamikazes came in droves. To get to us, they had to get through the carriers and warships. The carrier planes met them as far away from the convoys as possible. The destroyers, destroyer escorts, cruisers, and battleships took over when they penetrated the convoy. The sky was black with flak, but as usual the Jap planes kept coming and coming. It never ceased to amaze me how they managed to get through that heavy anti-aircraft fire. Usually they zipped in at low levels so the guns of the ships were almost firing at each other. Some came in high, selected a target, and dove down nearly straight into it, slipping through the flak to smash into a ship in a giant fireball that usually inflicted terrible damage. Once the enemy planes made it inside the convoy air screen, the carriers and the transports were very vulnerable.

By the Spring of 1945, most Japanese planes were in the hands of inexperienced pilots. They often selected any ship they could get to, especially if they could not reach the ship they really wanted. Reports of enemy submarine activity were heavy, and some of the ships in the convoy reported torpedoes. The destroyers and destroyer escorts quickly dispatched enemy submarines or sent them back into hiding.

I remember when an LSD motoring directly behind the *Middleton* reported a torpedo on a direct intercept course for their ship. The young ensign who was Officer of the Deck on the LSD ordered a full right rudder—directly into the path of the approaching torpedo. Turning into a torpedo is an extremely hard decision to make, but it has to be made quickly if it is to be made at all. The natural tendency is to turn away from a torpedo, but the young officer determined the trajectory of the torpedo at two o'clock (less than 90 degrees off his starboard bow). It was a tense fifteen seconds aboard before the torpedo missed the LSD by a handful of feet. By turning into it, the brave officer saved his ship, much as Cdr. Mckay had done earlier for the *Middleton*. If the ensign had turned away, the bow of the LSD would have been in the projected trajectory for a longer period of time. That fellow was both brave and smart.

The weather was turning colder as the ship moved farther north. Everyone was wearing his heavy foul weather, fur-lined jacket on watch. On the 26th of March, the Fifth Fleet moved into the Ryukyu Islands and landed an expeditionary force on Kerama Retto Island, just off Okinawa and several smaller islands in preparation for the main landing on Okinawa. The Japanese threw a massive number of suicide aircraft at the fleet and damaged a battleship, cruiser, and several destroyers. These reports filtered back to the task force, which was less than a week away. It was a good indication of the reception we could expect. The next day we heard that suicide planes hit a carrier and several other warships. We also learned that B-29 raids against the Japanese mainland from Tinian had intensified. Ironically, both sides could now launch land-based bombers against the other. The men we landed on Kerama cleared out mines around Okinawa so our ships could come in closer to support land operations with naval bombardments. The big guns of the Navy, coupled with constant aerial bombardments, cleared an area for the main invasion force.

The task force pulled into position during the night of March 31 just off the southwest coast of Okinawa near Hagushi. I was preparing my boat for lowering just as dawn broke and the island materialized in front of me. I was surprised at the landscape. This was no jungle island like all the others. This was farm country. I could clearly see the fields on the slope coming down to the ocean. It looked like a patchwork quilt. It looked like home.

"H" hour was 8:30 a.m. Lucky 13 plowed through the surf full of young, anxious, nervous, but incredibly brave Marines. To our surprise, there was little or no resistance as I put my boat on the beach and lowered the ramp. The sound of explosions and gunfire accelerated once the ramp was down and the Marines charged out. I watched as the Marines fired at something in the distance, and could tell they were encountering return fire because they were seeking whatever cover was available. Still, the hot greeting everyone expected on the beach failed to materialize.

On the third trip into the beach, the control boat asked me to go back to another transport and help unload their troops. I moved quickly to the ship and pulled alongside. Tex and Bill took the cargo net into the boat and troops started coming down. They were Army, and it took all of five seconds to figure out they were inexperienced. They had entirely too much gear on, and their backpacks looked too heavy. They also looked scared and sank down low into the boat. Once loaded, I sped off to the designated beach. Although the beachhead had been established, the fighting beyond the beach was becoming intense. The sound of explosions and gunfire was much heavier during this trip than the previous two. When we hit the beach Tex lowered the ramp. None of the soldiers moved.

"Let's go!" yelled Tex. "Get moving! Now!"

The soldiers remained in the boat, squatting low, looking at one another, but not moving. I moved over next to them. "Get off my boat! We have to get out of here!"

Some of the soldiers looked at me with eyes the size of saucers. Still they did not move.

"Damn it! If you don't get off," I threatened, "I'll turn our 30-caliber on you! You are endangering this boat! Now, let's go!"

This time they started moving. First one, and then another, and then all of them filed out of the boat and ran for the nearest cover. As I backed off the beach, I knew I would never have used my gun against American troops. I also wondered whether any of those Army boys I made get out bought the farm on Okinawa. I still think about it today.

During the first day there were several air attacks and kamikazes hit another U.S. battleship and several larger landing craft and destroyers. Before nightfall, the U.S. forces captured and secured two airfields. The relatively light resistance to the landing allowed the Americans time to establish a large beachhead and offload heavy equipment to repair the airfields. All of the boats worked through the night unloading men, supplies, and equipment.

At midday on the second day, I pulled alongside the *Middleton* and a jeep was lowered into my boat. Four guys who appeared to be troops clad in fatigues climbed down the cargo net. I didn't recognize them. One burly guy sat on the engine hatch with his rifle across his lap. I was about to tell him to get down in the boat when I realized who it was: Jack Dempsey. The other three guys were his public relations aides, complete with cameras and gear.

"Shove Off Cox'n!"

On the way to the beach the photographer snapped a dozen pictures of Dempsey. One included me looking at the camera with Dempsey sitting on the engine hatch with his rifle, and Tex in the background. The photo was released through ISN and AP and appeared in *Newsweek* and papers across the country. My mother recognized me in the picture and saved it. The caption read, "Dempsey goes in on D-Day."

The photographer recorded footage of the approach to the beach. Tex dropped the ramp once we hit the sand. We all got a good education in public relations. The photographer went out first and set up his camera. Then he asked Tex to crank up the ramp and wait. Battle-weary troops coming back from the fighting looked on in amazement as the photographer set up his gear. Once he was ready, Dempsey climbed up on the hood of the jeep and, with his rifle in front of him, nodded his readiness. The jeep driver yelled for Tex to lower the ramp, and when he did the driver rolled out of Lucky 13 and onto the beach—with the movie cameras grinding away. My aunt and mother, who both saw this on the newsreels, said they thought Dempsey was under heavy fire the whole time as the jeep roared out of the landing boat in the first wave of an assault landing. The men left their life jackets in the boat. As I pulled away from the beach, I picked up the life jacket Dempsey had been wearing. In the pocket was a tube of lipstick and a compact of face powder. I had never given any serious thought about the vanity that goes with fame. Even the "Manassa Mauler" wanted to look his best for the cameras.

The tides at Okinawa were so immense that the water line receded more than 100 yards when the tide was out. On the fourth

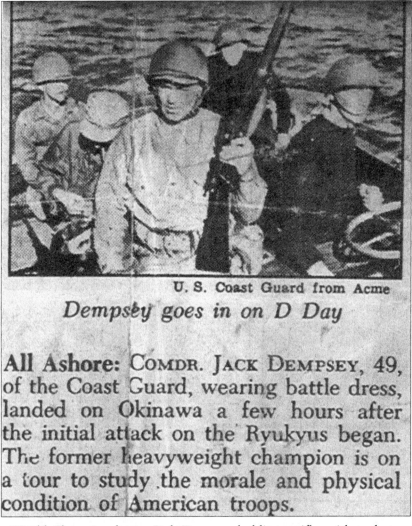

U. S. Coast Guard from Acme

*Dempsey goes in on D Day*

**All Ashore:** COMDR. JACK DEMPSEY, 49, of the Coast Guard, wearing battle dress, landed on Okinawa a few hours after the initial attack on the Ryukyus began. The former heavyweight champion is on a tour to study the morale and physical condition of American troops.

World Champion boxer Jack Dempsey holding a rifle, with author Ken Wiley (right) and Tex Lee (behind Dempsey's left shoulder).

day of the invasion I took in a load of low priority supplies to the beach. The boat control officer told me it might be the next day before we could unload. We could stay beached or circle around off-shore. Other boats were in the same situation. I don't know who suggested it, but we decided to let the tide beach our boats and wait it out. We pulled up as far as we could and let the water receded under us until we were high and dry. It was better sitting twelve hours than running around in a circle off-shore. At least we could some rest and we had a good supply of canned food and rations.

About 9:00 p.m. that evening the public address system on the beach blared: "Now, hear this!" began the Beach Master. "All hands are commanded to be on alert all night. We expect an all-out attack by the Japanese to retake the beach. Japanese aircraft with paratroopers have been detected heading this way. Expect kamikazes, suicide boats, and bombers. The main Jap fleet is also expected. You are to shoot anything you see in the sky and anyone who doesn't answer your challenge with the proper password."

We were stuck on the beach until the tide came back in. All night we listened to machine gunfire as various boats shot at shadows or one another. It was a long and tedious night during which Bill and I stayed glued to our 30-calibers while Tex served as lookout and issued or answered challenges with the red flashlight. The Japs never made an all-out attack against the beach, but scattered air raids kept the night lively. As the morning tides came in, I eased the boat into the water and vowed that I would never take the easy way out again.

We later learned that the Navy was meeting every movement of the Japanese fleet and aircraft with decisive countermoves. They engaged and stopped every major enemy thrust to repel the invasion, although we lost warships daily from kamikaze and suicide boats. The aircraft that slipped through also did damage to some of the ships in Task Force 58. Okinawa was different from other landings. The Japanese threw everything in they could from the mainland. The fighting on the land was about as intense as anything any American troops anywhere had ever experienced.

I remember the day we got word that Ernie Pyle, the popular war correspondent everyone loved, was dead. He was riding in a jeep with other men on an island off Okinawa when Japanese machine guns ambushed them.

Chapter 32

# Okinawa Shima

The light resistance to the initial landings on Okinawa was misleading. The Japanese pulled a sucker play on us, saving their strength for a final showdown. And they used everything in their arsenal to do it. We stayed on and around Okinawa for almost a month. Except for a few scattered hours, we spent the entire stay there on Lucky 13.

One day we had pulled alongside the *Middleton* to refuel and get sandwiches and coffee. The O.D. yelled down from the quarterdeck through a megaphone, "Cox'n from boat number thirteen! Report to the quarterdeck on the double!"

I climbed the gangway as fast as I could to the quarterdeck, saluted the flag and then the O.D. "Aye aye, sir!"

The O.D. was a young ensign named Murphy. "Wiley, I want you to take these five soldiers over to Ronta Island. It's about twenty-eight miles up the coast. Here's a map showing the location and your course," he continued, pointing to a map spread out on a table. "Our troops secured the island this morning and are still mopping up, so be careful. Lieutenant Wilson will go along with his five men." Wilson was a rugged looking soldier with a heavy black mustache. He nodded in my direction and I saluted him. "The Lieutenant will tell you more about the mission on the way," explained Murphy.

"Aye aye, sir!" I answered, saluting again before turning, saluting the flag, and moving down the gangway. The Lieutenant and the five soldiers trailed behind me.

It was not until we filed into the boat that I got a real good look at my new passengers. They were all rugged looking, small in stature with dark complexions. They were also traveling light—very light. These guys were experienced at whatever it was they did.

"Cox'n, shove off!" ordered Lt. Wilson. I pulled the boat away from the gangway and headed on a northerly course.

Tex and Bill were both curious, but they knew better than to ask where we were going or who we were taking there. They would know soon enough.

Wilson was standing in the cargo hold looking straight at me. It was rather unnerving. "What's your name, Cox'n?"

"Wiley."

I knew I was supposed to salute, but something told me not to. He smiled slowly, broadly. It was the first time he had cracked a grin, and I knew right then this guy was going to be all right.

"Look Wiley," he began. "I'm so damn tired of all this protocol shit that it makes me want to puke. My name is just Wilson, or Roy if you want to. We're all going to be together a few hours in this boat, and I think we ought to drop all the saluting and the other bullshit. Now, for your information, all of these men are officers—Army Intelligence."

As he let the news soak in, he removed the bars from his own collar and peeled off the heavy black mustache. My mouth fell open in disbelief. It took all of three seconds for him to look like a Jap. He laughed when he saw my expression. "Use, 1937, Japanese mother, American father, born and raised in L.A., but I can still speak the lingo. Watch this."

He motioned to one of the soldiers. The man broke out in what sounded to me like perfect Japanese. The other four men joined in, and as soon as you could spit, a lively Japanese conversation filled the gunwales of Lucky 13.

"They've all been through language school and since they each have some Japanese ancestry, they speak fluent Japanese," Wilson explained. "In fact, they even speak the dialect related to different geographical areas of Japan. I'm telling you this because we're going to change over to Japanese soldiers in this boat. It's important for our mission."

I nodded before shrugging. "Ok by me."

"We'll have to leave our uniforms and American possessions with you. We'll be on the island exactly nine hours. That should be 0200 in the morning. I want you to pick us up at 0200 just off the southern tip of the island." He pulled out a map, unfolded it, and pointed to the spot. "Don't mark it! Just be there. If there's heavy fire and we have to, we'll swim out to you. About 1,000 yards will be right if you can't come in to close safely.

"How will we know it's you?" I asked.

"We'll signal you by red flashlight," he replied. "Let's see, the password tomorrow is ORANGE and the answer is AID. That's if it's ok for you to come in. Come to think of it, you better lay off 2,000 yards until just before 0200, and then come in."

Tex, Bill, and I listened intently and absorbed every word. While Wilson lectured us, the other five soldiers changed into Japanese uniforms and applied make-up to their faces. They were really beginning to look like authentic Japanese soldiers. We all knew the only place on the island that had been secured was the beachhead. That meant these guys were going behind Japanese lines for some reason. I also knew that reason was none of my business.

"Any questions?" asked Wilson.

"No."

"Good. We'll leave our M-1s, BARs, and forty-fives here in the boat. Don't hesitate to use them if necessary," he said with a grin. I liked this guy.

Each of the "Japanese soldiers" took the .25-caliber Japanese rifles from a box they brought aboard as well as small Japanese pistols. Now they were full-fledged Japanese soldiers.

"How are you going to get through our lines?" Asked Tex.

Wilson raised his eyebrows and shrugged as if to say, "I don't know." He cleared his throat and answered, "The Beach Master has a platoon waiting for us on the beach. They will escort us as prisoners down the beach to the front lines. We'll take it from there." Bill, Tex, and I just exchanged looks. These guys had guts.

Wilson shifted the subject. "You might as well know this, since you're involved and you could meet a suicide boat in the morning.

We think they're coming from this island, but when the Japs see they're going to lose it, they'll move them somewhere else. We think they may have thirty or forty suicide boats in an island base with a hidden channel leading out to the ocean. Our job is to destroy the base."

"With what?" asked Bill. "You don't have enough explosives on you to do that."

"No, but those boats do," he answered. "We'll use their own explosives if we can, so if you see a big boom about midnight, you'll know we were right and hopefully successful."

"What if they move out before you get there?" I asked.

"Then we're just too late. So far, all of their missions have been a few hours after midnight. We don't think they'll come out to go on a mission before then. They may decide to move the base to another island, but you'll notice that we have a whole bunch of DEs, LCIs, and PTs patrolling off that island, and they're watching real close. Of course, we need a landing craft to come in for us. That's where you come in."

"We'll come for you. Don't worry," I said.

"How many Americans do we have that can penetrate Jap lines?" asked Bill.

Wilson smiled. "I don't know the exact number, but not many. In fact, it was hard getting this group together. With everybody looking the part and speaking Japanese, we have a real good chance of pulling something like this off. We all went through special training together. We're a team. If you spot one soldier who makes you suspicious, you might question him, right?" I nodded and Wilson continued. "If there are six of them talking and laughing, would you give it a second thought? Besides, if we are exposed, there are enough of us to put up a pretty good fight!"

"Makes sense," I answered. "How did you ever get together?"

"The Army scanned everyone's personnel records for some Japanese ancestry and ran a background check on our loyalty. Special Forces weeded us down to a few who qualified. A major came up with the idea of a group penetration. We did it first in New Guinea, then again on Saipan, Leyte, and Luzon. Each time was for a different purpose, though."

"Did you run into any problems?" Bill asked.

"Yeah, just about every time!" laughed Wilson. "The biggest problem was on Saipan. We joined up with a Jap patrol and told them we had escaped from the beach. We didn't know it, but they were getting ready for a Banzai attack on the Marines at the airfield. Before we knew it, there were several hundred Japs around us. We could not leave now—that would have been unthinkable for a Japanese soldier tasked with the great honor of dying for his Emperor. But if we stayed we would have to charge with them straight into the 2nd Marines! These guy would have thought we were Japs. It was an uncomfortable position."

"I'll say," I answered as Bill issued a long, slow whistle. "What did you do?"

Wilson heaved a sigh. "We took the coward's way out. When the Banzai attack began we were the first ones hit. We bravely fell in our tracks and the rest of the Japs ran right past us. As soon as they went by, we crawled for the rear and then ran like hell!"

"What about the time on Leyte when we were trying to make contact with the guerillas?" commented one of the other soldiers. His name was Woods. "We had one of the guerillas with us who was supposed to identify us to the others. When we met Japs, we passed him off as our prisoner, but one Jap officer was so infuriated at the guerillas that he drew his pistol and shot and killed him before we could do anything to stop him. That left us in one hell of a mess. We finally came upon their hideout in the mountains and were sitting there watching them for a distance and talking about how we could expose ourselves without being killed. We recounted the execution of the guerilla, too. Suddenly, a voice rang out from the nearby jungle: 'Lay down your guns.' It was in perfect English."

"Wow," said Tex. "What happened next?" The story was enthralling.

"Several voices in broken English chimed in: 'Throw down your guns. Hands up!' To me it sounded more like Filipino than Japanese," continued Woods, "but we did exactly as told. A young man with an automatic weapon, apparently their leader, stepped out first and asked us who we were. We introduced ourselves and while we were talking, fifteen or twenty Filipinos filtered out of the surrounding brush."

"What about the Jap uniforms you had on?" I asked.

"Those were a problem," admitted Woods. "Their leader asked about them, and we told him we were dressed this way to penetrate the Jap lines and that we had one of them with us. Their leader interrupted and told us, 'Yes, we heard all of your conversation. No single Jap could have ever spoken such perfect English, let alone an entire group. I am so sorry to hear about Ramon. They will pay for that. Come with us until we can make contact and verify who you are.' We all breathed a sigh of relief," admitted Woods.

Wilson picked up the story. "When we got in their camp, I explained our mission to them. We wanted all of the guerillas to unify and help set up a coordinated series of sabotage and attacks. Garcia, the leader, assured me they would help us. In about an hour, one of his men came back and whispered something to him. He turned to me and said, 'Lt. Wilson, your story checks out. Welcome to our camp.' I couldn't believe this," continued the Lieutenant. "They had checked us out in an hour, through Jap lines, without a radio. He never told me how and to this day, I don't know."

"Tell them about Luzon, Lieutenant," Woods urged. "That's the one I still get shaky just thinking about."

"Yeah, let's hear it," urged Bill.

"We were part of First Cavalry and went in with the fourth wave," began Wilson.

"First Cavalry, Fourth Wave? That's who we took in to Lingayen," I cut in. "Are you the guys who went down and liberated the Japanese Prison Camp?"

"Yes, and the Colonel sends you his regards," smiled Wilson. "In fact, he was the one who recommended you and your crew for this mission."

Bill, Tex, and I shared smiles and nods.

"Well anyway, we went in just as soldiers in the First Cavalry," continued Wilson.

When we got down close to Manila, we broke out front, killed a few Japs for their uniforms, and went down to the P.O.W. camp. We infiltrated with the guards and they never noticed us. When the attack came, we planned to have the prisoners coordinated so they could keep out of the line of fire and we could do our attacking from the inside. We were supposed to tie white handkerchiefs around our arm so our own people wouldn't shoot us. Well, wouldn't you know it? The Japanese had treated those prisoners badly. They were in such terrible shape, half-starved and little more than walking skeletons. They had been tricked so many times they didn't believe we were Americans! They thought we were a bunch of Japanese trying to tell them to follow them when the fighting started. They thought it was another death march, and they were the hostages. I really couldn't blame them, either.

Wilson sighed, shook his head, and continued:

Anyway, that part of the plan wasn't going so well. We managed to put explosives at the gates and station ourselves in some strategic positions. Most of the Japs pulled out before the attack and only a small number remained. We were really afraid that the prisoners would give us away since they didn't believe us, but they didn't. The trouble came when one of the Japanese guards heard us talking to some of the prisoners—it was Jenson and me. The Jap challenged us and had us at bayonet point. We tried talking to him in Japanese to smooth it over, but he was suspicious. He marched us off to his commandant. Of course, he didn't know there were six of us, so Murphy here followed until we were out of sight, snuck up behind him, and killed him with one swift knife thrust. Now, of course, we had to dispose of the body. If we left it, they would suspect the prisoners and kill them. So we pulled down his pants, dumped the corpse on one of the latrines, sat him up on the throne, and tied him there so that he looked like he was doing his business. No one ever questioned him and he stayed there four hours until the attack came.

"Wow! Ya'll sure live dangerously," Tex drawled.

I was really hoping for another story, but by this time we were approaching the island and a beach patrol boat challenged me. Tex answered the challenge and we headed toward the beach. There was very little surf and the landing was uneventful, the nose of the LCVP sliding smoothly onto the beach.

"Wiley, you better call out for a Sergeant Magee," ordered Wilson. "I don't think we ought to go charging out of here in these uniforms just yet."

"Ok," I answered. I looked about and shouted to one of the beach party, "Sergeant Magee? Is there a Sergeant Magee?"

"Magee? Yeah, he was just here." The soldier approached Lucky 13. His eyes nearly bugged out of his head. "Geez!" he exclaimed. "You guys got those six prisoners without any guards?" He leveled his M-1.

"It's O.K.," I answered quickly. "Just get the Sergeant over here quick."

Within a minute or two the Sergeant and about fifteen men walked up to our boat. "You Wiley?" Magee asked.

"Yeah. Are you Magee?"

"That's me," he answered loud enough for everyone to hear. "So these are the prisoners I'm to take up to Major Randall on the front line?"

"Yes, these are the ones," I replied.

"All right! Fall in!" yelled Magee.

The "prisoners" filed out of the boat and the American soldiers closed in around them. As they disappeared into the distance, I looked at my watch. It was almost 1700 hours. We had nine hours to wait. We stayed on the beach about half an hour while I talked to some of the beach party. The fighting in the center of the island was fierce. The wounded were pouring back to the beach. I knew we could make the south side of island in about two hours, even by swinging out wide enough to miss any shore fire.

We carried several loads of wounded out to the ships and at 2200 hours departed on our "mission." The weather had changed and the water was choppy, the swells building to disquieting size. It's a good thing we gave ourselves plenty of time because it took a lot longer to reach our rendezvous point than I was expecting. Finally, I reached a spot about 2,000 yards due south of the point of land we had already christened "Pick-Up Point." I circled Lucky 13 slowly at idle speed, watching the shore closely.

A flash caught my eye. Deep in the island, a giant mushroom of flame rolled slowly upward hundreds of feet into the sky. After a few seconds the sound of the massive explosion reached our ears.

Wilson and his men found the base, which thanks to them no longer existed. I checked my watch: it was ten minutes after midnight. All three of us kept our eyes glued on "Pick-Up Point." The cloudy sky made it very dark. It was difficult to see anything. After about an hour Tex yelled out, "Red Lights flashing!"

All of us read the password, but it seemed to be coming from a moving object: a boat. Now we could hear it. A small speed boat was approaching.

"WILEY, COMING OUT TO YOU," flashed the code.

We picked up the boat visually and then a second one following close behind. The boats were exchanging gunfire. I kicked the LCVP into gear and tore out to meet Wilson and his comrades. Bill and Tex were mounted and ready on the .30-calibers. As the first boat drew near, the second one slowed down. They had spotted us. Bill gave them a blast from the 30s and they turned around and headed back for the beach.

Wilson and his men pulled alongside us. "Thanks!" he shouted. "Quick, give us our guns! We're unarmed!"

Bill and Tex passed over their rifles and BARS. "Follow me!" Wilson ordered. "I think I can catch them, but I may need your firepower."

Wilson pulled away and gunned his boat after the Japanese. We followed as fast as we could. Wilson and his men opened fire at the Japs, who returned it with interest. Some of Wilson's bullets found their mark and the explosives in the small suicide boat detonated in a giant fireball. They were still several hundred yards off shore.

Wilson slowed down and I motored alongside. "I think that's the last of them," he said.

"They got out chasing us before the base blew. Can you get this thing aboard?" The speed boat was about 18 feet long, an easy fit for the LCVP's personnel-vehicle well.

"We'll try," I answered.

I put the stern out to the current and lowered the ramp. All of the soldiers came aboard and, with the help of heavy lines, maneuvered the speed boat until it was up on the ramp. Then, all as one, we pulled it in.

"Careful!" called out Wilson. "It's still got its explosives in it."

"Oh, great!" exclaimed Bill. Tex laughed.

Incredible, I thought. These guys were playing around with that other boat and exchanging heavy gunfire. They could have gone up in smoke and flame any second. With everyone helping, we got the suicide boat inside and the ramp closed and headed back home.

Wilson and his men found the base and decided to escape in one of the boats so Navy Intelligence could examine it. Because they looked like Japanese soldiers, two of them stayed back in case there was any trouble, while the others worked on the boats. Sure enough, the ones working on the boats were caught red-handed after they had planted the explosives and set a timer to detonate them. They were disarmed and being marched to a holding room when their buddies jumped the guards and an opportunity arose to escape.

Wilson and his men ran to the speed boat and made their getaway. The Japs sent several armed guards in another boat after them. They barely got away before the base exploded. There were about thirty-five or forty suicide speed boats in a marina-type harbor, explained Wilson, each filled with enough explosives to blow up a sizeable ship. The chain reaction of explosions shook the whole end of the island. The only boats that remained intact were Wilson's and the pursuing enemy speed boat. The chase wound its way down the narrow river inlet, choked by a hail of fire from the pursuing boat whenever the stretch of river was straight enough to keep them fleeing Americans in view.

"Thank God for the bends in the river," Wilson commented dryly. "The Jap boat made a turn too wide once and ran aground. That helped us gain a bit on them. It's a good thing you guys came in to meet us, though. Those thirty calibers knocked them back on their heels, and when you armed us, it was an entirely new ball game. Murphy was a much better shot than they were. He hit the bang box."

"If you don't mind, Wiley, we were told that if we were lucky enough to get one of these boats out in one piece, we should bring it back to the LSD," explained Wilson. "They have a complete shop to dismantle and analyze it. There are a lot of things we can learn that will help us in the future when we go up against these babies."

We left Wilson and his men with the captured boat aboard the LSD. As we were pulling away, Bill said, "I sure as hell knew we had brave guys, but I had no idea we had people like that on our side.

And boy, they sounded more like Japs than the Japs do! How ya' gonna' know who to trust?"

"Yeah, I wonder if the Japs have anything like that. Hell, Miller, you ain't much bigger than a Jap. Are you sure you're from Ft. Worth?" said Tex, who laughed at his own joke. I joined him.

"Well, one thing's for sure," shot back Bill. "Nobody could mistake that red hair and freckle face of yours for a Jap."

## Chapter 33

# Confusion on the Road

The road to Tokyo was built by island-hopping—wresting specs of land away from the Japanese one by one, and moving our airfields closer and closer across thousands of miles of ocean. Each step gave us a launching point to reach the next step. Along the way we bypassed most of the Japanese-controlled islands, taking the most strategic and leaving others cut off. Eventually we were within easy striking range of the Japanese mainland.

We traveled in convoys and carried troops, equipment, and supplies. For the transports, supply vessels, and escorts this meant lots of two-way travel in an area of the world still heavily populated by Japanese. Even with all of our overall success there was the constant danger of air raids, torpedoes, mines, and suicide weapons of all kinds. The campaign to Okinawa, the doorstep of the Japanese mainland, brought home the difficulties that awaited us.

Ray Kreckel was a big guy, about six-three and 225 pounds. He had played football at Massillon, Ohio, a school recognized nationwide for its football achievements. Massillon was the prep school for college All-Americans. Ray was a tremendous athlete. He was also one of my best friends. En route to Luzon, Ray, Doll, and I attended a briefing on suicide boats. The words of Lt. Munger still rang in our ears: "The suicide actions of the Japs that we saw at Saipan and Tinian were makeshift more than carefully planned. The

Japs used anything they could lay their hands on, and it was probably spontaneous rather than well planned. In any event, I think they learned something. If a man is willing to die, he has a much better chance of taking out his target. We have word now that what we saw in the Philippines, Leyte, was much more planned that Saipan. The Japs are losing now big time, and they know it," continued the Lieutenant. "For people who are fanatics about the supremacy of their country, this is hard to take. You saw how many of them committed suicide rather than be captured alive at Tarawa, Kwajalein, and Eniwetok. Remember the Bonsai attacks on Saipan? By the way, you also remember that we always take less than two percent of them as prisoners. The reason is that they plan to either win or die. We now know they are just planning to die."

"What do you mean, Lieutenant," someone asked.

"They have special schools for their pilots, where they are taught to fly their airplane loaded with bombs directly into a ship," he explained. "Their flight is a one-way ticket. They have a ceremony, which is equivalent to a funeral, for the pilots before they take off. There is no plan to return. To return would be the ultimate shame."

Lt. Munger continued: "Now they have formalized the human torpedo, the dreaded Kaiten. Each Jap sub carries several of these and several Kaiten pilots, specially trained to ride the torpedo and guide it directly into a ship. There is no return for these Kaiten riders, either, but it is a great honor to be one of them and the line of volunteers is long."

We just shook our heads. Listening to such things was still incredible, even after all we had experienced.

"Now we come to the one that affects us the most—the suicide boat," continued the Lieutenant. "Instead of using the slower barges, the Japs have fast 18-foot speed boats. These boats are twice as fast as our landing craft and are loaded in the nose with TNT and in the stern with depth charges. That packs a real wallop. We can expect an all-out effort this time. They've had a little time to get their so-called 'Special Forces' organized."

"There should be plenty of them because they think we're going to hit their mainland," I said."

"Yes, and we need to learn your daily passwords and practice our own morse code," answered Munger. "Your lives will depend on it. You already know how devious they can be, so don't trust anybody."

"I saw one of those speed boats at Leyte, when the ships were out," said Ray. "It looked like the boat races. This patrol boat was after him and he was running off and leaving it. The patrol boat was shooting fifties, too, and I swear the speedboat was outrunning the bullets."

"So what happened to him?" I asked.

"Well," replied Ray, "he was circling around trying to get a line on the ships, but the escorts were keeping him out. He had no place to go. He finally just headed in toward a destroyer and they hit him with their Pom Poms and exploded him before he could do any damage—but man he was fast! It was so dark I could barely see, but it looked like there was only one man aboard."

"That's all it takes," said Doll, "but I'll bet he can't outrun my fifties."

After the meeting the three of us walked down to the crew quarters talking about the new Japanese weapon. When we arrived, O'Neal, Bryan, and Bill Miller joined in.

"They say that's what got that tanker back in Leyte," Bryan said. "The ship saw him coming and just didn't have time to shoot after he failed to answer the challenge."

"Well the *Monroe* shot up some of its own boats coming in because they didn't answer the challenge," Doll added.

"They reacted too fast. You know, this damn war is getting too dangerous for me," said Bill. "Whatever happened to the good 'ole days when your enemy was always the Japs? Hell fire! Pretty soon they're gonna' infiltrate our chow line and we'll have to answer a challenge to get a stale bologna sandwich!"

"Did you hear what Tokyo Rose said last night?" I asked.

O'Neal piped in. "Yeah, she said that after the Philippines, we should know that the Japanese will never surrender. She said her brave men were jumping at the chance to die for the Emperor as long as they can take an American ship with them."

"One thing's for sure," I replied. "If we see one of those things, we better knock it out fast, or it's liable to take a whole ship with it."

Custer had walked up during the conversation and chimed in. "It'll be open season on the kamikazes and all suicide boats, so long as you don't leave your own mission undone. But there's one thing I want you to remember. These guys are fanatics. Don't take any chances. Some of those Japs speak pretty good English and they'll try to trick you. Ask some of the guys from the *Hunter Liggott.*"

"What's that all about?" I asked.

"At Guadalcanal, their boats tried to infiltrate ours at night by speaking in English. They yell, 'Hey Mac! You got any chow aboard? Want some good chocolate?' Or maybe, 'Hey Joe! You guys from the *Liggott?*' I'm telling you right now that if you want to stay alive, use the password first, then any other questions you want to throw in. If he's a Jap, the longer you make him talk, the sooner he'll screw up."

"Right," several of us said simultaneously.

"There was a Cox'n who went into the dock one night to pick up some Marines who were supposed to be there," continued Custer. "Well, he didn't know it, but the Japs had overrun it and captured the pier. When the boat came in, the Cox'n gave a signal and instead of giving the correct response, someone on the pier said, 'It's O.K. Come on in,' in perfect English. The Cox'n stopped about fifty yards off and asked, 'Why didn't you answer my challenge?' The Jap responded in perfect English, 'Hell, Mac, I forgot what it was, but you can come on in. There's just me and Hewley in here right now.'"

Custer paused a moment to let it sink in. "Do you get it? They wanted the boat, or they would have already opened fire. The Cox'n was almost convinced, but he decided to check a little further. 'I want to hear from Hewley,' he said. The Jap answered, 'He's asleep. Now you don't want me to wake him up, do you?'"

"This is creepy," said Bill.

"Yup, and often deadly," shot back Custer. "Well, this began to make the Cox'n nervous, so he said, 'Who pitched for the Dodgers in last year's world series?' There was a long pause before the Jap answered, 'Joe DiMaggio.'"

"Joe DiMaggio!" we all said in reply.

"Well, that did it. The Cox'n put the power to it and headed out amidst a hail of bullets. He got away, but only because he wouldn't give in too quick. If you're in doubt, and you have the time, keep 'em talking. They'll screw up sooner or later."

"How do you think they'll do it this time?" I asked Custer.

"They've got a base hidden somewhere in the area. They'll probably come out at night. Remember on Saipan when six of them came out? Well, they'll send 'em out about a half a dozen at a time. That's plenty to raise holy hell with the fleet. They'll have us shooting at each other again and they'll be hitting in all these different areas at one time. That's why our escorts will have to really be alert and keep them from penetrating. Our biggest problem is going to be when we're out of the anchorage on special missions or just routine trips," Custer continued. "We're liable to run into 'em at any time. Remember that they don't want you, if they can get a ship. That's one small advantage."

The informal strategy session ended when General Quarters sounded. The Officer of the Deck came on the P.A. system: "General Quarters! General Quarters! Now hear this! All hands man your battle stations! All hands man you battle stations. Boogies reported at ten o'clock!"

We grabbed our life jackets and helmets and Doll, Kreckel, and I took off for the ward room, which was our standby station. "Here they come," said Doll. "It's beginning again."

From the wardroom we could step out in the passageway and see the convoy on our port side. Anti-aircraft fire was already speckling the sky. There were two Zeros about 600 hundred feet passing above the convoy from ten o'clock. They split apart and one passed right over the *Middleton* while the other turned and headed out at about seven o'clock. For a second I thought he was aiming for us, but it became clear his victim was one of the transports behind us. I watched as he selected his target and rolled over amidst an almost solid sky of black anti-aircraft fire. He climbed as he began his roll, then suddenly flipped over and headed straight down. I had seen it a score of times. The battle had come down to a fight between a single Zero and the ship's gunners. If they didn't shoot him down, in a few seconds many of the men on the ship would be dead.

Every gun on that transport was locked on that screaming Zero, as were a few other guns firing from nearby ships. It seemed impossible the Zero could fly through it. Everyone who was watching held his breath. I know I did. Finally, just a second or two before the Jap would have hit the transport, part of one wing ripped away. The Zero was so close to the transport that his flight path was not substantially altered. It veered slightly and almost missed, but finally impacted against one of the bridge's gun pits. Our hearts sank as we watched the ensuing explosion. It was as if someone had ignited an ammunition dump.

"Jeez, I think that's the *Calloway*, isn't it?" asked Doll. The rest of us just shook our heads. With all the smoke and flame we couldn't be sure. "It is. It's the Calloway," Doll said adamantly. "I wonder if Blaine's O.K." Blaine Collins was one of our friends who transferred from the *Middleton* to the *Calloway*.

Fortunately the last second damage to the Zero prevented even more injury to the ship. Still, many men were killed and wounded in the blast, and once the smoke cleared we could see a raging fire and a tangled mass of steel where the left side of the bridge had been. Now the fire had to be put out or the transport would be a total loss.

I took a deep breath and said a quick prayer for those poor guys. That's how fast it happens. One second you are watching events unfold as if in a movie theater, and the next second you realize you're in the movie and about to be killed. There were no guarantees out here—only a thin line between life and obliteration. That Jap pilot did exactly what he wanted: kill himself and as many of us as possible. It was simply unthinkable. How could we hope to win against that? That mind set changed all the rules of warfare. We had won everything so far because we had superior equipment and forces, but these suicide fighters evened the odds some. Right there I became convinced it would take us ten years to subdue mainland Japan. I remembered as a kid reading in history class that early Texans never really defeated the fierce Comanche Indians. Unable to convert them, they were forced to eventually killed them all. That is what we're going to have to do to Japan. In the meantime, I thought, they will extract thousands more American lives.

Doll, Ray, and I watched the crew on the injured transport use fire control hoses and fight like heroes to subdue the flames. They eventually brought the flames under control and saved their ship.

We later found out that our friend Blaine Collins was one of the twenty men killed by the kamikaze.

# Chapter 34

# Forty-Eight in Diego

We were still at Okinawa in late April 1945 when I received orders to return to the *Middleton*, where Lucky 13 was hoisted aboard. The ship was pulling out during an air raid and everyone was at battle stations. A large flock of Jap planes had penetrated the defenses in an effort to reach our transports. Several destroyers and escorts escorted the convoy of transports.

The harbor quickly filled with smoke. When the smoke began breaking up I could see a destroyer off our starboard bow and another just ahead of him. Both were firing anti-aircraft guns at Japanese aircraft. The Japs dropped their bombs and I saw the first hit right in front of the destroyer off our bow. Then a second, third, fourth, and fifth as the bombs fell into the water, each one closer until the last struck just off the destroyer's stern. Everyone waited for the sixth bomb, which would have been a direct hit. It never came. I shook my head and sighed. How many times had we seen such a fine line between destruction and safety, life and death? If that plane had one more bomb, or had started dropping them a second later, the result would have been more dead Americans. Like life, war was utterly unpredictable.

The convoy pulled away and headed back to Pearl Harbor. On the way back we learned Jack Dempsey had stayed on the beach a few hours, interviewed some troops and the beach party, and returned to the ship. The next day he was flown to Guam and then back to the States.

I was hoping we would get some time in Honolulu so I could see Lori, but the *Middleton* only stayed in Pearl Harbor two days before sailing for Hollandia, New Guinea, to bring troops back to Pearl Harbor. Hollandia proved a sad and unforgettable experience for all of us. Our assignment was to help the Army load a convoy of ships. We worked around the clock. About midnight, I was working on the beach when I heard a loud crash. An Army Tank Lighter rammed Henry Perkins' boat. Henry had served with Doll on his boat as one of his bowmen. Someone told me he was badly injured and in the hospital. It hurt just to hear the news.

Henry T. Perkins was from Dallas. We had been together since boot camp. I knew his cousin, who lived in my hometown of Itasca. Henry joined the Coast Guard when he was 16-years-old by lying about his age. He had an old guitar and constantly made up songs and sang them to us. His latest composition was about a fictional trip back to the States he called "Forty-eight in Diego." It was a catchy tune, and he had everyone aboard the *Middleton* singing it. Henry died early the next afternoon. We buried him at the Army cemetery on Hollandia with a full military funeral. I was one of the Pall Bearers and fired an M-1 Garand rifle over his grave.

When we returned to Pearl Harbor, rumors began circulating that we were going back to the mainland. Once we pulled out of Pearl, Cdr. McKay got on the P.A. system and announced the *Middleton* was heading for San Diego for a week of long overdue repairs. Everyone would receive a 48-hour pass. We were all excited by the news, but it was a little creepy. Many of us exchanged glances. It was almost as if Henry had known. It was a simple tune with only one verse, but "Forty-Eight in Diego" hit the all-time best seller list on the *Arthur Middleton*. Everyone was singing,

> Forty-eight in Diego, had a great time,
> Forty-eight in Diego, women and wine,
> Told all the bartenders, set 'em up Joe
> Loved all the ladies, but never told them so,
> Told all the mothers, sorry gotta' go
> Oh, forty-eight in San Di . . . e go!

"Think of it, Wiley," Doll said. "Forty-eight hours of our own in the good ole U.S.A. Boy, look out girls, here we come!"

To say that everyone was excited was the understatement of all time. This was stateside, something we had all longed for and waited in anticipation of for all those months and for some of us, years. We were going home—even though it was not really "home." By this time in my life anywhere in the U.S.A. was home.

Although it was now May and we were off southern California, the weather was very cold. Those long months in the South Pacific had thinned a lot of blood. We wore our fur-lined foul weather gear while on watch.

Doll, Bill, and I were in the second group to get liberty. That meant we would be in port two days before we could go ashore. This allowed me a chance to call home. My mom and dad wanted to come to California to see me, but I told them that there wouldn't be time. The trip from Texas would take at least two or three days, and we would be pulling out within a week. It's hard to crowd that much into a short telephone conversation, but we sure did. Mom explained how surprised she was when she spotted me on a newsreel with Jack Dempsey, and that Troy was volunteering to go to the Pacific now that he had served two tours in Europe. Tom Hollimon, one of my closest friends from Itasca, was stationed in San Diego aboard a cruiser and mom gave me the name of his ship. Vic and Betty were in South America. I missed everyone so much I ached.

San Diego was a sailor's town. I located Tom and had a nice visit with him. Everything a sailor could want (and I mean everything) was available. Doll, Tom, and I tried to take it all in. We met and dated some nice girls, walked in beautiful parks, played around in amusement centers on the beach, and more. My girl was from Oklahoma and she worked at a J. C. Penney's store. We bar-hopped and nearly got into several fights. We sure packed a month of activities into a 48-hour pass, but it ended all too quickly. Doll and I both felt like we had accumulated enough experiences now that we could hold our own when the old salts started spinning yarns about their many ports of call.

After just one week we shipped out on the *Middleton* for Pearl Harbor, unloaded troops, and set out again for San Diego for another "Forty-Eight in Diego!" This time, Doll and I took a train to Los Angeles and went to Hollywood. Girls there were different than they were in San Diego. I don't think I had ever seen so many beautiful girls walking down Hollywood and Sunset boulevards. Most had on the shortest of shorts and halters and, with their California tans, looked like goddesses. Everyone was friendly, too. Wherever we went people offered to buy us drinks. The five ribbons and six battle stars we wore proudly on our blouses were like a bugle blast announcing our arrival.

# Chapter 35

# Stateside

After another week or so in San Diego the *Middleton* made another run back to Pearl Harbor, where we unloaded troops and equipment. Much to our surprise and delight, we headed back a third time for the West Coast. This time the port was Los Angeles, where we were told the *Middleton* would go into dry dock for more extensive repairs. How could the news be any better than this? Rumors really flew about extended leaves for everyone. Surely if the ship was going into dry dock, we would get a long leave?

When Custer posted a list on the bulletin board assigning 26-day leaves to everyone in the boat crews, I thought the yelling and screaming aboard our old ship would drive us all deaf. The days we spent sailing for aboard the *Middleton* were wild ones indeed. Doll was in the first liberty group this time. Bill and I were assigned to the second group. Life aboard the ship during dry dock was different. Liberty was plentiful with 48 hours on and 48 hours off. I visited my relatives around Los Angeles and spent a lot of time with friends having a good time.

It seemed to take forever, but it was finally my turn to go home. Bill and I caught a train together. The round trip cost for service men was only $38.00. As the train rolled across California, Arizona, New Mexico, and Texas, I saw the western United States for the first time. The mountains and deserts were beautiful. The train ride was exciting at first, and then simply exhausting. The weather was hot and we were grimy from the soot that blew back from the coal-burning steam engine and the long hours without a bath. It took two full days to reach Ft. Worth. Even so, the scenery was magnificent and I relished every minute of the trip home. I had been to the far side of the world, seen terrible things, and here I was again in West Texas.

I took a bus home to Itasca. I walked down the same streets I had played on as a young boy growing up in this small central Texas town. Many people shot me a double look and when they recognized me, rushed over to welcome me home. I would be lying if I told you it didn't feel good. Many boys were coming home now, and each one was the talk of the town. I had been gone for nearly two years, but after what I had seen and done, it might as well have been a century. Everything was different now. Itasca was the same—but it wasn't. My world was different and I was suddenly unsure of my place in it.

My reunion at home was fantastic. When I found out I was coming home, I sent my mother a simply five-word telegram: "Have coconut pies ready Tuesday." When I arrived, there were four fresh pies ready to be eaten. My mother was the world's best cook, and since we had such a large family, she enjoyed cooking for us.

It was early June 1945. Germany had surrendered a few weeks earlier. The end of the long and terrible war in Europe had everyone in America breathing a sigh of relief. However, everyone expected the war in the Pacific to go on for a long time—and maybe many more years. I fully expected to go back and join the massive task force we all anticipated would be heading for the invasion of Japan. I had very little enthusiasm for it now, especially after spending time back home, so I decided to make the most of every minute.

My parents had aged a lot during my absence. I talked with my mom about Joe, but my dad couldn't speak on the subject. He had received a letter from Joe just before his last mission. Joe told him that on each mission they lost as many as fifty percent of their bombers. He wrote my dad that he did not expect to come home. It was very hard for Troy Wiley, Sr. to understand, and he never accepted or got over his son's death. For the first time in my life I felt the helplessness this fine man felt, as only a parent could feel. He had five sons. Four of them were in the military and the young one still at home would have to serve his country soon. One had been taken away from him, and there was nothing he could do to change that. Dad would have given his own life for any of us.

My mom filled me in on extra details about Joe's final mission. My brother Troy, who was in England, had talked with some of the airmen from Joe's squadron. His plane, a B-17, had been hit by anti-aircraft fire. According to an eyewitness, it was a direct hit and there were no parachutes, which meant there were no survivors. Joe died over Holland, along the bombing route into Germany where their mission was to destroy a heavy industrial area that made equipment for the Nazi army. My mom was a strong person and she accepted Joe's death, even though I know it devastated her until the day she died. My dad was never the same man after receiving the news.

I walked to town. It seemed so small now, this town that had been my life. I knew every house on the way. I knew every store. I went to "Woods," the favorite hangout of the young people. "Woods" was a pharmacy complete with marble counters and white stools and tables. A group of young people invited me over as soon as I walked in.

The twenty-six days I spent in Itasca was an entirely different way of life for me. The ship, my friends, and the war slipped away a little more each day, even though I knew I would have to leave home and return to the only way of life I really knew. I went out on a date almost every night. It seemed like there was always a get-together at someone's house or at some local function. The popular music at the time was a complete surprise to me. A song about "mares eat oats and does eat oats and little lambs eat ivy" was all the rage. (I couldn't understand the words, either.) The song we all loved in the service was "We'll Meet Again. Don't Know Where, Don't Know When." It signified the times perfectly because we were always on the move and friends passed in and out of our lives. I thought of Lori. I thought of Henry. I thought of many people.

All too soon it was time to go back. It was nearly July 1945. I would be twenty next month. Franklin D. Roosevelt was dead. Harry Truman, who was relatively unknown, was now the President of the United States. The war in Europe over. World War II was entering its final stage in the Pacific. That's where I was going.

My brother Troy had completed his twenty-five missions and volunteered to stay for ten more. He flew those and then volunteered to serve in the Pacific. My older brother Vic was in Argentina with his family, attached to the U.S. Embassy. Bill and I had agreed to meet in Ft. Worth to make the journey back to California together. We had many stories to exchange as the train pulled out of Ft. Worth and headed west.

When we got back aboard the *Middleton*, another surprise awaited us. Custer had posted a list of men transferred to shore duty: everyone was on the list.

The next night, Doll and I were leaving the *Middleton* for our last night of liberty when a familiar voice spoke up behind us. "Hey guys, wait up a minute." It was Custer and he was in his dress blues. I suddenly realized that I had never known Custer to take liberty. In fact, I had never seen him in a dress uniform. Doll and I looked at one another, shrugged, and stopped while Custer approached.

"If you don't have plans," he said, "I would like to buy you both a steak dinner." He watched as our eyebrows arched in surprise. We both nodded our approval. He broke the awkward silence. "I guess you guys have a lot of reason to hate me, don't you? I was pretty rough on you sometimes. Maybe this will help to let you know that I really liked both of you."

I didn't know what to say, and a small lump formed in my throat. Doll broke the silence. "For my part, I'm proud to have had you for a leader and I want to thank you for getting us through the last two years and for being a friend. I'm sorry that we're having to part."

I nodded my head and added, "That goes for me to. I feel lucky to have served under you, sir."

"Well, they say that you have to hate the person you work for, and I figured if the truth were known, most of you did!" I suddenly realized how lonely it must have been for him aboard the *Middleton* all those many months.

"I'll tell you something else," I said. "Every man in the boat division feels the same way we do. For what it's worth, 'Well done!'" We all laughed.

We enjoyed the steak dinner, talked about what we were going to do with our lives, and drank a few beers. Of all the people on the ship, Custer decided to spend the evening with us. It was a night I'll always remember.

When we returned to the ship I walked slowly on deck and climbed aboard Lucky 13. The men of the *Middleton* (there were no longer any boys on this ship) were going stateside. I would finally be able to do all of the things I had been deprived of for so long. There would be girls of all types, but I no longer wanted to build the stories sailors liked to share in their bull sessions. I wanted my dream to come true. I wanted that dream girl to materialize. But I was no longer in a hurry. When the war was over I planned to go college, play football, become an engineer, and then marry that special girl.

The experiences of the past two years flooded over me at that moment: the *Middleton*, Cdr. McKay, Lt. Hoyle, Custer, Ken Riley, Bill Miller, Tex Lee, Charlie Doll, Tex Thornton, Henry Perkins, Blaine Collins, and even Capt. "Vell Done!" Svensen. Every one of them and hundreds of others had contributed to my life. I sat there for the better part of two hours and relived much of our time together. In the dim light I could still make out the small caliber bullet holes in the plywood fence above the armor plating on the port side we had received at Enewitok. I thought about the crease in the valve cover Bill had straightened out in the Philippines, and the strafing holes we plugged up after we got back on the ship. No one would ever know the story of how these things had occurred. I so wanted to thank Chris-Craft and Gray Marine Diesel and tell them how well #PA-25-13 had performed.

It was about midnight when Doll came looking for me. "Hey Wiley, you can't take it with you." His voice was nearly a whisper.

I sighed, leaned forward, and patted the gunwale where I had painted the name "Jean."

And then the words I had heard so many times slipped from my lips: "Vell Done, ole' buddy, Vell Done!"

# Postscript

So many people touched my life during World War II. Unfortunately, postwar life was hectic and many of the threads that bound us together severed during peacetime.

Charles S. Doll was my best friend aboard the *Middleton*. He left the service and went to college at Southern Florida. Doll enjoyed a long career with General Electric. Today, he and his wife Caroline live in Harrodsburg, Kentucky, near their four children and their families. We have stayed in touch over the years and reminisce of the days and years that made such an impact on our lives. In a recent conversation we talked about Henry T. Perkins. "Perk" was Doll's bowman on Boat 29 until his death in Hollandia, New Guinea.

Billie "Bill" L. Miller was my Motor Mac who experienced so much of the war with me on Lucky 13. We first met when we joined the Coast Guard. There were five of us altogether who left Dallas for boot camp in St. Augustine, Florida. We were all just seventeen. The other three were Bob Horton, also from Ft. Worth (Pascall High), John Ligon, and Lynn Britton from Sunset High in Dallas. We joined together, went through basic training together, through landing craft school together, and remained generally together throughout the war (although Bill and I were assigned to a different ship). Bill and I were discharged together, attended the same junior college and played football on the same team in Hillsboro, Texas. Bill married Jon Anne and spent the rest of his life in his beloved

Carter Riverside area in Ft. Worth. We stayed in touch often. Bill never lost his sense of humor. He was awarded the Navy and Marine Corps medals for rescuing a bunch of sailors from a burning LCI that had been hit by mortars at Eniwetok. When asked why he did it, this was his response: "Well, it was like a multiple choice test with only one answer." That was Bill Miller.

The last time I saw Bill we had lunch in Dallas. We talked about the 5-inch gun the Japs kept rolling in and out of a cave to try to get the boats coming through the pass in the reef, and how the U.S. destroyer sitting offshore was trying to catch him with its 5-inchers when he rolled out. "That bastard might not have been such a good shot," laughed Bill, "but he was sure good at dodging that destroyer's guns! It was like the Keystone cops." Our talk included the suicide boats and our narrow escape when Bill's red flashlight wouldn't work. "You know, Wiley, we were just a bunch of damn kids. I don't know how we won that war." My friend passed away in Ft Worth, Texas, about ten years ago.

Bob Horton went back to his job with MKT Railroad in Ft. Worth, married, raised a family, and passed away at an early age in the 1970s.

John Ligon returned to Dallas and became a star baseball catcher at Southern Methodist University. The team also had a center fielder named Doak Walker (a future NFL inductee to the Hall of Fame). John married and later moved into a career with the Security Forces at LTV.

Lynn Briton married and opened a jewelry store in Corsicana, Texas.

Tex Lee, my bowman in Lucky 13 from Lubbock, Texas, disappeared after the war in that giant melting pot of people scurrying to pick up lost lives. I never saw or heard from him again.

Custer, the NCO in charge of our boat division (I never knew his first name), took Doll and me to dinner the night before we left the *Middleton*. I never saw him again. That was true with so many of the men I shared years of my life with. Cdr. Hoyle, the Beach Master, Cdr. McKay, executive officer, and Capt. Sveret Olson, Bob Baker, Ray Breland, James O'Neal, Tex Thornton, Red Myers, Wendel Lloyd, John McKim, Bob Johnson, Jim Murray, and the rest of the 500-man crew of the *Middleton* were left behind as I moved on to the next phase of my life. This was typical of the time and environment we lived in. The war threw me together with people I did not know, sent us to places we had never been, and separated us suddenly never to see one another again. We learned always to look forward. All we wanted was to survive the war, get back home, and pick up where we left off. We didn't fully realize that the years changed on both ends.

One person deserving special recognition for all that he did during those years was the combat artist Ken Riley. Ken was a seaman first class and a shipmate. He did the series of fifty-two artist illustrations, some of which appear in this book. All of his drawings and illustrations were alive with action. He had regular duties aboard ship like everyone else, was a member of the Beach Party, and went in with the first wave of every invasion. He was in the thick of the action. Ken received national acclaim for his drawings and the mural on the wall at the Coast Guard Academy. After the war he drew for the *Saturday Evening Post* and became famous for his Western art. He is living in Tucson, Arizona.

Some of the girls I met during before and during the war (and are mentioned in the book) deserve some follow up. Jean was the childhood "sweetheart" I named my boat after. The timing was never right for us. Her long red hair and freckled face carried me through many a sleepless night over miles of ocean. She dated and met new friends in her hometown in West Texas all through her teenage years, and I met and dated girls in California after getting back in the U.S. while awaiting my discharge. We continued to correspond, but we did not see each other. She married someone a year or two after the war. Many years later, I ran across her in Dallas. Ironically, the girl I eventually fell in love with and married, as well as one of our four daughters, has similar features.

Lori, the gorgeous nurse in Pearl Harbor we used to keep in front of the door so we could see the outline of her body through the light, vanished after the war. I longed to see her again in Honolulu, and looked forward to our night together at her apartment where she invited me to stay. Unfortunately, I never got back to Honolulu. We both wanted companionship at a time when we both needed it, but I think deep down we knew it would never go beyond that. I hope she has had a good life. She was a nice girl and deserved one.

Marcia, the Filipino school teacher, was a true friend I was glad to help in a distant land. I never saw her again, but I can still clearly see her face and hear her voice. We had a song from that era that summed up all of the many goodbyes and quick departures. It went like this: "We'll meet again, don't know where, don't know when." It was a way of closing when we knew our paths were pointing in different directions.

When I got out of high school, I wanted desperately to go to college and play football. Like my older brothers, I couldn't afford it and I was from such a small school that I couldn't get an athletic scholarship. All during the war I never lost sight of my ambition to go to college and become an engineer. (Thank God for the G.I. Bill, which allowed me to do this.) I wanted to have the fun that I missed as a teenager.

I attended junior college in 1947 in my hometown of Hillsboro and played football. We won our championship and went to the Junior Sugar Bowl. It was there I met Fran, the girl I would one day marry, on a double date arranged with my brother. Fran was living in a room in the same rooming house as my brother and his wife. My brother and his wife arranged the "blind date" for me. The night went well and we dated often after that. We married in December 1949 and moved to Denton, Texas, where I began my career with the Soil Conservation Service. We have four daughters, each as pretty as their mother.

I was the fourth of five brothers in military service during World War II. Rounding out a family of eight was one sister named Ailene and my parents, Troy and Dora Wiley. I authored a manuscript entitled "Gold Star Mother Praying for The White Cliffs of Dover," which I hope to publish soon. Vic, my oldest brother, went into the Army in 1938 and married Betty Dubler while stationed at Sandia Air Force Base in Albuquerque, New Mexico. Joe, the next in line, joined the Army Air Corps and was stationed with Vic, whose squadron was scheduled to go to the Philippines. They were on an unarmed troop ship one day out of Pearl Harbor heading for the Philippines when the sun rose on December 7, 1941. The ship sailed quickly for San Francisco, where both Vic and Joe volunteered for a pilot training program. As I related earlier, Lt. Joseph W. Wiley, co-pilot on a B-17 with the Eighth Air Force, was killed on January

30, 1944, on his fifth mission over Germany. He is buried in the Army cemetery in Holland. Maj. Victor D. Wiley was assigned to the Embassy Service in South America during the war. He performed several assignments in Europe and Asia after the war and retired in the mid-1950s. He continued his career as an executive with a large defense contractor. Vic had two daughters and one son.

Troy, Jr. (M/Sgt. Troy O. Wiley), third in line, joined the Army Air Corps in 1942 and attended gunnery school. He was assigned to the Eighth Air Force and sent to England. He arrived there just nine days after Joe was killed. He flew twenty-five missions as a top turret gunner on a B-17, and then volunteered for twenty-five more. After his thirty-fifth mission the war in Europe ended. Troy, who is credited with shooting down the first German jet fighter aircraft, was awarded the Distinguished Flying Cross and five air medals. Troy married Edith McClung of Hillsboro, Texas, and stayed in the Air Force with the Embassy Service. He served five foreign tours. He and Edith adopted an Austrian baby girl and then had a daughter of their own. Troy's second wife Irma, born in Czechoslovakia, moved to Germany in the 1950s and was a victim of the aftermath of WWII. After a successful career with his own insurance company, Troy and Irma retired and live on the Guadeloupe River in Sequin, Texas.

Bill (Billy D. Wiley) joined the Army at the age of 18 and served during the Korean War. Bill and his wife Sue Schrieber of Grandview, Texas, live in Edmond, Oklahoma. They have three sons.

Since I am one of the characters in this book, I guess I should update my own story before closing this account. I have retired four times and it just doesn't work for me. I went back to school at Oklahoma State University to finish my work toward an engineering degree and went to work for LTV, a large defense contractor. The company diversified into commercial areas and I was in charge of new business. I retired after twenty-two years as vice president of marketing and vice president and general manager of one of LTV's divisions. One of their subsidiaries (Siemens, USA) called me back in 1975 to help market automated mail sorting machines. After four years, National Presort hired me as executive VP to get its products into the marketplace. Eleven years later I retired, but keep getting offers to do studies and analysis of mail operations.

Unfortunately, Fran and I divorced after twenty-eight years of marriage. My work required a lot of travel (about seventy-two trips per year) and she wanted a different life. I married Deane Osborne and continued consulting work for seven years. We organized our own company, D & K Wiley Enterprises, and have lived in her home in beautiful Mountain City, Tennessee, for the past sixteen years. I spend a lot of my time writing and dabbling with new ideas.

World War II made such an impact on my life that I remember it in vivid detail. In 2004, I began my latest venture, a grass roots project to put local veterans video museums in the community of their heritage. We are working with WWII veterans first, for the obvious reason that we are all double parked. It is a volunteer program and there is no cost to anyone.

I believe every life is a story worth telling, and it is impossible to record in a single book the events we experience. I have begun a volunteer program to make available the life stories of veterans on DVD. We use old photos of the veteran and his family, friends, news clippings, documents, public domain information, and non-copyrighted music and narration. We advocate Local Veterans Video Museums and provide copies to the veteran and his/her family. Local High School students often do the interviews and make the DVDs, so there is no cost to the veteran.

I hope you have enjoyed the story of my service and of all the brave men and women who gave up so much to help preserve the freedom and gifts we have in this wonderful country we live in. They say "freedom is not free." Whoever coined that phrase knew what he was talking about.

Appendix

# A 1944 Roster of
# the *Arthur Middleton* (APA-25)

This appendix of names was prepared from an official Coast Guard roster of those who are listed as having served aboard the *Arthur Middleton* in 1944. As with nearly every roster ever created, it may well be incomplete, may include misspelled names, or may include the name of someone who did not serve aboard the *Arthur Middleton* in 1944. My hope, however, is that someone, somewhere, finds it useful.

Adams, Horace D.
Adolphson, Arthur W.
Albrecht, Henry K.
Anderson, Charles E.
Anderson, Malcolm M.
Andrews, Bernard H.
Bahm, Richard J.
Baum, Clavis W.
Becker, Robert M.
Bower, Arthur, J.
Brockman,Fred B.
Burgess, Perry E.
Burton, Clyde R.
Butler, Larence G.
Callow, Charles W.
Campbell, Donald E.
Carolino, Pedro O.
Carroll, Lloyd D.
Catayas, Andres C.
Catucci, Dominic

Chapman, Harry
Chappell, Raymond C.
Chausmer, Bernard
Chester, Richard L.
Choina, LeRoy A.
Clark, Bertie C.
Clark, Clarence C.
Clemans, George A.
Clore, Leland W.
Clow, Fred C.
Cobb, John J.
Coleman,  Earl L.
Collier, Jack A.
Collier, Jr, George W.
Comstock, William E.
Connelly, Jack R.
Cook, James J.
Coronado, Basil C.
Correll, Gordon K.
Cory, Paul

Costa, John J.

Costigan, John E.

Cox, Robert C.

Cragg, Ralph

Croall, Milton L.

Crumpton, Ralph C.

Custer, Dale C.

Czerwinski, Henry F.

DaCosta, Albert R.

Davenport, King J.

Davidson, Arthur R.

Davidson, Elton E.

Davis, Harold B.

Davis, James W.

Davis, Jr, Clifford D.

Davison, Donald W.

Deason, Charles L.

DeBoer, Delbert E.

DeBoer, Lloyd R.

DeBruyn, Allan B.

Dees, Noel D.

D'Elia, Peter A.

DeWitt, Franklin M.

Dichiara, Robert M.

Dickey, Gilbert W.

Dishrow, Flloyd H.

Divine, George F.

Doll, Jr, Charles S.

Donicht, Jack R.

Dooher, Thomas A.

Douglas, Ogre P.

Doyle, Alexander L.

Driscoll, Richard J.

Dupre, Jr, Julius J.

Dutton, Robert M.

Elmore, William A.

Ernst, Robert O.

Espinosa, Benjamin P.

Evans, William A.

Evdokinoff, John

Farmer, James P.

Farrell, James T.

Farrington, Elmer E.

Felix, William H.

Ferguson, Marvin R.

Ferrara, James S.

Fiedler, Gustev J.

Fitch, Jesse, C.

Fitzgerald, Thomas F.

Flanagan, Eugene L.

Flanery, Richard E.

Frakes, William A.

Frans, Melvin A.

Fraser, Colin D.

Fredrickson, Lee E.

Fuller, Billy J.

Fuller, Burt P.

Fulmer, Max J.

Galahan, Billy T. L.

Gallivan, Timothy L.

Gamble, Clinton W.

Gans, William J.

Garrett, John B.

Garrison, William G.

GebHart, Richard C.

George, Paul K.

Gibellino, Jr, John

Gibson, Thomas E.

Girouard, Joseph T.

Gleason, Jr, Friend W.

Goates, James W.

Goines, LeRoy A.

Good, Edgar F.

Goss, John G.

Grant, Felix E.

Gratton, Ray A.

Gray, Wallace R.
Green, Bruce A.
Greene, Bluego
Guerrero, Macario
Gunderson, Daniel C.
Gunderson, martin H.
Guthrie, Floyd H.
Hackett, Walter M.
Hal, William A.
Hamilton, Albert J.
Hamilton, Buster R.
Hamlin, Eugene K.
Hand, Robert B.
Haney, Charles C.
Haney, Gerald A.
Hanson, Dick
Harity, Bernard J.
Harris, Emmett L.
Harvey, James D.
Hatcher, Lloyd D.
Hayes, James N.
Haynes, Thomas M.
Heaton, Richard F.
Heinick, Harold L.
Heldt, David R.
Helvik(?), Howard
Hemmilla, Lewis H.
Hendricks, Lorange R.
Herman, Joseph M.
Hickmon, William A.
Hicks, Chalres W.
High, Eugene F.
Hill, Albert T.
Hill, J, Robert.
Hillman, Ralph J.
Hinkey, Robert H.
Hinkle, Byron L.
Hodge, James A.

Hoffman, Elder W.
Hogan, Thomas H.
Holden, John P.
Holderby, Robert A.
Holland, Clifton H.
Holland, John M.
Holt, George W.
Hon, L.
Hooper, Edward
Hopkins, James H.
Hopson, —
Hormath,—
Hormell,—
Hoyle, Robert
Hudson, —
Hug, Donald
Hughes, —
Hulse, —
Huotte, —
Huseby, Morris
Inkland, —
Irvin, Milton A.
Iverson, Oakely K.
James, —
Jamieson, Shelby C.
Jarvis, Douglas H.
Jaynes, —
Jenkins, Clark L.
Jennings, John E.
Jensen, Evan A.
Jensen, Harald M.
Jensen, Ralph S.
Johnson, Edward F.
Johnson, H.
Johnson, John M.
Johnston, —
Johnston, Robert
Jones, —

Jones, —
Jones, —
Jones, John M.
Jones, O.
Jones, William M.
Kallard, Robert D.
Kantl,—
Kanz,—
Karz, —
Kaylor, Howard D.
Kelley, Thomas D.
Kemp, Daniel R.
Kennett, Edward J.
Kenney, Francis J.
Kenney, Jr, Albert W.
Kerr, Douglas S.
Kerwin, Fred V.
Kibbe, Malin E.
King, Arnold K.
Kitchel, William E.
Klander, Albert
Knight, Harold
Knight, Lynn W.
Kolar, Jr, Philip M.
Kummer, Roy R.
Kurucar, George H.
Lahaderne, Bernard P.
Laidlan, Lansing S.
Lambert, Robert M.
Lampieah, George
Landis, William H.
Landsberg, Robert R.
Lane, Anthony J.
Langbert, Keith R.
LaPalme, Allan E.
Larson, Howard E
Latimer, Ralph S.
Lawrence, Joseph

Leaf, Harvey E.
Leathy, Joseph R.
Ledfeler, Urial W.
Lee, Hoy
LeFever, David S.
Lemke, Jr, Edward F.
Lewis, Roscoe W.
Likbeck, Robert C.
Lim, Lee Y.
Linquist, Emil J.
Lisle, Robert G.
Liverman, James
Lloyd, Wendell M.
Longhire, James C.
Losfeler, Raymond L.
Luke, Gean S.
Lynch, John P.
Lyons, Theodore R.
MacAloon, Jack R.
Macomber, Frank S.
Maddox, Boyd C.
Magnus, Flloyd L.
Malloy, Jr, Joseph F.
Marks, Frederick N.
Marshall, Warren E.
Masoner, Vurture A.
Masters, Granville L.
Mayberry, William H.
Mazer, Nathan
McCrea, Felix A.
McCrory, Francis H.
McGrath, William H.
McKay, Donald E.
McKean, George W.
McKim, John F.
MckKinnon, Thomas N.
McMeans, Clifford E.
McMullen, William L.

McVeigh, Edward J.

Melton, Jack H.

Mendoxa, Rosario E.

Meyer, George H.

Miller, Billy L.

Miller, Howard C.

Miller, James E.

Miller, Jesse D.

Milligan, Donald B.

Millovancevish, John E.

Mills, John H.

Montgomery, Charles M.

Morse, Gene L.

Morse, Lynn F.

Mounts, Jack

Muffelman, Jr, William F.

Mull, Donald

Mullally, Leonard A.

Mullaney, James

Muri, Sanford H.

Muriekes, William J.

Murray, William J.

Muskat, Morris S.

Musson, Robert M.

Myers, James A.

Nadeau, Thomas E.

Nastor, Isidro

Nave, Chester F.

Nelson, Donald

Nelson, Robert G.

Newel,, Phillip G.

Nichols, William J.

Nolan, Earl L.

Nyberg, Carl M.

Nygren, Vincent A.

O'Brien, William P.

O'Connor, Harry

Olivas, Joseph A.

Olsen, Severt A.

Olson, Russell I.

O'Neal, Roy D.

O'Neill, Lee W.

Oringer, Walter H.

Orr, Norman D.

Orr, Robert F.

Osborne, William H.

Osterloh, Walter F. H.

Otto, Florian J.

Owens, Howard

Palmer, Elmer E.

Pankey, Howard M.

Pasch, Russell L.

Paulsen, Lawrnece P.

paulson, Erik E.

Pennington, Jr, John W.

Pereira, Mitchell A.

Perine, James F.

Perkins, Henry T.

Perrin, Carol T.

Perry, Wayne R.

Petersen, Harold A.

Peyton, Henry H.

Phillips, James E.

Pickford, Billy J.

Pimentel, Marion N.

Podmore, Francis H.

Poteete, Woodrow W.

Potts, Samuel J.

Powell, Jr, James N.

Powell, Robert E.

Powers, Jr, Samuel L.

Presthold, Gordon C.

Prichard, George W.

Prouse, Donald R.

Przykopawski, Henry

Pyetzki, Rolland R.

Radetzky, Nicholas

Radoff, Allen A.

Rahm, Lester S.

Rainey, George A.

Raustadt, Dwain L.

Reichert, Rudolph E.

Richardson, Edwin F.

riley, Kenney P.

Riley, Letsser H.

Robbins, Oscar P.

Robertson, Ralph J.

Rohne, Evan H.

Rousseaux, Ralph A.

Rudyk, Theodore

Ruotsala, Walter J.

Russell, Jr, Dean F.

Ruthenbeck, Lloyd W.

Ryan, Robert C.

Ryman, Jr, Frank L.

Sauerforn, Josef

Scharbach, Cletus J.

Schempf, Wayne A.

Schmoot, Wilbert M.

Schneider, Bernard J.

Schnurr, Pete P.

Schnurr, Toney E.

Sea, Nelson E.

Sealabrina, Daniel J.

Sears, Howard S.

Senior, Norman C.

Shallow, William J.

Shane, Robert A.

Sheets, Wilber D.

Shepard, Dale F.

Sherstad, Carlyle R.

Shields, Ralph H.

Shupe, Jay B.

Silvestro, Michael A.

Sivori, Lloyd V.

Smith Jerry G.

Smith, Frank E.

Smith, Jr, Stnaley S.

Smith, Ladell

Smith, Richard E.

Sparks, James P.

Spawr, Arvil D.

Speck, Russell M.

Sponer, Darwin W.

Stabler, Harold L.

Stamey, Elbert E.

Standlee, Raby D.

Stansbury, Phillip C.

Staples, William F.

Stark, Robert F.

Steele, Charles M.

Stensater, Norman H. C.

Sterrenburg, Gerlad R.

Steuer, Edison C.

Stigall, Orville R.

Stocchini, James A.

Story, Wayne S.

Strickland, James D.

Strunk, Robert K.

Studley, Orville J.

Sularz, Henry A.

Sumner, Marvin

Sutton, Robert G.

Sykes, Robert A.

Symes, Herbert S.

Tabiolo, Esteban

Taggard, Thomas D.

Tannner, Lyman D.

Taylor, Joe

Taylor, Williem E.

Tedder, Mark T

Thomas, William E.

Thornhill, Richard W.

Tingvold, John E.

Tonel, Leopado, T.

Torak, Jr, Michael G. A.

Trokey, Raymond L.

Trotter, David B.

Tuchtenahgen, Glenn J.

Valenta, Raymond F.

Van Dorin, George L.

Vance, Harry H.

Vandeleur, Jr, John S.

Venturo, Andrew R.

Villanueva, Domingo, A.

Votaw, William H.

Wagner, George E.

Wagner, William O.

Walker, Robert LaRoy

Walz, Richard C.

Wanamaker, Jr, William G.

Wanless, Paul C.

Ward, Raymond M.

Warner, Lyman D.

Warner, Robert

Watson, Horace W.

Watson, Robert C.

Weekley, Jr, A. F.

Weidner, J. C.

White, Raymond J.

White, Robert G.

Wicks, Charles

Wiley, Kenneth E.

Williams, Gordon S.

Williams, Theodore E.

Williamson, John A.

Willis, Nelson E.

Wilson, Donald, E.

Wilson, John G.

Wilson, Randall E.

Winegardner, Dean S.

Wisniewski, Harry S.

Wizland, George S.

Wooley, Earl K.

Wurts, Jr, Burkhardt

# INDEX

*Arthur Middleton*, USS (APA-25), xiii, 65-66, 104-105, 111, 113-114, 117, 120, 124, 126-127, 139, 172, 176, 178, 180-181, 197, 221, 305-307, 309, 312-313, 315-316; development of the attack transport, 6; assigned to, 67, 68-70, 72-73; Kwajalein, 76, 83-84, 86; Eniwetok, 87-89, 91, 94, 96-97; Guadalcanal, 132; Saipan, 142-145, 149-151, 158, 162; ships gunnery, 186-188; Philippines, 199-202, 207-208, 212, 214-217, 219; Leyte, 229-230, 232; Luzon, 235, 237, 238, 242-243, 248, 252-253, 258; New Hebrides, 268; Manus Island, 269, 271-272, 274, 276-277; kamikaze, 278, 280-281, 283; Okinawa, 287, 303-304

Baker, Bob, 160, 187, 215, 316
Baker, Sam, 106, 129
Ball, Lucille, 175, 263-264
Blair, Billy Buck, 20, 23
Blissett, Wilma, 269-270
Borneo, 263-265
Bradley, Boone, 9
Breland, Ray, 129, 316
Britton, Lynn, 24, 25, 27, 30, 49, 66, 315-316

Cahill, —, assigned to the *Arthur Middleton*, 69-70; Kwajalein, 77, 79, 80-83; Eniwetok, 88, 90, 93-94, 96
*Calloway*, 139, 304
*Cambria*, USS (APA-36), xiii, 5-6, 58-59, 61, 63, 65-67, 70, 74, 77, 87, 117, 216
Camp Lejune, North Carolina, 44-46, 49, 51, 54, 67, 124
Catalina (seaplane), 221-277
*Cavalier*, USS (APS-37), 117-118
*Chase*, 6
China Clipper, 221
Chris-Craft Boat Company, xvi, 2, 4, 249, 313
*Climber*, 6
Collins, Blaine, 51, 53, 55, 304, 313
Cooper, Eugene, 253
Curtiss, I. C., 9
Custer, Dale C., assigned to the *Middleton*, 67-69; Kwajalein, 77, 79, 80, 82, 84; Albert Ellison, 105; joining the ranks of King Neptune, 126; Guadalcanal, 129; Tokyo Rose, 136-137; Saipan, 151-153, 162; suicide boat, 171; Philippines, 204, 214, 216-219; Catalina incident, 224; Leyte, 229; Luzon, 241-242, 249-251; New Hebrides, 264; Okinawa, 302-303; going home, 309, 312, 313; post-war, 316